EXPLORE

STORIES OF SURVIVAL
FROM OFF THE MAP

EXPLORE

STORIES OF SURVIVAL FROM OFF THE MAP

EDITED BY JENNIFER SCHWAMM WILLIS
ADRENALINE SERIES EDITOR CLINT WILLIS

MAINSTREAM
PUBLISHING

EDINBURGH AND LONDON

Adrenaline® and the Adrenaline® logo are trademarks of
Balliett & Fitzgerald Inc. New York, NY.

An Adrenaline Book®

First published in Great Britain in 2001 by

MAINSTREAM PUBLISHING COMPANY (EDINBURGH) LTD
7 Albany Street
Edinburgh EH1 3UG

ISBN 1 84018 490 6

First published in the United States by
Thunder's Mouth Press
841 Broadway, 4th Floor
New York, NY 10003

and

Balliett & Fitzgerald Inc.
66 West Broadway, Suite 602
New York, NY 10007

Series Editor: Clint Willis
Book design: Sue Canavan
frontispiece photo: © Chris Rainier/Corbis

Printed and bound in Great Britain by The Bath Press, Bath

For my parents, Ellen and Jay,
who let me wander and always welcome me back.

contents

viii **photographs**

I **introduction**

7 from *The Lost Tribe*
by Edward Marriott

45 *An Evening Among Headhunters*
by Lawrence Millman

57 *Lost City of the Lukachukais*
by David Roberts

75 from *Antisuyo: The Search for
the Lost Cities of the Amazon*
by Gene Savoy

85 *Cahill Among the Ruins in Peru*
by Tim Cahill

115 from *Farthest North*
by Fridtjof Nansen

139 from *Snow on the Equator*
by H. W. Tilman

159 from *In Trouble Again*
by Redmond O'Hanlon

193 *Unknown Interior of America*
by Alvar Núñez Cabeza de Vaca

217 from *The Dogs of Paradise*
by Abel Posse

229   *Bikpela Hol*
       by John Long and Dwight Brooks

247   *Crazy in the Congo*
       by Michael Finkel

271   from *The Indian Alps and How We Crossed Them*
       by Nina Mazuchelli

285   *Arctic Discovery*
       by Lawrence Millman

289   *Upland Stream*
       by W. D. Wetherell

309   from *This Wild Darkness*
       by Harold Brodkey

321   from *Mountains of Tartary*
       by Eric Shipton

335   **acknowledgments**

338   **bibliography**

p h o t o g r a p h s

7   Young Jivaro tribesman
    © H.E. Anthony/Courtesy National
    Geographic Society

45   Headhunters with weapons
    © H.E. Anthony/Courtesy National
    Geographic Society

57   Cliff dwellings
    © Galen Rowell/Mountainlight Images

75   Vilcabamba, Peru
    © Hiram Bingham Collection/Courtesy
    National Geographic Society

85   Pre-Incan ruins
    © Allard Collection/Courtesy National
    Geographic Society

115   Ice Drifts
    © Galen Rowell/Mountainlight Images

139   Ruwenzori
    Courtesy National Geographic Society

159   Central American fer-de-lance
    Courtesy National Geographic Society

193   *Theatrum Orbis Terrarum:* Map of
    Florida and the Gulf of Mexico
    © Tony Arruza/Corbis

217   Fleet ships of
    Christopher Columbus
    © Bettmann/Corbis

229   Entrance to underground cavern
    © Thomas R. Fletcher/ Stock
    Boston/Picture Quest

247   Killer bees swarm around
    Hank Morganstern
    © Chris Anderson/Aurora

271   Himalayan range
    © Galen Rowell/Corbis

    Baffin Island
285   © Galen Rowell/
    Mountainlight Images

289   Trout Stream
    © Jeff Greenberg/
    RAINBOW/PictureQuest

309   Boy on raft
    © Steve Maines/Stock,
    Boston/PictureQuest

321   Mountains in the Kashgar Range
    © Alison Wright/Corbis

introduction

My palms are clammy. My heart is racing. I am alone. In the dim light, through my half-closed eyelids, I can make out several enormous gray shapes.

It is 1964. I am seven years old, and I am standing in the Hall of African Mammals in the American Museum of Natural History in New York City. The shapes that loom before me constitute a herd of elephants. Can I walk into the hall with my eyes wide open? Or will today be like other days, when I turn my back to the herd and edge past them, taking care not to look behind me? If I can manage to confront these huge silent creatures, I will have earned the right to travel into the world beyond them—a world of tigers, dinosaurs, and birds of paradise; of fur-clad Inuits and half-naked Amazonian Indians who crouch beneath ferns.

Looking back over the years, I wonder why those elephants frightened me so much. Was it their sheer size? I think it was their unnatural silence. They seemed so ready to lumber off their platform, to step over the red velvet barricade and head on down the hall, their massive hips swaying. I could not believe they would never move, or breathe—that I could never make contact with them.

• • •

I think exploration is about contact, about looking for connections between here and there, between past and present, between the individual and the universe. It is a way to confront and then overcome our fear of the unknown. It is Tim Flannery searching in New Guinea for a bat from the Ice Age. It is Lawrence Millman dining with headhunters in Ecuador. It is Gene Savoy seeking an ancient city in the jungles of Peru. It is Christopher Columbus looking for a New World. It is Eric Shipton exploring mountains in China for the sheer pleasure of being in them.

David Roberts once made an expedition to Mali on the trail of a long-gone race of people who used mysterious means to gain access to their cliff-side burial sites and granaries. "That we made no real dent in the enigma deepens it," he wrote of the trip. "We had ventured into the unknown, coming home not with answers so much as with a renewed sense of wonder. What more can one ask from a journey?"

Some travelers believe that they can remain aloof from their journeys of exploration. They seek to recast the unknown, or the different, in images of their choosing. But explorers worthy of the title inhabit their experience, no matter how difficult or threatening, and come to know its value. Young Edward Marriott endured just such a painful awakening during his time among the Liawep, a primitive tribe living deep in the jungle of New Guinea:

> "Although I had gone as an impartial observer, I knew the Liawep had seen me as something quite different, and on their territory their beliefs counted more than mine. With no recourse to science they believed that everything happened for a reason, that disasters were brought about by evil forces. Death, they believed, happened for a reason. When five people died in the storm they searched for a cause, and the finger pointed at me. . . . Somewhere inside me I knew there was truth in this. Despite protests from my rational mind, I felt culpable."

The explorer's mind ultimately is open to the unknown and the unfamiliar. It is open to whatever is, and this openness can bring great joy as well as pain. Dr. Thomas George Longstaff, who climbed and explored in the Himalaya half a century ago, put it this way in his 1950 memoir, *This My Voyage*:

> "Since happiness is most often met by those who have learned to live in every moment of the present, none has such prodigal opportunities as the traveler. . . . So long as he loses consciousness of self and is aware in all his senses of the present scene, almost any part of the world is as good as another. Mountain or desert, it is all one."

We are natural explorers, born to experience wonder. We start at birth exploring ourselves; babies spend hours observing their own fingers and toes. We gradually widen our circle of interest to include the people and the world around us. When my oldest son was five years old, we walked home from his school every day up the same Brooklyn street. I would pull him along, always impatient to get to the next thing. One afternoon, though, I gave in to his rhythms, his sense of adventure; I let him lead me home. He looked in windows, balanced on ledges, and clambered onto the shoulders of an enormous bronze bull that stood proudly in someone's front garden. My son was completely absorbed and entirely happy.

Exploration is as much a state of mind as a condition of place. Travel writer Lawrence Millman understands that context can sometimes force us to see something ordinary in a new way or simply guide us to appreciate it, and to see it more clearly:

> "In travel, as in life, context is everything. It's not likely that anyone would pay much attention to a traffic jam in Manhattan, whereas a traffic jam in Tiniteqilaq, East Greenland, would be a remarkable event, maybe even a disturbing one."

Some discoveries do occur in far-off places and alien surroundings. But other discoveries take place in our backyards, provided we are open to them. W.D. Wetherell sets out to explore a small stream behind the woods near his house in New Hampshire:

> "I'm not sure what prompted me to do it; it was close to dark and the stream was more shreds and tatters than definite flow. But the future has a magnetism all its own, and there in the twilight, in the mountain stillness . . . I was more attuned to it than usual, and it would have taken a deliberate act of violence not to have given in to its pull."

Still other discoveries are made when we journey inward and are present for what we find there. The novelist Harold Brodkey, dying, wrote these words:

> "I don't know if the darkness is growing inward or if I am dissolving, softly exploding outward, into constituent bits in other existences: micro existence. I am sensible of the velocity of the moments, and entering the part of my head alert to the motion of the world. I am aware that life was never perfect, never absolute. This bestows contentment, even a fearlessness."

When I set out to edit this collection, I held a rather narrow definition of exploration. I expected heroics—searches for lost cities, encounters with danger, great suffering—and I found all of that in these stories. John Long dives to the point of no return in an unexplored underground river in New Guinea. Fridtjof Nansen leaves his ship in 1895 to fight his way toward the North Pole by dogsled and kayak. Alvar Nunez Cabeza de Vaca in the early 16th century spends eight long years wandering the American southwest, subject to starvation, slavery, and loneliness.

But the stories offered much more than heroics. A broader definition of exploration began to form in my mind and in my heart. I came to agree with Eric Shipton, a great explorer of the 20th century, who wrote about these matters when he reflected on his life of adventure:

> "There are few treasures of more lasting worth than the experiences of a way of life that is in itself wholly satisfying. Such, after all, are the only possessions of which no fate, no cosmic catastrophe can deprive us; nothing can alter the fact if for one moment in eternity we have really lived."

What do these explorers seek—and what do they find? Like the rest of us, they crave adventure and its essential elements: contact and wonder. Shipton's friend and frequent companion H.W. Tilman was 79 years old when he was lost at sea on a sailing expedition to the Antarctic. Some years earlier, he offered this advice to a man who asked him about expedition logistics: "Put your boots on and go!"

—*Jennifer Schwamm Willis*

from The Lost Tribe
by Edward Marriott

Edward Marriott (born 1966) in 1993 became the first white man to visit the Liawep, a "lost tribe" living deep in the New Guinea jungle. He hoped to find there an innocence to contrast to the ills of his own modern culture. Instead he found men like Herod, the village's native hell-fire-and-brimstone missionary, and Fioluana, who had expectations of his own. This passage finds Marriott planning his departure, unaware that the Liawep aren't finished with him.

I had begun to notice great birds circling, gathering after the storms had passed. I imagined them to be vultures, but that bird was unknown here. They were huge and black-bellied, with wings like claws; a giant bat's reach. But then I saw one land and settle, smoothing itself, straightening its neck, looking out of the lower branches of a tree. It was just a hornbill. Somehow, up in the sky, it had looked like death approaching. Now that it was down I could place it. It fixed me with its tiny oil-black eyes, turned its head slowly, cocked its beak, and took off. The noise of its wings was like beaten leather.

The weather was willful, erratic. At night the rain wheeled about crazily, coming after dark then in flashes or quiet and steady, like sleep, through the night. Evelyn, Herod's daughter, was weakening and would not take milk. She lay in his lap, or close to his wife's breast, with the blackness outside, and mewled and puked warm, translucent vomit that dripped through the floorboards. Herod believed she had malaria and asked me if I had any medicine. I had quinine and

Fansidar, packed in Goroka, but Herod had already dispensed quinine and I hesitated to offer Fansidar, a malaria antidote of such power that, so I'd been told, to take it more than three times would be fatal. Evelyn was not yet one and, although she wouldn't eat, her eyes were still bright and her forehead felt peach-warm, not fevered. So I did not mention my Fansidar. Instead I gave her two chunks of my last chocolate bar, in goodwill, as she would be sure to reject it.

Herod's concern for Evelyn had overtaken his antipathy toward me. He wanted to take her to the doctor at Wanakipa and, desiring us as traveling companions, pressed us to start back, too. Despite all he had done to stand in my way, I began to warm to him again. My feelings for him had oscillated as violently as his moods—from belligerence to a kind of warped affection. He was no longer the obstructive priest, but the worried parent. He stared at the fire, twisting his beard in his fingers. It was a long way, he said, and with rains like these he did not want to walk it alone. Elisa would stay at Liawep and keep the fire burning.

The carriers made no secret of their boredom. While I scuttled around gathering information, they sat and smoked in Herod's house. They had no interest in the Liawep, only a morbid fascination with their history of brutality. Once or twice one had expressed an opinion, but these were couched as complaints. Why were we staying so long? Didn't I know the Liawep were dangerous? What did I expect them to do all day long?

Dunstan, taking my side, became less and less genial. "Look, you guys," he spat, after a week of such lethargy, "what are you doing sitting around?" No one stirred. Someone coughed, irritable. Since waking, none had moved more than a few feet. "Hey, come on! Why don't you go and make a garden for Herod? Why don't you go and hunt wild pig?" There was a dusty shuffle as they tailed out of the door.

Later I saw them sitting on a tree stump by the church. Only two—James, the boy, and Miniza, the oldest, with his goatee and easy giggle—had done as Dunstan said. They had taken a bushknife and were somewhere down the jungleside, slashing away at the undergrowth, clearing ground for a garden.

When we approached the others by the church, Dunstan said, "You're still here, you guys. What did I say?"

Only Dison, who had grumbled all the way from Wanakipa and was sure to grumble all the way back, spoke. "I washed *masta's* trousers this morning," he said, rolling a cigarette. I was *masta*: Dison was old enough to regard the old colonial form of address as appropriate; all the others called me by my name. I had not asked him to wash my trousers. Dunstan had suggested it, anything to alleviate Dison's lethargy. Now he was holding it against us. He coughed out *masta*, like something was stuck in his throat.

The tension eased after my food was finished; the carriers eyed me less resentfully. I had bought for three, and we were eight, so naturally I had rationed them more than I had Dunstan or myself. Dunstan had fewer qualms about this than I. He told me not to worry. "Before, *kiaps* ate their own food also. Only they lazy guys. Don't worry, we eat the rice and noodles."

Nonetheless, when we made tea, we'd pour the water into the three cups, squeeze out the tea bags, sprinkle on the powdered milk and pass them round. The same with the white plastic salt grenade. Each of them would pour out a tiny pyramid into the middle of their dark palms and lick it off in one lisp.

Since learning we were planning to leave, Fioluana's interest in me had become insistent, as if he was worried I'd escape without knowing the rest, everything he'd held out this long to tell me. He eyed me desperately. I was prepared to do whatever he wanted; I owed him that much.

He arrived at Herod's house early one afternoon. The day was hot and close, with a naked, eye-frying sun and a hot wind stirring, a sure sign of wild storms to come. I was sitting on Herod's veranda with Dunstan and Titus, enjoying the shade. Fioluana propped one leg on the veranda, attempting a macho carelessness, and screwed his mouth into a pained grin.

"You will come?"

This was my part of the bargain. He wanted me to see his house and discuss his future. His eyes were set on the far horizon, on the promised land described by Jack and Yasaro. I nodded, and followed him away, taking Titus as translator. Dunstan, who had begun slipping into lengthy homesick reveries, waved us away, his mind on his wife and sons and the baby that was due any day now.

Fioluana moved fast. The climb to his house, around the shoulder of the mountain, cut through untrod jungle. Without a path, I slipped constantly, flailing out for creepers to stop the slide. Fioluana beat ahead with a bushknife. I had to run to keep up. Twice, breathless, I skidded across the mud on plate-leaf. Further in, where the jungle was deepest and coolest, we came to a fallen trunk that crossed a gully. The memory of my previous falls came sweeping back. I rested while Fioluana went ahead, steeling myself.

Halfway across the trunk, Fioluana turned and swung me a vine. I caught it and pulled down; it stretched elastic from some treetop far above. I held it tight and walked fast along the trunk, determined not to fall too far behind. I scuffled along as Fioluana had done and jumped down the other side, congratulating myself at having escaped an indignity I had thought inevitable. My complacence came too early. I landed on sugary topsoil, both feet kicked from under me, my bottom hit the mud and I began to slide. Panicking, I flailed my arms furiously. A vine caught my elbow. Laughter bubbled from above.

By the time I had struggled to my feet and climbed to where I'd fallen, Titus and Fioluana had composed themselves, their mouths set politely straight but their amusement visible in their bright, vivid eyes.

"It's not far now," Fioluana reassured me, checking the skid marks up my side. "We will go slow."

Ten minutes later we broke into a sunny clearing. There were two houses in the center, one broken-backed, with only rafters and torn-out walls remaining and half the steps to the veranda missing. The other was newer, but by no means immaculate. One corner of the roof, an overhang, had been blown through, as if hit by lightning. Leaves drooped in a tattered fringe. A woman was sitting in the crippled house, her legs hanging through smashed floorboards. She hauled herself upright as we approached.

This was Fioluana's wife, the woman who'd been in church; her skittish tattoos, etched inky blue over each temple, marked her out. She watched us with narrowed pillbox eyes and greeted Fioluana timidly. She wore just a grass skirt, newly made, with the grasses still pale green. She crawled out from under the ruined house and led us across toward the other.

Fioluana became suddenly, nervously voluble. They were both his houses, he babbled, the old one and the new one. Abused by rain, which soaked and swelled, and by sun, which dried and cracked, bush houses did not last long. The older of the two was only five years old.

The newer, barely a year old, creaked and groaned as we climbed the steps. There was a tidemark, charred firesmoke where the roof met the wall. The door was tiny, and I had to crouch to pass through. In the buffer corridor lay an old dog, graying round the chops. It growled as I approached, but its heart was not in it and, by the time I stepped over its back, it managed only a benign sniffle.

Inside, the house was as dark as every other house I'd visited; faces blushed and bloated by the light of the fire, giant shadows loomed across the walls. Fioluana's wife was kneeling on the other side of the fire, her face turned away from the heat.

Fioluana rubbed his hands together: the novice lecturer on the first day of term. His daughters, he said, were the problem. They were sick. All the rain had brought fever. It made the air heavy and diseased. He spoke with conviction, forbidding dissent. He wanted to know what I would do.

I stepped around the fire to where his wife was hunched over. The younger girl cannot have been more than one; the other, still wearing the flowery dress she'd worn that first day in church, was older, perhaps four or five. They lay at their mother's feet, asleep. She lifted their heads gently, as if they were fragile china. They slept on, their woody skin pale and buffed with feverish sweat.

Their mother nodded at me, expectant. I touched their foreheads with my fingertips. I sensed the heat, busy and troubled, before my fingers reached the skin. I made reassuring noises; it would pass, I told her. Fioluana would not accept this: he knew I had medicine. I hedged.

I had already decided against handing over anti-malarial drugs to Herod's daughter, fearing she would not be strong enough to take the dose. The same applied here.

"Well, then, you must take them with you when you go back to the village. Tonight there will be a storm and they must not stay here." He stood very close, searching my face. "I am going hunting. You must watch over them until I return."

He took my elbow and guided me toward the door. The sunshine bleached the grass and the ruined house, throwing black shadows with straight-ruled edges. It was already well into afternoon, and the sky was clear. Storm? Today seemed the gentlest of all the days so far, the least likely to spoil thunderous.

He climbed down the steps. When I reached the ground he waved an arm under the house, indicating I should take a look. I kneeled. The earth was damp and fresh-turned. At the far side, half out of the shade, was a tobacco plant, the hairs on its leaves turned to gold scratches by the afternoon sun.

"What . . ." I half turned, unclear what I was supposed to notice, but Fioluana was already pressing in beside me, his hand gripping my shoulder. I could hear the soft rush of Titus breathing, as he crouched behind.

Fioluana dug his hand into the earth, squeezing the clod until it backed out through his fingers. This was Herod's doing, this piece of inexpert weeding. There had been plants here, ancestral tokens which brought luck in hunting. Herod had uprooted them all.

"And you let him?" I stared at him, astonished. Why not simply refuse? Herod could not have forced the issue; he would have been out-numbered.

"Because of my daughters." Fioluana shrugged helplessly. "Herod says if we go to church he will take them to Wanakipa when they are older. There is a school there. I want them to go to school."

I wondered if the handful of others who had appeared in church that first morning had been subject to similar bribery. With his methods exposed, Herod seemed a pitiful character, weak and corrupt. I worried over the violence of his coercion, the bold uprooting of all that held meaning. Had he left anything?

Fioluana pulled back and stood up in the sunshine, rubbing his knee like an old man soothing arthritis. He smiled bitterly. "We have thrown our things away." He made it sound as if the houses had been stacked with charms, objects to stroke for luck, everyday totems. There was one for each activity—pigs, health, children, hunting.

"Everything? You haven't kept anything?"

Fioluana held up his hand, silencing me. He led me around the other side of the house, to where the tobacco plant was stretching for the sun. He reached down and parted the leaves. Around its base was a dusting of tiny seedlings, as timid and fragile as day-old cress. These were from the plants Herod had ripped up; Fioluana had salvaged some seeds. When they were stronger he would replant them at the edge of the clearing. They would grow into a broad-leafed grass, with a gnarled ginger root. They smelled strong, he added, sniffing his fingers, chef like.

"I will not tell Herod they are there," he said, nodding grimly, as if already imagining the scene, Herod's frantic searching. "He will never find them."

Above us in the house I could hear Fioluana's wife moving about, collecting food for the night, wrapping her daughters for the journey. Fioluana stood up. There was one more thing he wanted to ask.

He delivered a speech so long, so punctuated by deliberate hand movements, that I imagined he had rehearsed it many times before. In his willingness to speak to me, to deal with my inquiries direct, he was, I reflected, unique among the Liawep. I remembered two men I'd met in the church a few days earlier: their reticence had been typical.

Nervous, they had wrapped their tobacco in leaves that were still too green and fizzed and spluttered near the burning tip. I had wanted to question them—these two were a father and son, and I hoped they would draw a picture of manhood and family life and the passing-on of knowledge, but all that came through was their fear of me. They had sat side by side, heads inclined identically, like two drab parrots.

The father looked the same age as the son, the only mark of his seniority a small bald patch, a sanded-away disc at his crown. His eyes were blunted: it was as if he had been looking at my eyebrows or my nose, afraid to fix me in the eye. He gulped air noisily as he spoke.

"A lot of people"—gulp—"are hiding from you, because you are a white man. White men"—gulp—"never come here." He had not understood why I was there; he thought I planned to "break up the mountain"; worse, that I had come to put them in jail. He covered his eyes with his fingers, like a child who believes no one can see him.

Fioluana was knowing, sophisticated, almost cynical by comparison. "We want modern things," he was saying, "things like you have, and like Peter. We would like a hospital, more bushknives and an airstrip." This, finally, was the real legacy of Yasaro's patrol: a want like the pain of hunger for the "better" life Yasaro had promised. Fioluana spoke greedily, his lips wet and full.

I stopped him: there was no room for an airstrip. But he had it all worked out. Had I not noticed that the houses were all built around the edge of the spur, that there were none in the middle, that the spur was fifty feet wide? Planes could land there.

He was overlooking the small matter of the church, however, that stood plumb in the middle of the clearing. I could not see Herod tolerating its demolition, and even then, even if he were persuaded, the strip would rate as an uncompromising test of a pilot's nerve, only navigable on the clearest, stillest days.

But to Fioluana these concerns seemed like excuses not to fulfil his wishes. With my white clout, I should effect change. "If we build an airstrip, we can move the church further up the mountain. No problem. You will tell the government these things?" Was this not Peter Yasaro's responsibility, rather than mine? But he said Yasaro had been away a year now and would not return. They'd built a helipad and still no one had landed. Besides, Yasaro wanted them to move, and they would not leave their houses and their gardens. So, under duress, I promised, because he wanted me to, and felt immediately hollow, knowing my word would carry no weight and that his hopes would go unrealized.

We were pitched against each other. The more I equivocated, the surlier he became. He clapped his hands and shouted up at the house. It was clear, after all the help he had given me, that he hoped for more than thin excuses.

His wife appeared on the veranda, the elder girl cradled close to her neck, arms pinned in, limp by her side. She trod gingerly down the narrow boards to the steps, hunkered forward protectively. She had slung a deep net bag over her shoulder and it hung heavy over the small of her back, weighted pregnant with the sleeping baby. She looked us over, then craned her head toward the sky above. The wind was picking up. She trod uncertainly on to the first step, muttering something over and over.

Titus bent toward me. "She says the storm is coming. She can feel it."

Fioluana stood at the bottom of the steps and lifted his sleeping daughter off his wife's shoulder on to his own. He held the back of her head and she slept through. He consulted intently with his wife. She nodded soberly, turning occasionally to us.

Fioluana walked over. "Titus," he said, "you will look after my daughters?" He did not look at me. Titus nodded dumbly, his mouth ajar. I wanted to ask Fioluana more—where did he plan to leave us? What should we do for his family?—but he was already striding toward the edge of the clearing, slashing ahead with the bushknife, scything impatiently with his free hand. His wife trod blindly after, following his tracks out of the clearing into the jungle.

We seemed to be returning a different way; although I was incapable of telling two stretches of jungle growth apart, we were definitely losing height now. On the way over we had kept high, dropping into Fioluana's clearing only near the end. So now we should have been climbing. I worried silently. Every ten minutes there would be a long arcing cry, the animal call of Fioluana far ahead, spurring us on.

Through breaks in the jungle canopy I saw clear blue sky being slowly tarnished by advancing storm clouds. It had looked so settled all day; now black was nosing in steadily from the north. Slowly, the forest was darkening, shadows and colors merging into a rotten mud-green.

Ahead there was a clearing; a bright patch a hundred yards on. There was rising smoke and voices. As we neared it seemed there were a hundred of them, all male, barracking and clamoring to be heard. Fioluana was standing silhouetted at the edge of the clearing, striking his bushknife into a tree trunk.

"This," he said when we reached him, "is where I stay. You go back to the village."

His wife reached up to him to take the girl, but she had already woken, her eyes wide and surprised. In the clearing there were fifteen, perhaps twenty men, some the hunters I'd met the first day, others I did not recognize. They were building a fire, milling around, turning toward us, laughing and jabbing their fingers in our direction. These were the men Fioluana was to join hunting. They would not return to the village for a day, perhaps longer, depending on their success. They were men together—hard-hearted, competitive, edgy.

I walked toward them, stepping clear of the deep grass, to say good-bye to Fioluana. This would be the last time I'd see him; we would likely leave the next day to begin the long journey back. I reached out to embrace him, but he recoiled and looked around anxiously. Confused, I offered my hand instead. He squeezed it once, then slipped free.

"You go now." He looked into the sky. "The storm is coming. Take my family to the village." He turned, paddling his hand in the air, dismissing me.

I watched him leave. He stopped by two men who were bent over the carcass of a pig, a rope around its neck and its face swollen tight with blood. They looked like cheesemongers with their long bushknives, heads down, bottoms in the air, tanket leaves in a spray like the tall feathers of ducks disappearing underwater.

Titus fussed with my sleeve, anxious to be off. But I wanted to watch for a bit longer, observe these preparations for the chase. Through this break in the jungle the view stretched for miles, down toward the valley which curled away with the river, a snake groove through the jungle. Again I noticed the sartorial debris of Peter Yasaro's patrol. He must have distributed clothes with abandon. There was one man, his face tarred with charcoal, under whose uniform profusion of tanket leaves, a pair of ladies' knickers, frilly-bordered, sagged over his muscled buttocks and bunched around his genitals.

Two men tore the carcass open, breaking its back, forcing the legs outward till the long rib fingers looked like the bones of a wrecked galleon. Another man was building a fire, making a firebox with rocks around a circle of cold ash. At his feet lay the squirreled body of a *cuscus*; half the arrow, torn off, was still bolted in its side. It had round, trusting eyes popping in surprise, and soft, expensive-looking fur, demerara-colored.

Their behavior puzzled me. Would they take this meat with them, or was it just for tonight, a kind of celebratory supper? I picked out two of the hunters I'd met before and approached to ask, but Titus would not follow. He folded his arms and ground his heel obstinately in the dirt.

The hunters were all watching me; they had stopped laughing now and were waiting to see what would happen. I smiled falsely, and began to back away, but my foot caught against a log. One of the butchers pulled his knife from where he'd wedged it in the earth, cut off a strip of pork and held it out toward me. Someone else laughed, a poisoned rattle. Everything moved very slowly, as if this had all happened before; far off, torn pennants of rain were sweeping across the mountains. I took the meat, inclining my head in gratitude. It smelled of death. The men stared at it with hungry dogs' eyes.

The smell clogged my nostrils. I passed it on to Titus, who took it greedily, forgetting for that instant the compulsion to leave. He stripped it with his teeth and ran his tongue over his lips. A crumb of fat lodged in his beard.

Fioluana stood up from the fire, a butchered joint, the skin burnt and peeling like a tire frazzled on scalding blacktop, gripped clublike in his hand. He trod toward me. I looked around for Titus, but he was leading Fioluana's wife to the edge of the clearing, the elder girl cradled against his shoulder. I began to retreat, fearing this unaccountable change in Fioluana was something to do with these men all around. It was his bald, macho edge, reserved for posturing in front of his fellows. It scared me.

He swept his hand across the sky, across the great sagging canopy of rain, plump and low, which was already spotting the dust at our feet. He grunted a gravelly order, and pointed toward Titus. I understood nothing of what he said, but the meaning was clear. I turned away.

Titus was waiting for me at the edge of the clearing, sheltering behind a wall-smooth tree-trunk. He walked on when I reached him, throwing short-tempered explanations over his shoulder.

"Em laik yumi go. Family bilong em sik. Ren i kamdaun."

But this was only the half of it. There was more here neither of us understood. Why had Fioluana turned so cold, so suddenly? Was it an anger born solely of disappointment? And the others—why had they acted as if they had never met me? It was as if I was a complete stranger once more. I might as well—for all they seemed to have absorbed— have been a miner out to exploit them or a government officer tracking down inmates to fill his jail cells. I had expected the stereotypical remote tribe, children touching my white skin, old women perplexed by my blue eyes, but the Liawep had confounded me. They feared me because they did not understand me; I feared them for the same reason. They believed I was there to break their mountain. I'd now heard that several times, from different sources. In deference, to counter this fear, I had treated the mountain as they did. I nodded to it as I walked up the village: the priest to his crucifix. And in truth it frightened me.

When I looked back one last time, Fioluana had turned to rejoin the butchers. Desperate now for an amicable resolution, I waved, trying to transmit a relaxed chumminess. Two of the men noticed me and alerted the others. They swung around and stared. I tried again. Fioluana lifted the haunch to his face and sank his teeth into the bubbled skin, tearing out pink, half-cooked flesh. He sucked it from the knuckle in oily swabs. I waved again, trembling now, but this time they mimicked me, giving precious, girlish waves. I felt beaten, overwhelmed, sick, and frightened.

I had arrived prepared to feel pity for them, to examine the changes being wrought on their lives, but they were stronger than me, more insolent and proud. They were too much for the neighbors they'd coolly massacred; they were too much for Herod, who struggled to make them believe; and they were certainly too much for me. Cast out, I felt an unexpected brotherhood with the priest. It was not what I'd expected to feel, but it was real enough. It gave me comfort that I was not the only outsider.

Now they were driving me out, laughing cruelly, drunkenly. "Bye! Bye! Bye!" they parroted. As we climbed into the jungle and I looked back one last time, one of the butchers stood up. He was shouting something, I couldn't hear what. In his left hand he flashed the bushknife. In his right he held the haunch, a hefty triangle of meat. His hand was dark with blood, running in oily tracks down his arm.

I ran into the jungle, after Titus, tripping in my panic to get away. Heaving asthmatically, I fell in behind Fioluana's wife climbing slowly on Titus's heels. We were heading straight up now and I'd lost my bearings. I had no idea where the village was, the river, or the mountain. Underfoot the ground crumbled wet and sugary, overlaid with leaf-mold and rotting pulp, the smell so strong and sweet it was like these were bones we were walking on, mashed to fertilize a vegetation already grown monstrous. I wanted to be free of it, to walk in a field of grass, but all around there was jungle, endlessly deep, endlessly high, closing in and cutting out the light. The sky was now as dark as over-ripe fruit, but still, somehow, the rain was holding off. Titus kept turning to soothe us. "Not far. *Longwe liklik.*"

We rested only once. Titus, ever the peacemaker, tried to engage Fioluana's wife in conversation, but she was too absorbed in her children, rocking the elder girl in her arms, her dress rucked up around mud-crusted knees, to respond. Empty eyed, he turned to me.

"I'm sorry. *Mi no save.*" He reached for my hand. "When I was a boy and the first white man came to my village, my father ran off to hide in the bushes. He covered himself in mud and stayed in the bushes until the white man had gone. It is the same here, with you. *Wankain long* Liawep. White men are different from black men."

• • •

It was dusk when we reached the village, the mountain buried under cloud, the jungle all around a deep black-green. Up the river valley there were brushes of rain, spilling from low, torn clouds. I prayed we might be spared the worst—it had held off this long.

Titus, convinced the storm was about to break, hustled Fioluana's wife and her children to the nearest house, fifty yards across from Herod's, near the bottom of the spur. I followed, eager to help, but felt already redundant. The woman opened her bag as she stumbled forward, lifting her naked baby clear. Titus set the other girl down at the base of the house's steps. She stood unsteadily, gazing with eyes gone smoky with fever. I remembered how bright she had been before, how she had flirted with such charm, as light as the breeze; now there was shadow around her eyes and her skin was dully bruised. I would bring her painkillers later, I decided. It was all I had that I was sure would not cause her greater harm.

As we lifted them on to the veranda, Titus stroked the back of her head. Her mother pushed past, steering her toward the door, clutching her baby underneath its bottom. At the door a face appeared—the old yellowed man, his skin still jaundiced with saffron mud, the color now dissolving in streaks down his cheeks. He looked from me to Titus, his eyes goggling enormous. As the woman approached, he retracted his tortoise neck and disappeared into the dark.

It was the noise I heard first—the hungry-belly rumble that always presaged the most violent storms. The rain started moments later. We ran for Herod's house too late, and were drenched in seconds.

Outside the house Herod was struggling in the mud. In his rush to get to cover, he'd thrust his Bible in his canvas satchel without buckling the strap and, as he'd swept the bag away, the Bible had fallen out, splayed open, face down in the mud. As we skidded past him he was cursing and groaning.

I stopped on the veranda and watched him peel it open; there were clayey globs stuck to the pages. He smeared it across his T-shirt, where it left a mud-red skid. We watched him, shocked.

"Go on, go inside," he muttered, angry at his clumsiness. Rain was spotting his shirt, flattening his hair, running down his forehead and into his eyes like sweat. He shook his head bitterly and followed us.

It was a dreadful night, which Herod spent in flight, running between his house and the other, fifty yards across the spur, where Fioluana's wife and his sick children lay coughing in the dark, around the fire. He began to turn delirious himself, repeating over and over that they had malaria. "Malaria, malaria, all of them malaria." Each time he returned to us, squeezed together, close to his fire, his eyes seemed madder, his face more drawn. His legs ran with mud and rain and his feet slopped dark wet footprints across the floor. He washed his hands obsessively, frantically scrubbing them under the curtain of water that poured from the roof.

We spoke very little. Elisa, Herod's wife, was waiting for two boys to return from hunting. She became increasingly fretful. "They're young boys," she kept repeating. "Where are they?" Herod soothed her, saying they were not so young and they knew the jungle and had often hunted alone. "But what if they get caught?" she butted in. "Or what if the bridge falls in? What then?" She seemed constantly close to tears.

I worried about the river filling with rain, turning wild. The niggardly Dison, the most cautious of the carriers, wanted to know what we'd do if the bridge was down. So far none of us had dared bring this up, as there was no answer. If the bridge had collapsed we could not cross the river; it would only take us under. I felt too weak to swim floodwater.

"We could build a raft," Dunstan suggested. This had become a refrain. He pushed his baseball cap back on his head, the peak cocked skyward. Fear made him look like a young boy. It was comforting to discuss this, something real. All else fogged and dissolved under scrutiny. I tore a piece of paper from my notebook and dug around for a pen and drew the kind of raft in which I wanted to cross the Lagaip.

It looked more like a jetty, adrift from its moorings. At the front, two tiny stick figures prodded the water optimistically with long poles. The sides were tree trunks, bound one on top of the other. The middle was a vast expanse of planking, the size of a small dance floor. It looked unlikely to capsize.

Dunstan squinted at the picture and half shook his head, half nodded. "We'll see. Tomorrow we see." He returned to his cigarette, which had cooled. He had not smoked when we set off. His wife hated it. Now he was smoking as much as the carriers, but his lungs were unused to the uncured roughness of bush tobacco and he coughed windily.

"I'm not going on your raft," Dison said abruptly. He was sitting back from the fire, his face in shadow. "Dangerous." He almost whispered.

"And what will you do, then, when the bridge is down and we cross on a raft?"

"*Mi no save.* I can't swim."

I kept looking at my watch, obsessively, unnecessarily. It was eight thirty-four. Lightning was somewhere close, the gap between light and sound was narrowing. It had been far off for some time; now it was closing in on us. The rain was hissing and boiling on the roof and drilling wormholes in the mud.

I stood up and walked to the door. It was utterly black outside. Fifty yards across the square I could see the rain-blurred outline of the other house, where Herod was praying for the sick children. I squinted into the gloom, but could only see what was near, the ditch around Herod's house stirred up and flowing, thick like gravy.

Then, from clouds so low they seemed to squat on us, lightning spat out. It was close, just up the jungleside, on the edge of the mountain. The thunder broke slowly; I could feel the shape of it, edgy and precipitous, like crumbling rock face. It shook the house and I felt it in my chest, tight like a drumskin. The lightning tore the sky and I could see every house, the church's roof flattened, running with water, streaming off the fringes, and Herod, caught in the strobe, electric white, midstride, running back across the mud, crouched over, his Bible crooked under his shirt. Then it went black again and there was only the slap of Herod's feet in the mud and he appeared, suddenly, in the firelight. He jumped on to his veranda beside me, shaking himself like a dog, water spraying off his hair, pouring down his face. "My God," he said, heaving. "What a night."

I followed Herod inside. No one spoke; they were staring into the fire. Only Dunstan looked up. "What do we do?" he said.

"I don't know. Pray?" It was only half a joke. I had prayed ever since we'd entered the jungle. I would twist my wedding ring and pray that I would see my wife again; I prayed that we would bring good, not evil; I prayed we would all get out alive.

Following the etiquette, Dunstan prayed first for the sick children, that they would sleep through this night and wake to sunshine in the morning. He prayed for Herod's baby, Evelyn. He thanked God for our food and for enabling us to meet the Liawep. Then he prayed for us, for our safe return home, for our deliverance.

Outside, the sky moaned and heaved and split open and the lightning carved through the night. It was closer. Elisa covered her baby's ears too late and Evelyn started wailing. Titus had his fingers in his ears and was shaking his head. Herod stood up again, unable to relax.

"I'm going over to the other house," he said, the Bible in his fist. "If I don't go and pray, they will die."

Herod had complained about this house before; the family that lived there was "like stone" to his message, and had never been to church. Cynically, it looked as if he was using Fioluana's daughters' illness as an opportunity to take the others his God, with the drama of the wild storm as backdrop. This time Titus and Dison ran across with him. They had sat too long and Titus, I fancied, had become rather fond of Yawali, Fioluana's elder, flirtatious daughter, whom he had carried through the jungle earlier. He wanted to hold her hand and nurse her.

The lightning was becoming more frequent. It seemed to center on the mountain, building with intent. It never seemed possible it would just blow over; there was something evil in it that silenced us all and was turning Herod into a madman, King Lear in the mud outside, railing against it. Dunstan, with superb irrelevance and a gravity that embarrassed me, was telling Andrew that I no longer wished to be called *masta*. I had told Dunstan this two days earlier. It was too late to change anything; I was simply sharing my feelings. I did not feel like a *masta*, that was all. I never wanted him to turn it into a command.

Dunstan had nodded and said he understood. "Yes, it means rich foreigner, and you are not rich foreigner." Now I could hear him say the same to Andrew. "You must not call Edward *masta*. It is for patrol officer or rich foreigner." Ironically, the more I had shied from the role, the more Dunstan had assumed it. The less I exercised my will, the more he cracked the whip. He had become quite a bully. "Why haven't you made a fire?" he would spit, or, "Cook now. We want to eat." This time Andrew puzzled over his words. His cigarette tailed a thin blue line to the ceiling. "Yes," he repeated, "not *masta*." He looked over Dunstan's shoulder and saw me watching him. He spoke more softly and his words sank in the storm.

It was nine-thirty. My watch was steel, with a link strap, and I wondered vaguely whether it would attract lightning. I unclipped it and laid it on the floor. I wanted the night to be over, but it had only just begun. If I went to sleep, perhaps I would wake when it had passed. It seemed a good idea. I left Dunstan and stepped into our room, untied my shoes and slipped, fully dressed, into my sleeping bag. I lay on my back with my head on my clothes, packed into a roll, socks gray and gritty with mud, trousers and T-shirts with the fug of the jungle on them, the clog of warm compost and decay.

I lay there, thinking about the smoke Herod had seen curling from the top of the mountain. Perhaps the mountain was volcanic. I'd once seen pictures of Mount Sakura-jima in Japan, with a thorny crown of broken-veined lightning, a mad Einstein head of hair. The swirling ash, I remembered, generates its own electricity. Perhaps that was happening here.

Over our heads the clouds heaved open again. Lightning bull-whipped. Please, into the jungle, I prayed. Save us. Beside the fire Dunstan and the others were silent again, waiting, while the night spewed and foamed.

I tried to remember what I knew about lightning. There was some comfort in facts. It loves golfers, I knew, especially the way they stand alone on the fairway, raising steel clubs to the sky, or huddle under trees when the rain comes down. It looks out for swimmers, too, in open-air pools. Lifeguards watch the storm approach and clear the pool when it's a mile off. Each flash crackles with hundreds of millions of volts. Planes usually escape, singed a little at wingtip or on the ends of their noses; the current passes through them to ground.

Ball lightning is more of a mystery. At the Royal Astronomical Society in London on 25 January 1952, members held what they billed as a "geophysical discussion devoted to the subject of thunderbolts." It was an excitable meeting. One speaker stood up and described a plane trip he had made in the late summer of 1938. He had been flying over the Toulouse Gap in a BOAC flying boat, on the way to Iraq, when a fireball flashed in through the cockpit window, burned off the pilot's eyebrows, burst through the forward passenger cabin and exploded in the rear cabin, just beside his seat. At the same time, the hotel in Marsellies where the passengers were to spend the night was hit by lightning and burned to the ground.

I lay inside the mosquito net. It seemed safer, somehow, sagging over my middle, almost touching my face; like being in a coffin. I think I slept, despite the fury outside. It was like trying to sleep backstage at a heavy-metal concert or, worse, lying down on stage, in front of the drum kit, and wondering why sleep didn't come as the guitarists axed out colossal earthquake chords. The thin bamboo wall behind my head was soaked. Water was coming in everywhere. The floor, too, was damp, but it was hard to see whether it had leaked from above or been sucked up from below. Herods house was hammered into the side of the mountain, just off the edge of the spur, and with each thunderclap it seemed to slide further downhill, toward the edge of the jungle. I slipped into half-sleep, dreaming of the bridge, of finding a lifeboat by the river with four scrubbed lifeguards who would guide us up the gangplank to safety.

I woke to a thunderbolt so violent I thought lightning had torn into Herod's house. I sprang from my bed and became entangled in mosquito net, tearing it away from me, off my face, only to find it manacled around my feet when I tried to stand. Across the square, through the fuzz of the rain, there was a single, demented scream. Dunstan and the carriers stood up from the fire, chattering in panic. As I struggled with my shoes I could hear them clatter to the door, trying to work out what had happened. Someone was out in the rain, running our way, screaming as loud as the thunder. He stamped on to the balcony and I could hear it was Herod, shouting as if he was in a hurricane and we were offshore: he shouted like a deaf man would shout, unable to hear himself. Still half drugged with sleep, it made no sense. Was he berating the carriers for having soaked up his hospitality but given nothing in return? And if so, why would he choose now, late at night, as we were being tossed about by the storm? His screaming sparked hysteria. Dunstan and Titus tried to shout above him, to make themselves heard, and I could hear Elisa moaning, "God, oh God." Then, as the thunder broke again, they ran out into the storm, shaking the house as they jumped, leaving only Elisa's pained thin cry and me, struggling to free myself from yards of cream muslin.

Moments later Dunstan was back alone. He bent down in the doorway to our room, blocking out the light from the fire. He was in silhouette. His beard was dark, oiled, tight; I could see every hair. "Edward, Edward." His voice was high-pitched, unbroken. He spoke in a halfway whisper, insistent. "There's been lightning and it struck the other house, the one with the sick children." He caught his breath, sucking in air in great gulps, wheezing with the smoke.

"The children?"

"Fioluana's wife, his daughter, three more *pikininis*. All dead."

"Fioluana's family?" This was not happening.

"I'm frightened," he said. He took off his baseball cap. I touched the back of his hand. It was cool.

He stared at the floor, pulled at his beard. "You, you stay asleep," he said. I was fully dressed, but he couldn't register this: his mind was scorched by what he had seen.

The noise seemed to have abated a little. It was still raining, but quieter and steadier. There was still lightning but the thunder jumbled like loose machinery and felt more like background, less like artillery, less like looking down the barrel. Herod came smashing back into the house as I stood up. He slipped on a wad of mud and hit the doorpost. He was still shouting, pointing to his ears this time, shaking his head.

"Come on!" He waved his arms wildly. His tongue was pink and glistening. He spat as he shouted. He was uncontrollable. "They need help, come on!" And he turned and swung on the doorpost and ran out into the storm again. Dunstan followed him and I followed Dunstan and suddenly we were out there, in complete darkness, racing across the mud toward the other house, flogged by the monsoon-warm rain. I brought my flashlight and the white spot made everything around it blacker. I trained it on Dunstan, on his frantic pedaling heels, and ran.

Inside the house there was no fire. Herod was shouting and pointing. I handed him the flashlight. He aimed it at the roof. The beam veered around crazily, like an anti-aircraft spotlight.

"There!" he yelled. "It come in there!" For a second he held the flashlight still. There was a tear in the roof, like a rock had fallen through, but singed and tasseled like burnt straw at the edges. He swung the torch down to the fire. "BOOM!" He raised both arms to describe the explosion. The light skidded across the roof.

I made Herod shine the flashlight at the floor; I'd seen something. He pointed it and its beam picked out two small bodies, on their backs, their hands half raised to their faces, frozen in death like bodies at Hiroshima. Behind them, against the wall, was the old man, his head sunk in yellowed hands and his back curled forward, the back of his neck visible, the skin pulled tight and onion-shiny over his spine, rocking himself slowly "I'm sorry. I'm so sorry," Dunstan mumbled. He stood behind me, rubbing his forehead. "I'm so sorry for what has happened."

Closer to us, almost at our feet, was the body of a woman. For a second I failed to recognize her. She, too, was on her back, legs apart, feet near the fire. My foot was near her head. I stepped back. Herod shone the light on her face. Her eyes stared. Blown petals of white ash covered her skin and the floor. Beside her lay the naked bodies of two little boys, three or four years old, clutching each other. The woman wore only a grass skirt; her breasts were full and nipples rude and pronounced as if she had been breastfeeding. Then I noticed the starfish tattoos on her temples: Fioluana's wife. Her mouth, which earlier had been pursed with the worry of the coming storm and her shivering, fevered daughters, now hung wide open, white ash icing her lips and tongue. I looked around for her children, but was distracted by the sight of another woman, crouched against a far wall, rocking a tiny baby I guessed was Fioluana's youngest. The woman rolled her head, mumbling incoherently. Herod bent down to talk to her. She did not look at us. She wore a T-shirt that looked burnt, but it could have been dirt. Five people dead. Only three survivors.

"I was there," Herod said. He had calmed down and was no longer screaming. "There, in the door. I pray for the sick children. Then BOOM! BOOM! This light comes through the roof like a waterfall. BOOM!" His Bible was on the floor where he had dropped it. Through the hole in the roof rain fell like sequins in the flashlight's beam, spangled, sprinkling the ash, spitting on the last hot logs. One of the little boys, who lay with his arm over the other's waist, had broken his nose. It was crooked, squashed sideways, a teardrop of black blood in the nostril.

I grabbed the flashlight back, desperately hoping that Dunstan had been mistaken and that Fioluana's elder daughter had survived, but I was unable to fix on anything; faces loomed at me, puffy-lipped and blue-veined, like drowned men dragged to the surface. I felt Dunstan's hand on my shoulder; I must have been swaying, about to fall. Then, as I turned, I saw her, half underneath another girl, on the far side of the exploded fire. It was as if they'd been thrown into each other's arms. Her dress was askew, crumpled like burnt paper, torn half off her neck; the soles of her feet were flayed and bleeding.

Minutes passed. Herod ran the light around, like a circus master of ceremonies at his chamber-of-horrors sideshow. No one spoke and no one moved and there was something reverent about that, although I knew I was intruding, and I grieved for Fioluana—both his pretty ones, only the baby saved. Our thoughts went no further than the house; we stood silent, remembering. Then the storm came back. Lightning lit the house through the hole in the roof, then thunder, like the start of a rock slide, shook us to action. "We can't stay here." Dunstan turned for the door. "Not in this house."

Herod held out his hand to the woman by the wall, but she looked at where the fire had been, and where the rain fell softly, and did not respond. Her hands were held around the baby's chest, circling it with no break. The baby's eyes were open and staring at somewhere above her head. Herod reached down and took her hand. He slipped his fingers between hers and the baby's belly and lifted her hand away. "You must get up," he coaxed softly. "It is not safe here." She shook her head but Herod persisted. He reached down and took the baby and her hands reached up with it, even though it was not hers. Herod lifted it away, above her head, and gave it to Dunstan. Then he reached for her hands again. There was dust in her hair, as if she'd been near a falling building. She let Herod lift her and, when she was standing, fell back against the wall again. There was no urgency: she moved slowly, as if half frozen. She had calmed Herod. We were in the center of the storm, still. Destruction had brought an uncertain quiet.

"You come, too," Herod said to the old, yellowed man, who was coiled up into himself against the far wall. Herod had the light in a pool at his feet and he walked through the white confetti ash. The man was the grandfather of Kesime, the other girl who lay dead at his feet. He looked as if his world had been destroyed, that nothing remained. Herod cupped his hand around the back of his neck and I saw for the first time his tenderness. "Come, come, you come," he repeated, urging him to his feet by placing one hand under his armpit. The man responded as if to his mother's touch and rose weightlessly.

I stood and watched like a useless voyeur at an accident. Herod handed me the flashlight and told me to go first. I stepped out across the pale dusted boards on to the dark veranda. The rain had brought cold and I shivered. Herod ushered the broken people with him, the man and woman who had still not straightened, who bowed their heads against the storm. Dunstan followed with the tiny baby cradled into his shoulder, its face bright and pale. For seconds we stood together under the veranda as rain spewed off the roof's grass fringe, inches from our faces. Lightning barked out again to our left, halfway up the mountain. It lit the church and the mudbath across which we'd have to run to reach Herod's house. Everything was glossy with rain.

I expected Herod to run, but he walked slowly, holding the two sur-vivors on either side, cupping their elbows. I wanted to run back, but Herod asked me to walk ahead with the light. Dunstan alone scurried, bent over, his head and hands covering the baby from rain. I heard a clank and creaking of floorboards as he reached Herod's house. The droplets of rain fell fat and heavy on my head as we walked. We were soaked within seconds. I looked back once but Herod swept me on with his hand. I kicked out at every step to test the way, treading tenta-tively, but kept skidding sideways, the beam of the flashlight arching overhead and dissolving in the gray underbelly of the clouds, low over us like a marquee filled and sagging with rain.

Dunstan was handing the baby to Elisa as I entered and switched off the light. The carriers looked up at us for explanation. Then Herod walked in, followed by the two survivors. The woman looked up at the fire and collapsed on to her knees, then her side. She lay with her face against the floor, close to the fire, lips pursed fatly. In the light of the fire her face seemed blackened by smoke, as if she'd rubbed herself in charcoal. One breast hung low from her T-shirt, thin stretch lines in suspension. Her moans sounded as though her insides were creaking, straining to keep whole. Titus reached his long, thin arm out across the fire to touch her, but she drew her shoulders up and pulled her arms into her body.

The man wouldn't move from the doorway, even when Herod beck-oned him over to the fire. When at last he did, I could see that his back had been torn by the lightning. The skin hung away from the flesh like a strip of leather, exposing a wound as big as an outstretched hand in the small of his back, just above the tanket belt. It sweated like meat on a butcher's slab. He clutched one of the fire's corner posts as he lowered onto a tucked-under leg, keeping his hand on the post and laying his forehead on the back of his hand. He moved very slowly. He sat there, his eyes filmed over, unseeing, all vision inside, burnt tracks in his memory. The rain had made his chalked face run, like mascara tears. His granddaughter lay covered in white ash in the house on the other side of the village, her eyes still open and her arms raised to cover her face.

Out of respect for their loss no one spoke. The carriers' fear seemed to be that the lightning would now hit Herod's house. They'd absorbed his description of the explosion, the way the thunderbolt smashed through the roof and detonated in the fire, and now they were scared.

Against the fuzz of rain and the split and rumble of thunder the only sound was the pale whine of Fioluana's tiny naked baby, held close by Elisa, who had passed Evelyn, miraculously asleep, into Titus's big hands. She was too young to register what had happened: she just knew that her mother was not with her. No matter how she was rocked and soothed, she mewled like a lost kitten.

I was aching to obliterate this night. It was now well past midnight and I wanted to sleep, to wake up the next morning and leave. But it seemed too selfish at such a time, and instead I dug in my rucksack for my painkillers, the yellow prescription-only torpedo lozenges I'd been promised would dull even a broken leg, and handed them round. "Good medicine," Herod said, leaning over the woman on the floor. She did not move and he placed the pill between her lips and raised her head off the floor and waited for her to swallow, stroking her throat and speaking softly.

I gave one to the old man in front of me and he rolled it in the bowl of his palm, then pressed his hand to his face and leaned back against the pillar. "What about his back?" Dunstan asked.

What did I have to treat a back flayed by lightning? Clearly some kind of measure was required. I unzipped my First Aid kit and rummaged inside. It had been designed for day trips to the Lake District, for grazed knees and thistle-pricked fingers: I had not envisaged disaster. There were two long bandages, rolled tightly, secured with a square of adhesive bandage; a jangle of safety pins; a tube of Savlon; three Band-Aids; and there, at the bottom, a surgical dressing. It was wrapped in greaseproof paper, which gave it a 1960s feel, and was grayed and frayed at the edges. I cut it in half with nail scissors, the edge jagging into tiny crescents, and stretched it for size over the wound. I cannibalized the Band-Aids, cutting away the adhesive ends and throwing the spongy, honeycomb middles into the fire where they bubbled. I squeezed pure white coils of Savlon on to the wound and gently spread it over, covering the pink rawness. Dunstan sat beside me. Unusually, no one else showed interest. I found it therapeutic. I did not know why the carriers were so quiet or why they would not look at me, but feared they linked me in some way with the lightning. I busily played the doctor, trying to banish these thoughts. I tacked the dressing in place with the ends of the Band-Aids and it billowed outward, sagging away from the skin. It was a hopeless job.

Behind the house, not far down the jungleside, there was a crack and roar of a tall tree tumbling on to the canopy, taking others with it. It was not accompanied by lightning. I did not understand this storm. I did not understand why, when there were higher points, the lightning had hit the house. There were trees nearby that were higher; most exposed was the church. Even Herod's house was isolated. I moved closer to the fire. Herod and Elisa looked across the logs at me. "The other house," I said. "Why did lightning hit the other house?"

"Because," Herod replied, like one who has always known the answer, "they didn't believe in God."

"I'm sorry? You were in there praying, Herod, when the lightning struck. Your God was in there, too, surely?"

"I hadn't started when the sky came down."

"But still, you were there. You're God's man, Herod."

"I hadn't started to pray."

"But the people. You're saying it was their fault?"

"They do not believe in God. Yes, it is their fault. For months their hearts are like stone. The people in that house still follow the old ways."

"So He fries them. Some fucking God you have, Herod."

"What you say?" I'd spoken in English. His lips were wet and his eyes were burning. He was snorting through his nose. He understood the thrust, if not the words.

"I'm going to bed." I stepped back into our room, lay down on the mat and listened to the storm. The lightning had moved on. I could hear it crackling in another valley. Would it come back? Wasn't five dead enough for one night? I had closed off my capacity for horror to such an extent that the most real threat to us had not yet crossed my mind. Until Dunstan voiced it. From the anxious pitch of his voice it had been brewing for some time.

"Edward." He kneeled in the doorway. "I'm frightened." Until now, I'd unburdened my fears on him three times a day. This was the first time he'd expressed his. I sat up and looked at him, but the fire was behind him and his features were in darkness. He placed one hand on the floor to steady himself.

"The dead mama and the dead *pikininis*. The Liawep will blame it on us." He was whispering, trying to sound relaxed, but his voice quavered. "We come here, and this happens. I'm frightened they will come for us."

This made perfect sense. I'd blocked out the thought with the immediacy of the survivors' needs, but there was an awful logic to it. It would compound Fioluana's distrust of me; I was thankful, cowardly, that I would not have to face him. Against him and the hunters we would have had no chance. I tasted sourness at the back of my throat. Instinctively I put my hand to my mouth.

Dunstan reached out for me. "I shouldn't have said anything, but we people say what we think." He paused, and added ludicrously, "But don't worry. You go to sleep."

He apologized again, but the thought was out and free and could not be locked away. It was his country, he had grown up with revenge and death and I'd grown up with democracy and dialogue. My instinct counted for nothing. I suddenly saw our time here for what it was. The Liawep had not wanted me to come; they had not wanted to answer my questions; they did not regret my departure. And now this. Everything happens for a reason, they believe. This had happened because we were here. That was what they would believe and now I, too, feared it was true. At home I would have dismissed these thoughts as foolish superstition, but such skepticism now seemed empty and irrelevant. Nothing was the same here. I lay back on top of the mosquito net and it tore away from the wall and flattened under me. The storm had stilled. In the quietness I could hear the carriers talking.

"Now He's killed them, He's stopped," Dunstan said, getting off his knees.

The carriers' voices were rumbles too low for me to understand. Only later, when we were safe, did Dunstan tell me of their discussion. Andrew and Titus were both set on going, disappearing into the jungle right then, five hours before dawn. They were convinced that, when dawn came and the news of the deaths ran around the village, the warriors would come for us. Dunstan defied them to leave. "We're men too," he had said. "If they come we can look after ourselves. If they want to throw a bushknife at us, we can throw one at them, too." He had persuaded them that the warriors would not hear of the deaths until they returned from hunting. That gave us a day's start. I lay down knowing nothing of this. To me the whisper of their voices was soothing, but I wished they were lying near me. Only the smell and warmth of other human beings would keep off the fear of death. I was convinced, as my brain turned in on itself and every thought curdled, that I would not live, that I would be carved up. What would I do if they burst in now? I knew I would not fight. For the first time I wished they were model Christians, with love and forgiveness tattooed across their knuckles, stamped on their foreheads. In that shameful moment I wished that Herod had had more success.

I slept for minutes, perhaps half an hour. I woke violently from a ghoulish dream, feeling my face. Dunstan was bending over me. "Shhh, shhh, you were shouting out." I struggled to sit up and found I had dribbled down my chin. I looked up at him. He reached out his hand. "We leave today before light, yes?" he said.

"That's not right. If we run it's like we know it's our fault." Already I was feeling like a fugitive.

Dunstan disagreed. "If we stay it's the same. Why would we stay and say sorry if it wasn't our fault?"

"But they'll catch us. There's no way we can outrun them in the jungle. It's their jungle, not ours."

He snorted. "It's our jungle, not yours. We are men, too. We can run."

This was the result of a compromise hammered out with the carriers. We would all leave together, but not until dawn. If we went when it was dark, Dunstan had told them, we'd easily get lost. They had agreed, but throughout the night they had pestered to be off.

Herod was elsewhere. In the stillness after the storm he sat in the other house, conducting a sleepless vigil with the bodies, praying for their souls. He did not move them or close their eyes. He left them where they were. He knew that, in the morning, the house would be full of people crying and staring and that, for a week, the dead would not be touched.

We all prayed that night. The hypocrisy no longer bothered me. While Herod's wife prayed for the life of the tiny baby she held and Herod prayed that his sinners would be spared damnation, I prayed for our safe return. No one slept; for almost five hours we sat around the fire, blindly feeding it logs, uttering banalities. Near the tail end of the night we had a visitor. The beaten-out bark that served as a door shifted and grated on the floor and I saw hands at the top, fingers folded over, lifting it up and across.

It was the chief. He came into the room and looked across our faces; he was the sheriff, his cell full of cattle rustlers. But his face was set and I could not see whether he felt grief or anger, whether he sympathized or held us to blame. I became suddenly edgy he'd brought the hunters, back early from the hunt, and that our time had come, but he was alone. He stood and watched us, then stepped behind us, around the wall, to Herod's bedroom. He bent over and his tanket leaves shuffled.

There was a clink as he picked up Herod's kerosene lamp, its glass fogged and oil-speckled. He held it up and the metal tinked as he turned and left the house with it.

A long while later he returned it, stepping in, just around the corner of the door, not looking at anyone. The lamp glowed faintly and there was a thin splish of kerosene as he put it down, lowering the handle slowly, careful it did not rap the metal base. He left it glowing and, as he turned, his shadow lurched across the ceiling.

At five, my brain fogged with a night of adrenaline and guilt and fear, Dunstan announced our departure. There was no sign of dawn; light would not start leaking into the night until six. Dunstan, calm until now, became frantic, bundling his clothes, my clothes, anything he could see, into his rucksack. The sudden panic made no sense.

"We go now. Now, before it is light." He was trying to force one foot into a still-laced baseball boot. He was ramming it in, over the tongue. He gave up furiously, throwing it to the bottom of his rucksack.

The carriers saw us move and were up and ready. They had nothing to pack—no changes of clothes, no sleeping bags, no soap powder. Their supplies of tobacco and newsprint were close to exhausted and would be stuffed into a pocket, or under a belt. Titus had a string bag, bulbous with sweet potato, hoarded hopefully.

Herod shuffled back in. He sat down next to the fire, took a stick and pushed around in the ashes, but the glow had gone and he turned up only light puffs of cool ash. He looked drained and broken. Through these days I'd felt everything for him—most often hatred and contempt—and now my sympathy surprised me. Though I despised his primitive evangelism, I could see he was suffering.

"Herod," Dunstan said. He broke off his desperate packing and leaned over. "We're going now, brother."

Herod grunted. He was drawing a circle in the ash, around and around the same groove. He'd dropped his plan to come with us: he'd stay until the dead were buried.

"We think that if we stay they will come for us," Dunstan said.

"True," Herod said. He did not look up.

Dunstan led the way almost at a run, quitting the house while I was still fighting with my rucksack, forcing the drawstring tight over a tangle of clothes and debris it was too dark to identify. I thrust the bag, straps flapping, at Andrew, and he bent down and reversed his arms through it. I followed him out, the last one to leave. Dunstan was already out of sight.

It was dark, but morning was coming. It was the torpid half-light of dusk, only colder and more lifeless. A gray light was leaking upward in the east, into clouds which sat low over the mountains. Behind us as we fled was Mount Woraitan, hidden in heavy cloud. Everything hung low, the color of old meat.

I broke into a run, struggling in the darkness and mud. As the ground dropped away into the jungle I looked back one last time. I could see the roof of the house, its wound like a soldier's chest shot open. Herod stood alone in the middle of the helipad, watching us go. His arms hung by his side; his face was undertaker-grim, camouflaged with mudsmears. I looked for grief, anger, even relief at our departure, but he was beyond emotion. I raised my hand to wave, but he seemed not to see me.

We ran and ran and ran. For an hour or more it was dark in the jungle, until the morning warmed slowly through. We struggled to see in the half-light and the mud was thick and cold and cloying. On the way to the Liawep we had stopped to point out flowers, or birds, or stamped-in pits where wild pigs had rolled, but now we moved silent and grim. Ahead I could see the carriers twisting down the mountain, their backs issuing steam, breath hissing and heaving, a mule train on a cold, high morning. Dunstan was far down, out of sight, speechless and determined. We stopped for the first time two hours later, at the bottom of the mountain, down by the river that fed the Lagaip. I felt ludicrously awake, my ears like antennae. I kept hearing whispers in the jungle about us, or the shuffle of wet leaves, and jerked about, expecting to see warriors charge out of the bush.

Dunstan looked over my shoulder, hunted. Above, the sky was lightening. "We have to keep moving."

"Do you think they're after us?"

"Not yet, but soon." I did not like to see him like this. I missed his jokey carelessness.

The first day of flight was the worst. Along the river, down to the Lagaip, the banks had crumbled and what had been dry land was now part of the river, split into grass islands and trees, water swirling a foot up their flanks. I waded after the others, emerging on to land again with my shoes splodged with leech blood and leeches hanging like deflating balloons from my ankles. By early afternoon we reached the Lagaip and passed the camp where we'd built a shelter on our last night in the bush.

The bridge, incredibly, was still there. It had slipped perceptibly and hung, disheveled, in the water, probably a foot under in the middle. It did not look safe, but it was there. Dunstan and the carriers were grinning madly.

We sat and rested. I handed around my glucose candy. The carriers thanked me but waited for me to go first. The candy dissolved tastelessly and fizzed like sherbet. They swallowed theirs hurriedly, wiping their mouths on the backs of their hands.

Dunstan rolled himself a cigarette. "I thought they might try to cut us off, up there." He looked past me, up the mountain. "Now we are at the river they can't cut us off. They have to catch us."

I took off my shoes to cross the bridge and laced them around my neck. In the middle, the water came up to my knees. When I lifted one foot to step forward it was knocked sideways by the current. The bamboo underfoot was slimy and almost free of support. The vines that lashed it to the handrails had mostly swollen and split away. Standing on the far pylon, I looked at the joints. The criss-cross of vine ropings were all coming loose. The bridge was unraveling itself. When the others crossed, it floundered and creaked. It was a sinking ship, half down, the deck swimming.

We climbed and fell and talked little. I followed closely behind Andrew, or Dunstan, or whoever was leading. At one point we were joined by a hunter, who carried his arrows in one hand and a small, glass-eyed pig in the other. He climbed with his toes deep in the mud and I walked right on his heels. He smelled of firesmoke and week-old sweat.

Through the jungle I saw shadows, like deer moving through twilight woodland, only half there. I shouted ahead, for the carriers to stop, but when they turned, the shapes stilled. At the front of the line, Dunstan was growing impatient. *"Hariap. Yumi go."* He leveled his bushknife through a tangle of creepers and stamped on.

I peered again through the gloom, convinced I'd seen the Liawep that they'd finally caught up to us. Fifty yards off, through hanging vines and mushrooming vegetation, I saw movement again. I ran after Dunstan and pulled him to a stop.

"They're here," I heaved. "Look."

He turned. The shapes were clearly men—fifteen, perhaps twenty—coming straight at us.

"Oh God." Dunstan scratched his head frantically.

"Quiet," Titus broke in, crouching down. *"No ken mekim nois.* It's the hunters."

There was no use running, as they were twenty yards off and closing. I was convinced they had come for us, and yet their voices were raised, almost jubilant.

Fioluana was at the head, yelling my name. He disappeared into a gully and clambered out toward me, flashing a spear above his head. He was distinguished by his mud-discolored shorts; the hunters who followed him all wore tanket leaves. As he closed, I noticed the slaughter hauled by the others: bony black-skinned pigs, koala-cuddly tree kangaroos, cockatoos and parrots in bright bunches, like prize vegetables. The hunters gathered around us.

Fioluana looked us over, muddied and exhausted, and grinned. Dunstan and Titus grimaced nervously back. Fioluana stabbed his spear in the ground and approached Titus. He stretched out his arms and embraced him. I saw Titus's eyes: wide and alert, scanning the warriors, while Fioluana's closed in ecstasy.

Fioluana moved toward Dunstan and me, and shook our hands warmly, with respect. He was pleased to see us, he explained. The hunt had been a fierce success—he gestured around the warriors, laying the spoil at their feet—and now they were returning to the village. Had we left this morning? I nodded.

"You walk fast. You must leave very early." He grinned uncertainly, unsure why we had not greeted him more fulsomely. "Why did you leave so early?"

I looked at Titus. How to answer? With the truth—that the storm had killed his wife and elder daughter, and we were on the run, fearful the Liawep would hold us responsible? Titus returned my gaze, his eyes dark, regretful pools.

Dunstan stepped forward. "We wanted to get back, to start early. *Meri bilong mi wetim pikinini.* My wife's expecting a baby." He patted his stomach, rolled his eyes. Fioluana spluttered out laughing. Not for the first time, I was struck by Dunstan's unnerving plausibility. Lies came easy, despite his gentle, pious demeanor.

The hunters watched in silence. When we had left Fioluana with them the day before they had been roused and belligerent. Now they took us in soberly, their heads erect, as if they knew our secret. One of them, I noticed, had been wounded, a machete-slash across his thigh. The skin had torn open, and the wound looked wet and taut. He saw me looking at it and glared back: a challenge, insolent and proud.

Fioluana was rubbing goose bumps off his forearms; it was still early morning and the jungle was cold and wet. His initial cheeriness had hardened. He could sense our reticence and did not trust it.

"We are going to the village now."

We nodded in unison.

"My family? You took them to the house?"

"Yes, yes,' Dunstan put in. "We're just tired. It's a long way. *Longwe tru.*"

Fioluana laughed, relieved. He turned and walked toward one of the hunters, who gripped a piglet by its hind legs. He took the animal and handed it to me. It had stiffened; its hair was sparse and wiry. It would help us get to Wanakipa; we looked thin and hungry. He sucked his cheeks. One of the hunters laughed harshly.

We watched them go off, the hunters lumbering big-boned after the sylphic Fioluana. When the jungle had swallowed them again, and their voices were tiny and far off, Titus turned to me, his hand over his mouth.

"Oh my God," he breathed. "*Mi sori.* What have we done?" I shook my head in reply, despairing of our cowardice, yet no longer surprised by it.

"It's okay, Titus," Dunstan soothed, misunderstanding Titus's disquiet. "We're on our way home. They'll never catch us now."

His assurances came too easy, and he knew it. They could reach the village in six hours, gather the rest of the men, and return for us. They moved twice as fast through the forest; they could, if they wanted, cut us off long before we reached the safety of Wanakipa.

The afternoon became evening and the sky cleared and gathered again. Fear kept our pace from slackening. We came out of the canopy, briefly, on to a ridge where we could see back across the Lagaip to Liawep. The sky hung too gray to see the village. Over the mountain blackish cloud billowed and rose. While we watched, lightning exploded somewhere inside.

What was it about that mountain? In my search for an explanation for the disaster I returned again and again to the mountain. I had feared it from the first. It had seemed a calculated presence and I had never felt easy with it. Dunstan believed it was a volcano; Herod had seen it cough forth smoke.

Something came back. One day, Dunstan and I, feeling the dirt behind our ears, ingrained up our legs and backs, had walked up the mountain to wash. We'd not gone far, just to the nearest stream, but as soon as we'd undressed, rain came spattering down through the trees. I scrabbled with the soap and pulled my clothes back on, half-soaked. Dunstan had pulled his shirt on with soap still frothing in his armpits, in bubbles on his chest. Now, long after, he admitted he'd been afraid the volcano would split open. "Volcano or landslide," he said. "One or the other."

His fears were more grounded than mine. In my mind, the mountain had become a malevolent beast. It had drawn the storm not because of its size but because it was evil. I had come to fear it because the Liawep feared it. I remembered Peter Yasaro's comment, filed to his superiors, that they should stop the Liawep worshiping the mountain. These deaths, then, were the mountain's response: cavalier, disregarding of the sanctities. If I lived there, I would surely have worshiped it. It was real and magnificent and, unlike Herod's God, did not have to be conjured to life on bended knees. More than this, though, it moved. Later, I discovered it sat on a fault line between two tectonic plates. It shifted, it issued smoke, it spat tongues of fire.

We reached two houses on a crest, built recently in new gardens. We had stopped here on the way; it was here we'd met the Liawep boy and marveled at the bananas, great fat sausages they'd insisted on baking green. This time there were thirty people sitting around a fire as darkness fell. They'd just eaten, and scattered, astonished to see us.

I took off my shoes and a crowd of children gathered around. We had climbed up and down, immune to hunger, for fourteen hours.

Behind me, coming into the clearing, were Titus and Miniza. They knew some of these people—the old man with a downturned pig's tusk through his nose, the man with the steel axe—and had gossiped with them on the way over. Now, disaster survivors making the most of the drama, they stumbled into the clearing, groaning, knees buckling. The crowd was hushed to silence.

Titus performed first. He rubbed his left eye and limped heavily, wincing every time he trod. He struggled to the nearest log and lowered himself, the old soldier, the suffering visible in his eyes. A little boy started to giggle, but was silenced by two adults. Miniza staggered up afterward, leaning on his hip, his face twisted with pain. He sank to the ground at Titus's feet and buried his face in his hands. It was an astonishing change from the morning, when they'd been almost jaunty. When we'd crossed the river they'd run, jumped, even joked.

The end of the day was a reddish rim over the far mountains and the sky rose overhead through deepest blue to tar black. With Titus and Miniza groaning, insensible, it was left to Dison to tell the story. A space cleared around him and he swung from Titus and Miniza—his props, proof of the catastrophe—to the mountain, across the deep valley. He pointed to it, squaring his body, facing it. When he shook his fist in the air and raged, the audience stared mutely. When he screamed out the sound of the thunder, they turned as one to the mountain, struggling to understand. Dison spoke in Hewa and, although I spoke not one word, I could understand everything. It was a morality play in another tongue; it followed a scheme we all understood. When he finished he sat beside Dunstan and put his head in his hands. No one spoke for a very long time.

An Evening Among Headhunters
by Lawrence Millman

Travel writer Lawrence Millman (born 1948) has made a career courting adventure in far-flung places. He went to the Ecuadorian Amazon in hopes of "a rendezvous with the fabled Jivaro", a tribe of headhunters. His companions on this dubious journey included ethnobotanist Paul Cunnane, who was eager to sample a powerful hallucinogenic potion. It was reputed to put the Jivaro in contact with their ancestors—just the fate that Millman wished to avoid for himself.

WHACK! WHACK! WHACK!

Osvaldo's machete came down with lightning rapidity on yet another hapless snake. Then he proceeded to cut it into halves, thirds, quarters, and eighths, as if he were slicing carrots for the stewpot. Thus far he'd dispatched at least two dozen snakes in this fashion. Fer-de-lances, bushmasters, even the harmless glass snake—they were all candidates for his egalitarian blade. In his enthusiasm, I think he must have done away with several liana vines and serpentine creepers, perhaps even a few epiphytes, too.

At last I got a little upset with his sanguinary behavior. I told him that he was disturbing the jungle's ecosystem by killing all these snakes. But Osvaldo, for all his virtues as a guide, was not what you would describe as an eco-minded individual. He replied:

"Have you lost a son to the bite of a bushmaster? I have lost such a son, and I am now making the snakes lose their sons. Surely you understand, Mr. Larry?"

I understood, more or less. And from then on, I kept my mouth shut about snakes. But not, definitely not, about mud. For this was the rainy season in the Ecuadorian Amazon, and the country through which we were traveling—the country of the *untsuri suarä*, or Jivaro— was not only very dense jungle, but also very dense mud. The Amazon jungle has often been described as an orgy of green. At this time of year, however, it was an orgy of brown.

For five days, our little expedition had followed a vine-choked trail that seemed more like an obstacle course than a trail. One step forward usually resulted in either being swallowed up by the mud, strangled by a vine, gored by a thorn on a vine, flayed by a gauntlet of branches, skidding backwards, skidding sideways, or even on occasion skidding down the steep embankment into the Ungamayo, a river luckily piranha-less.

On the other hand, the Ungamayo wasn't *candiru*-less. This made any type of river dip, intentional or otherwise, a hazard. For the candiru is a fish that makes the better-known piranha seem as innocuous as a Barbie doll. Also known as "the toothpick fish," it swims up the urethra and then extends its spiny retrorse fins, whereupon it becomes agonizingly undislodgable. If you don't get to a hospital right away, your bladder will burst. And if you don't happen to be anywhere near a hospital, your only recourse is to find someone capable of administering last rites.

The balsa log bridges we came upon seemed to have been designed for river dips of the unintentional variety. We were convinced that they'd been coated with grease just prior to our arrival. In trying to cross them, we must have looked like a parade of spastic tightrope walkers. On one of these crossings, our ethnobotanist Paul Cunnane slipped off the log and landed with a splat in a pool of blackish ooze, only to reappear a few moments later looking as if he'd just lost a skirmish with a mud slide in his native California.

"Goddamfuckinsonafabitch!" Cunnane yelled. (Or something equally passionate. I wasn't taking notes at the time.)

"Ah, another expletive for our peerless guide," declared Petrie.

Osvaldo, part Jivaro and part Ecuadorian, was very eager to learn
English language swear words on the assumption that they would
come in quite handy if he ever went to America. Every time one of us
swore, he would politely ask for the words to be repeated. Then he
would repeat the word or phrase himself, the better to remember it.

Ever onward into the jungle we slipped, skidded, slopped, and fell,
swearing and then swearing again for Osvaldo's benefit, a quartet of
white men en route to a rendezvous with the fabled Jivaro. At this rendezvous, Cunnane planned to drink *natemä (Banisteriopsis caapi)*, the
hallucinogenic drug that puts the Jivaro in touch with their ancestors.
He hoped to get in touch with a few of their ancestors himself, and
then write up the encounter for his ethnobotanical journal.

None of the rest of us was into drugs, at least not with the same
degree of scholarly rigor. Petrie, an anthropologist, preferred lascivious
subjects like puberty rites and genital scarification. Lethbridge was a
British Columbia museum curator who wanted to purchase a few
chonta palm *cerbatanas* (blowguns) and curare darts, perhaps a
shrunken monkey or sloth's head as well, for his special collections.

As for myself, I'd joined the expedition for what is commonly
referred to as "the experience." Jack Petrie, who'd invited me to come
along, had been a friend of mine since college; he told me that the trip
would be, as he put it, "a perfectly splendid ordeal." My previous trip
had been a trek into the Labrador outback; a trek where I'd gotten lost,
been eaten alive by sky-darkening clouds of black flies and mosquitoes,
and strained at least two ligaments. This jungle adventure, Petrie
promised me, would equal and possibly surpass that one for sheer
physical discomfort.

And discomfort there certainly was, especially when we stopped. It
was then that endless relays of konga ants would come up and pay
their respects to us.

"Osvaldo may not like snakes," Lethbridge observed, "but he doesn't
seem to mind konga ants at all. You'll notice how he always picks their
campsites for our campsite. . ."

Lethbridge did not have a very high opinion of konga ants. The words "genocide" and "holocaust" kept escaping from his lips whenever he mentioned them. But then none of us had a high opinion of konga ants. They'd get onto our bodies and clamp their pincers into some exposed bit of skin, then inject venom from a stinger in the rear of their abdomens. This venom, whose presence made itself felt for hours on end, served to raise the decibel level of our expletives several notches.

Petrie would try to keep up our spirits by saying that the bite of a konga ant was actually quite pleasant compared to the way we'd feel with a candiru lodged in the urethra.

But Cunnane wasn't having any of this optimism. Every time an ant bit him, he would subject the f-word to various permutations and combinations that I would not have thought humanly possible.

Osvaldo was thus highly versed in our vernacular by the time we reached a little clearing in the jungle. Here stood the fifty-foot-long *chacra* that was our destination. It was built of stout chonta palm staves set vertically in the ground an inch or so apart, with closely woven palm thatch for a roof. This roof rose to perhaps twenty feet in the center. There were no windows, as the Jivaro think windows a needless extravagance, not to mention an invitation for four-legged and two-legged enemies to climb in.

We paused outside and Osvaldo shouted in falsetto: "*Whee-dee! Whee-dee!* There are five of us, and we are friendly." Then he waited, silently regarding but not removing a tapir tick that was crawling up his arm.

From inside the chacra came the reply: "*Whee-dee!* You are welcome."

And what if we had not been friendly? Well, it's been a quarter of a century since the Jivaro shrank down the heads of unwelcome guests to the size of softballs. At least it's been that long since they did it as an integral part of their culture rather than simply to stay in practice. But even then they didn't bother to shrink the heads of white men. For white men, they believed, did not possess souls. And if the whole point of headshrinking was to render your enemy's soul small and thus manageable upon its reincarnation, shrinking a white man's head was unnecessary, indeed wholly redundant.

So it was that we entered the chacra with a reasonable certainty that we would leave it with our heads still joined to our necks and likewise the same size as before.

Once inside, we hunkered down on log benches behind which stood a row of six-foot-long arrows with sharp curare-blackened tips. Osvaldo introduced us to the man of the house, Juanga. Juanga was dressed in green Adidas running shorts, a dirty polyester T-shirt that advertised the Galapagos, and Wellington boots. This wardrobe, Osvaldo informed me, was a present from the Belgian missionaries who occasionally dropped in on the Jivaro. Juanga's personal accessories also included a jaguar fang necklace. This, I assumed, was not a present from the missionaries.

We bowed our heads slightly toward him (shaking hands, Osvaldo had warned us, is a summons to a battle), and he bowed toward each of us in his turn. Half a dozen naked kids with bellies swollen over their malarial spleens, the resident shaman, Juanga's younger brother Cajeke, leatherfaced old men, women with drooping triangular breasts, even some abject and scrawny dogs—all of them studied us intently. With our bush costumery and various ethno-appearances, we were real weird, man.

Now Juanga's wife came over to us. She was dressed in a red loin-cloth and wore a pudding-basin haircut. She dipped a gourd in a bucket of *nijamanchi* (Spanish: *chicha*) and then offered it ceremoniously to her husband, who drank it and gave the gourd back to her, thus demonstrating for us guests that it wasn't poisoned. She filled the gourd again and this time offered it to Osvaldo, who drank it even as he took care to avert his eyes from her face. It is considered very rude for a guest to acknowledge a Jivaro woman.

Nijamanchi is home brew. *Home* brew. It's made from fermented yucca (manioc) root that's been chewed to a pulp by the woman of the house. The woman's oral bacteria contributes to the fermentation process, something which Lethbridge, for one, did not appreciate. When his turn came, he refused the gourd. In doing so, he used Latin names to invoke the wide range of germs, some lethal, others merely dangerous, that the brew doubtless harbored. But Osvaldo got back the gourd for him.

Lethbridge shook his head. "The number of parasite eggs in that gourd positively boggles the mind," he said.

"It is very bad manners not to drink," Osvaldo told him.

"And bad manners are a crime the Jivaro punish by death," added Petrie cheerfully. "In fact, you may even reawaken their headhunting urge."

Muttering to himself, Lethbridge drank.

Now it was my turn. The woman offered me the gourd, and I took a few tentative sips. Not bad, I thought. Not bad at all. It tasted like a marriage between buttermilk and beer, with a subtle aftertaste of spit. I slowly drank the contents of the gourd, and then the woman returned to the bucket and filled it up again. I tried to indicate that I didn't want any more, but that isn't easy when you're scrupulously looking every which way but at the person whose attention you're trying to get.

One thing about nijamanchi: it gives your bladder a full workout. Cunnane was the last to get the gourd. I waited until after he'd drunk and then I rose to go outside. And as I left the chacra, Juanga's youngest son got up and joined me. He was observing the Jivaro custom which requires that a member of the family accompany a guest to the lavatory (any area not under cultivation), and chat amiably with him while he answers Nature's call. The boy and I could not chat amiably since we didn't share a common language, but at least we were keeping up appearances.

When we returned to the chacra, the boy uttered some words in Shuar, the Jivaro language, to Osvaldo. Osvaldo turned to me and said:

"What's wrong with your penis?"

"Inertia, mostly," I replied.

"No, the boy says part of it is missing. He wonders if a *brujo* tried to get a candiru out and made a mistake."

As best I could, I explained the role of circumcision in my culture, citing studies that show circumcised males have lower rates of urinary tract infections and sexually transmitted diseases than males who have not undergone the knife. A look of incredulity crept across Osvaldo's face. Lopping off a man's head was one thing, but lopping off a portion of his virile member was quite another. I had no choice but to step back outside and expose myself. Osvaldo's incredulity did not go away.

"The foreskin is a relatively insensitive piece of skin," I told him.

"How would you know, Mr. Larry?" he said. "You don't have one."

In our absence the story of my missing foreskin had gone the rounds of the chacra. And upon our return there was a riff of giggling and glottal-stopping banter at my expense. A woman with a baby sucking at her breast was so convulsed with laughter that she almost fell out of her split-vine sleeping-net. Even a couple of naked toddlers were laughing and pointing at me. Evidently, it was not considered bad manners to ridicule guests if they happened to be, like me, freaks of nature.

"This guy's a laughingstock in his own country, too," said Petrie. Osvaldo translated for the others.

"You're going to get a very nasty letter from my lawyer when we get back," I told Petrie.

Meanwhile the shaman had gone outside with Cunnane and now he came back to report that Cunnane's member, unlike mine, was intact.

"Some of us happen to be circumcised, some of us not, and Mr. Cunnane wasn't, probably because his background is Irish," I explained. Osvaldo dutifully translated this statement, but I could have been talking about floppy disks or cast-iron flamingo lawn ornaments just as readily as ethnic differences. Among whites, the Jivaro make no distinctions. Except for me. I'd become an instant anthropological specimen.

The shaman said something to Osvaldo and gestured in my direction.

"The brujo wants to know whether you are maybe a type of homosexual person," Osvaldo asked me.

"I'm not any type of homosexual person. Why does the brujo think that?"

"Because there is an old legend among our people. Many years ago one of our gods was a homosexual person. He had a very long penis, maybe a hundred feet long, and he kept sticking it into other men. That way he could capture their souls and put them into a little box. The sun god Etsa decided that it was very wrong for him to do this, so he snapped some of his penis off. And the part he snapped off became the grandfather of all the poisonous snakes in the world."

"Please tell the brujo that my penis has not been snapped off by any sun god," I said.

Osvaldo related what I'd said to the shaman, who immediately replied in Shuar. Then Osvaldo said, "The brujo will be glad to restore your missing part . . . for a price."

"What price?"

The two of them conferred. Then Osvaldo said, "One stereo cassette tape recorder. Or maybe a bolt-action rifle."

Politely but firmly I declined the offer, though I must say that I was curious about what hocus-pocus, sleight-of-hand, or medicinal herbs the shaman would have used to restore my long-lost prepuce.

"The brujo says that if you die in this incomplete state," Osvaldo went on, "you will be reborn without a leg or an arm. And then when you are reborn after that, it might be without *both* legs . . ."

Now dinner was announced. This brought at least a temporary halt to the mockery of my anatomy. On the chacra's dirt floor Juanga's wife had set a couple of huge banana fronds, and we helped ourselves to a spread of piranha, yams, yucca, and taro root, all boiled in the same pot and tasting pretty much the same. The palm grub side dish I could have done without. But the entree, howler monkey roasted whole, had a gamey flavor which I found rather tasty. According to Petrie, this flavor was not unlike the flavor of roasted *Homo sapiens*.

He should know. Once, on a field trip to Irian Jaya, he'd unwittingly dined on chunks of a dead warrior whom one of his ethnosubjects had killed. The similarity of those chunks to monkey, which he'd eaten earlier in the trip, had proved to him once and for all the accuracy of Darwin's theories about human origins. Indeed, he often used this similarity as an opener when he lectured college students on evolution.

While we ate, Cunnane fasted. An hour after dinner, the shaman was ready with the natemä. Cunnane was instructed to remove his clothing.

"Have a good trip, pal," Petrie told him.

First Cunnane inhaled some greenish nasal snuff (*tsangu*), which made him grimace. Then he took a nip of natemä, which made him throw up. But this the Jivaro would argue was not so much throwing up as it is getting rid of one's evil spirits.

Cunnane took more nips and got rid of more evil spirits. His last batch of evil spirits were personally disposed of by the shaman, who put his mouth to Cunnane's navel, sucked loudly and then spat. This brought shouts of merriment from the kids in the chacra.

"Why are they laughing?" I whispered to Osvaldo. "Is it because they think it silly to perform this sort of ancient ritual nowadays?"

"Oh no," he said. "They do not think it's silly at all. They are laughing because they've never seen their brujo get rid of a white man's evil spirits before. Maybe they think it's a really big job. . ."

Thus purged of evil spirits, Cunnane drank a little more of the natemä, which he now seemed able to keep down. Then the shaman shook a dried barbasco sprig over various parts of his body and began chanting something in a voice that became increasingly eerie and distant, although once or twice it erupted into the roar of, I assumed, a jaguar. I noticed that his eyes were glazed, as if he'd previously been taking some of the natemä himself.

"By now you should be floating above your body," Osvaldo told Cunnane.

"I'm not floating anywhere," Cunnane replied, green tsangu slime trickling out of his nostrils.

"Then perhaps you are seeing some wild animals? A big jaguar, for example?"

"Nope, nothing."

Natemä has powerful hallucinogenic alkaloids which produce a narcotized state similar to the mescaline of the peyote cactus. A good trip often includes visions of fighting jaguars or other heroic beasts, followed by an audience with one's ancestors; a bad trip, visions of gigantic spiders with hairy twisted faces or perhaps snakes with human faces, followed by an audience with one's enemies. But as the evening wore on, it was apparent that Cunnane's trip consisted of nothing more dramatic than an upset stomach, of which he kept complaining. The natemä, he said, had the same effect on him as a greasy pizza. Petrie took his pulse. It was normal.

"You are *really* not seeing any jaguars?" Osvaldo said, a look of amazement on his face.

"None at all," Cunnane said.

Now Osvaldo and the shaman got into a discussion in Shuar. I assumed Osvaldo was telling him that he'd given his charge, instead of the usual ancestral fix, indigestion. Soon the discussion turned into an argument, which turned into a shouting match, at least on Osvaldo's side. The shaman himself only shrugged and shook his head decisively. So decisively that it sent a ripple effect through his whole body right down to his calloused feet, which he stamped angrily.

At one point I thought Olvado was going to hit him. Fortunately, he didn't. To hit a Jivaro shaman would be rather like decking the Pope. Very bad juju.

Osvaldo told us the problem. Cunnane had received only about one-third the recommended dose of natemä, which was not enough to get a konga ant high, much less a full-blooded ethnobotanist. The shaman was refusing to give him more because he had no idea what a white man could tolerate. White men, he said, were different from the Jivaro, and an overdose might scramble Cunnane's brains for good, possibly even kill him. And then the Ecuadorian government would not be happy.

"Who cares if the Ecuadorian government is happy?" said Petrie. "I mean, we're about as far removed from any political arena here as you can possibly get."

"The brujo cares," replied Osvaldo. "He went to jail some years ago because he took another man's head, and he does not want to go to jail again."

"Tell the brujo that I'll take full responsibility for anything that happens," Cunnane said.

But it was too late. The shaman had already gathered his effects into a vine-bound medicine-bag and recanted the rest of the natemä. I caught one last glimpse of his primal Asiatic face before he left. A face whose lines were folded and then folded again into a ruinous splendor. The face of a man much saddened by these headless modern times.

One by one, my companions turned in. Just before I joined them, I went outside to empty my bladder again. It was a very clear night, with the Southern Cross pinned three-dimensionally to the sky and the stars around it so bright that they seemed to hum with wattage. Monkeys screeched; frogs croaked; insects sang; and a small bird made a series of soft whisking trajectories above me.

This time my lavatorial companion was Juanga's brother Cajeke, a fiercely-painted man who looked as if his hobby was disemboweling grandmothers with his machete. And as I stood there relieving myself, suddenly Cajeke raised his machete.

Holy shit! I thought. He's going to reenact the myth of the sun god on my poor abused organ of generation. But then he brought the machete down with a WHACK! on a five-foot fer-de-lance which was slithering directly toward me from across the yucca plantation. Cajeke's blow neatly severed the snake, whereupon both parts writhed convulsively for a few moments and then grew still.

From now on, I decided, I'd always be grateful for the etiquette of headhunters.

Lost City of the Lukachukais
by David Roberts

David Roberts (born 1943) has published books on subjects that include his own path-breaking climb of Alaska's forbidding Mount Huntington in 1965 and the travels of earlier explorers Kit Carson and John Fremont. He set out in 1996 to unravel the mystery of an ancient lost city, once inhabited by the cliff-dwelling Anasazi. Roberts, armed with modern climbing gear and a passion for the Anasazi culture, searched for the legend's source among the cliffs of New Mexico's remote Lukachukais region.

T he Lost City of the Lukachukais—now there is a legend to conjure with!" wrote Ann Axtell Morris in 1933. "Of all Southwestern enigmas, it is the most mysterious. And of all Southwestern treasures, it is the most desired."

As Morris told the tale, in 1909 a pair of Franciscan missionaries set out from Farmington, New Mexico, determined to penetrate the red-rock wilderness across the Arizona border, beyond the soaring monolith of Shiprock. Among these canyons and mountains, which few Anglos had ever seen, lived unacculturated Navajos, whose souls the fathers hoped to save.

One night, as they sat beside their campfire, the Franciscans were startled by the disappearance of their Navajo guide. Minutes later, the man returned, carrying a huge ceramic jar under his arm. One of the padres recognized the jar as a masterly Anasazi pot, fired at least 600 years before.

The padres asked their guide where he had found the jar. The

Navajo would neither tell them, nor allow the Franciscans to purchase the object. But he told them of a trailless box canyon, seldom visited by Navajos, at the head of which, on a high ledge, stood a huge, pristine Anasazi ruin. From this site, the pot had come.

By the 1930s, when Ann Morris first committed the legend to print, the Lost City of the Lukachukais had become an archaeologist's El Dorado. The writer's husband, Earl Morris, one of the leading Anasazi scholars of his day, spent years looking in vain for the Lost City.

In another version of the legend, the fathers had seen the cliff dwelling from afar, comparing it favorably to the wonders of Mesa Verde, but had had no time to approach the ruin. On subsequent journeys, they had never been able to find the site again.

Morris's fruitless search had pushed him to explore the Lukachukais further. On rugged, month-long expeditions in 1930 and 1931, he had dug in a dozen caves, finding the pit houses, baskets, and spear-throwers of the Basketmaker people, Anasazi who lived before 750 A.D., ancestors to the more visible cliff dwellers. Morris's pioneering work in the Lukachukais promised to be some of the most important research yet performed in the Southwest.

But the legend of the Lost City receded further into myth. And Morris himself, after his death in 1956, took on a legendary aura of his own. His portrait on the cover of Florence and Robert Lister's biography of the man, in battered fedora and denim shirt, is rumored to have served as the model for Indiana Jones.

Long an enthusiast of remote Anasazi ruins, I had followed Earl Morris's footsteps across the Southwest, from Canyon de Chelly to Aztec Ruins to the Ute Mountain Tribal Park south of Mesa Verde. The legend of the Lost City had gotten under my skin. In obscure documents, I had found further clues to the whereabouts of the elusive cliff dwelling. I decided to round up a few cronies and make my own search for the Lost City.

By 1996, there was virtually no chance that a ruin as grand as Cliff Palace could have escaped detection for a century. But the Luka-chukais, spreading across an out-of-the-way corner of the vast Navajo

Reservation, remained one of the least-visited regions in all the Southwest. A glance at the maps made it clear that the range promised months of blithe exploring.

On the one hand, I hoped to find, if not the Lost City itself, the wellsprings of the legend. On the other, I would be happy to tread once more in the footsteps of Earl Morris. And in any case, deep in the Lukachukais, I would be hiking canyons still all but unknown to Anglos and to archaeology.

Before heading into the desert, I stopped in Boulder, Colorado, to meet Joe Ben Wheat. Eighty years old, a retired professor of anthropology at the University of Colorado, Wheat is one of the few colleagues still alive who knew Earl Morris well.

"Earl was a great guy," Wheat told me, "but he wasn't a bit like Indiana Jones. He was very careful and precise with language. Even in casual conversation, he measured every word.

"In the field, Earl had the instincts of a pothunter and the scientific control to make archaeology out of what he found. He just had this quiet ability. He knew who he was."

It was Morris's influence that had persuaded the young Wheat to become an archaeologist. "In his own quiet way, Earl generated excitement. You could feel the force of his intellect."

Yet from Wheat's recollections and the Listers' biography, I gleaned a picture of Morris as a melancholic who felt he had fallen far short of his goals. No one ever dug more sites than Morris, but, like many another archaeologist, he found writing an onerous task. Toward the end of his life, he was plagued with guilt over the fieldwork he had failed to write up.

Indeed, Morris never published any account of either his 1930 or his 1931 expedition in the Lukachukais. Much of the content of his Basketmaker discoveries thus died with him. And in this silence from the grave, the mystery of the Franciscan legend deepens—for Morris himself, as far as I could learn, never wrote a word about the Lost City.

My perusal of maps and museum notes had convinced me that the place to look for the phantom village was in a canyon called Tsegi-ho-chon. In the 1920s, Indians had told John Wetherill, the only trader in northeast Arizona, about this canyon full of ruins. Wetherill would serve a Morris's guide in both 1930 and 1931. And Charles L. Bernheimer, the wealthy New Yorker who bankrolled the 1930 expedition, wrote that the Navajo name signified "Ugly or Difficult Rocks." During my own trip, I was to receive a much richer understanding of the name.

With a pair of friends, *National Geographic* photographer Ira Block and horsepacker/amateur archaeologist Fred Blackburn, I headed south on dirt roads from a gas station on Highway 160, to make a two-day reconnaissance of Tsegi-ho-chon. Simply finding the canyon proved tricky: we got lost twice before pitching camp at sunset on the north rim of the defile.

During a long, marvelous next day, Fred, Ira, and I hiked fifteen miles up and down Tsegi-ho-chon and its tributaries. In these lower stretches of the canyon, an inch-deep stream meandered between parabolic walls, some 100 to 200 feet high, carved over the eons out of sweeping red sandstone.

Navajos today run sheep through the lower canyon, which is grazed to a dry stubble. Here and there we found what Fred called *jedi*—bright rags affixed to posts or fences to act as mystic scarecrows, charming the coyotes away from the sheep.

We found four small cliff dwellings tucked into south-facing alcoves in side canyons. But the glory of Tsegi-ho-chon was its rock art, carved and painted on the canvases of the enclosing walls. The oldest figures (usually those highest off the ground) had been limned by the Anasazi. Particularly impressive were a number of hulking humanoids with broad shoulders, triangular bodies, and huge dangling hands and feet. These, we knew, had been inscribed during Archaic and early Basketmaker times, before 500 A.D.

But there was also an abundance of Navajo rock art, more than I had ever seen before. Athapaskan nomads from the Canadian subarctic, the Navajos had entered the Southwest around 1400 A.D., a hundred years after the Anasazi had abandoned the Four Corners. Navajos may have penetrated the Lukachukais as early as the eighteenth century. Certainly in of the Navajo rock art we saw looked old. The artists' favorite theme was horses, lovingly etched down to the hairs on the manes. I was beguiled by a series of eerie *yei b' cheis*—sticklike supernatural beings in charge of corn and fertility.

At the end of our jaunt, we discovered a shortcut into the middle Tsegi-ho-chon, saving six miles of approach. As we walked back in the late sun toward our car camp, footsore but exhilarated, meadowlarks and white-throated swifts darted before our path. The cottonwoods were just beginning to bud, and a few globe willows in full leaf blazed like green balloons it floating in the air.

Our reconnaissance had saved us a lot of unnecessary toil. We had glimpsed the upper canyon. Sixty-five years after Earl Morris's last visit, our own probe into the Lukachukais was about to begin.

A few days later, we returned to Tsegi-ho-chon in full force. Joining Fred, Ira, and me were Bryan Harvey, a young videographer with whom Ira hoped to make a film about our trip; Dennis Gilpin and Kelly Hays, husband and wife archaeologists who had worked elsewhere in the Lukachukais but never explored this canyon; and Wilson King, our Navajo guide. We had recruited Wilson out of Cove, an idyllic little town on the other side of the Lukachukais to the south. Though his home lay only about eight miles from the head of Tsegi-ho-chon, Wilson had never been in this part of the country, nor had any of his friends. So tortured is the Lukachukai slickrock that it can take a journey of 100 miles to go from one canyon to another only a few miles apart as the crow flies.

Fred used his two horses to pack our considerable baggage: besides Ira and Bryan's camera equipment, I had brought a full rack of rock-climbing gear and two ropes, hoping to use my skills as an alpinist to reach the more inaccessible cliff dwellings. I knew from many previous trips to the Southwest that the Anasazi had been climbing geniuses, whose dwellings sometimes lay on ledges you could figure out virtually no way to reach today.

We loaded up Shamrock, a chestnut Missouri Foxtrotter, and Rico, a dappled gray-and-white Appaloosa, then set out on foot up the canyon. As soon as we passed beyond the range of our reconnaissance, we recognized an alarming fact. The inch-deep, steady stream we had strode along a few days before issued from a spring in the valley floor. Above the spring, the canyon was dry as dust. For four miles we hiked onward, increasingly conscious of a dawning thirst, as we found not a single drop of water. All across the Southwest, the previous winter had delivered almost no snow, and everyone was predicting a tough summer for cattle, sheep, and crops. We began to worry whether we would find *any* water—the irreducible sine qua non for desert survival—during our week-long journey.

The splendor of the canyon distracted us from our water anxieties. As we headed south, the surrounding walls grew taller, until 300 feet of surging rock—fins, towers, bulging domes—separated us from the rims above.

In six miles of travel, we discovered half a dozen Anasazi sites. Several of these were intriguing, and in one we had a sudden shock of recognition. The ruin, we realized, was the same one Morris had called Archers Cave. For the first time, we correlated our own position with the footsteps of our predecessors in 1930.

Archers was covered with both Anasazi and Navajo rock art: black, white, and yellow handprints; a great painted white bird that Kelly swore as a macaw, indicating Anasazi contact with Mexico; a memorable Navajo battle scene, replete with firearms and dead bodies; *yei b' cheis*, one of which Wilson recognized from the ephemeral sand paintings he had seen Navajo shamans craft; the inevitable horses; and even a 1920s jalopy, detailed down to the bulging headlamps.

The most striking feature about the ruin was a two-story front wall festooned not with windows but with small loopholes. Morris's party had named the site after these holes, imagining ancient warriors shooting arrows through them, but Dennis and Kelly argued that the loopholes more likely served as viewing tubes through which hidden dignitaries could watch some sacred ceremony in the plaza below.

We pushed on into the waning afternoon. At last a trickle of water appeared, seeping out of the arroyo bank on the right. But it was not a good place to camp. We hurried on up-canyon, mistakenly believing we would find water above. Instead Tsegi-ho-chon dried up once more.

At last we stopped to establish base camp. The site was sublime, at the junction of two tributaries with the main canyon, on a bench covered with sagebrush and greasewood. Two geologic anomalies—a toothlike pinnacle of sandstone, and a slender "needle's eye" arch—guarded our camp.

But there was no water. In the end, for the next week, Fred and Wilson had to ride daily a mile back down-canyon to the fugitive trickle, where they filled every water bottle we had.

That night, we sat around a small fire of greasewood branches, which burn hot and smokeless. Coyotes howled in the darkness. I felt a deep contentment in the knowledge that only a handful of Anglos before me had ever camped in this convoluted canyon, which we had only begun to discover.

Lingering late around the campfire, I was treated to Wilson's explication of all the shades of meaning embodied in the name of our canyon (which Bernheimer had breezily glossed as "Ugly or Difficult Rocks").

"Tsegi-ho-chon," Wilson said, pronouncing it with a Navajo inflection that defies transcription. "It means literally, 'It doesn't work any more.' But it also means, 'The rock that has been destroyed,' or 'The rock that has ruins in it.' Or even just, 'It's been ruined.'

"I guess I'd translate 'Tsegi-ho-chon' as 'Inside of a rock that was being ruined.'" Wilson stuck another greasewood branch on the fire. "Basically, it's like a scary place."

The next morning, we loaded daypacks with lunch, clothing, and bottles fall of precious water from the trickle, then headed up the main fork of the branching canyon. Fred and Wilson followed on horseback.

As we pushed south, the canyon narrowed around us and the walls soared to a height of 400 feet. In the distance, a deer traversed the draw; then a coyote loped across a slickrock stab, seemingly oblivious to us. Farther along, seven wild burros peered over the bushes to watch us pass. The day before, as we entered the canyon, a Navajo woman he met along the trail had told Fred about the burros. "They've been there for years," she said. "Nobody can catch 'em." Near its head, the valley made a sudden turn to the left. In a glance, I could see that Tsegi-ho-chon ended in a true box canyon, where vertical walls prohibited escape.

But it was not the canyon itself that took my breath away. One hundred fifty feet above us on the left, ranging across a long, concave ledge sheltered by a gigantic overhang, stood the rooms of a spacious Anasazi town. All the ruins we had seen coming up the canyon were dwarfed by this lordly village.

At first, the ledge seemed impossible to reach: beneath it, the rock caved away in yet another overhang. But as I approached the only part of the cliff that was less than vertical, I found exactly what I was looking for.

A series of shallow, cupped steps led up the sixty-degree precipice. The first several steps had been improved by moderns wielding metal tools. The remainder, above, had weathered over more than 700 years to mere scallops that would barely take the toes of one foot.

It was an Anasazi hand-and-toe trail, carved by some ancient engineer wielding a quartzite pounding stone. And it had once served as the ladder to the village, up which men, women with pots on their heads, and bare-foot children had scampered daily.

Nervously, I set out to climb the eroded staircase. Forty feet up, I nearly quit, for a piece of cliff had broken away, leaving three feet of blank rock. But the sight of the lofty city was too enticing. I pushed delicately on, until I reached the lip of the ledge.

My friends below heard my jubilant cries, and their envy forestalled more than a cursory visit. I climbed back down the hand-and-toe trail, dashed the two miles to base camp, retrieved a rope, and hurried back to the high cliff dwelling.

By early afternoon, after I had belayed each of my colleagues up the hand-and-toe trail, all seven of us stood in the magnificent ruin. There followed three hours of rapturous discovery.

We counted some forty rooms, of which a remarkable ten were kivas, underground chambers possibly reserved for religious rites. "This has to be the ceremonial center for the whole damned canyon!" Kelly exclaimed.

The ruin, to be sure, was no Cliff Palace. (The crown jewel of Mesa Verde boasts four-story towers and some 200 rooms.) But the site was so dramatic that I could well imagine early travelers such as the Franciscan priests sighting the stone-and-mud town from afar—perhaps from the mesa opposite—and being able to divine no way of getting to it. Perhaps here was the ruin that had given birth to the legend of the Lost City.

It was not so much the size as the exquisite preservation of the site that dazzled us. Of all its rooms, the masterpiece was a big, rectangular kiva with an intact roof made of wooden poles, shredded juniper bark, and mud; six pristine "banquettes," benchlike storage niches in the walls; and a perfect chimney, deflector slab (to regulate drafts), and hearth in the floor. None of us had ever seen a better preserved kiva.

Dennis was beside himself. "Holy mackerel," he whispered. "This is staggering. I feet this is exactly what the kiva looked like in 1275. This is just a treasure trove of information."

The rock art was as rich as what we had found at Archers Cave. And on one wall, we saw an inscription from the Bernheimer expedition, with the initials:

J. W.—E. H. M.—30.

We had found the record of Earl Morris's visit, sixty-six years before—as well as that of his peerless guide, John Wetherill.

That evening in camp, looking over my notes, I figured out that the cliff city on the high ledge had been named Promontory Ruin by Morris's 1930 team. But once again, the ambiguity of the record befuddled me. Had Morris speculated, as I would six-and-a-half decades later, whether an early glimpse of Promontory had inspired the legend of the Lost City? The only day-by-day account of the 1930 expedition I had been able to find was Bernheimer's typescript diary, which I had discovered in a museum archive. And Bernheimer never mentioned the Lost City.

The diary, however, disclosed other tantalizing hints. Before the 1920s, the Lukachukais had been off limits to all Anglos. In Tsegi-ho-chon, the expedition had felt sure, as Bernheimer wrote, that they had managed "to penetrate a canyon no white people had ever entered." Yet the party's Navajo guide told them about "a hunter by the name of Lang" who had tried to probe Tsegi-ho-chon around the turn of the century, only to be chased out by Navajos.

This scrap of diary entry set off bells in Fred's head. The passion of our horsepacker's life is to find inscriptions scrawled on Anasazi cave walls by the first Anglo visitors. Fred knew Charles Lang well—in fact, he had interviewed Lang's son when the man was in his nineties. But Lang himself, who had been a crony of John Wetherill, remained an enigma. What Fred wouldn't give to find some firsthand account of that daring solo thrust into the Lukachukais! Had Lang been the first white man to see Promontory Ruin!

In any event, it seemed likely that only a handful of Anglos had climbed up to Promontory since 1930. One of the finest Anasazi ruins any of us had ever seen lay in such an obscure place that it went years at a time without a visit.

Alone among the seven of us, Wilson had entered the ruin with misgivings. In fact, I had overheard him mutter, "I hope these guys forgive me."

The relationship of Navajos to the Anasazi ruins that are scattered all over their reservation is a complex one. These "houses of the dead" are not simply taboo for Navajos; an immense power for both good and evil haunts the crumbling room-blocks.

Beside the campfire, Wilson told us what had happened to him the year before. Hired as a worker on an archaeological dig in the path of a proposed highway, on his first day Wilson had unearthed the skeleton of a fifteen-year-old Anasazi girl. Two months later, he woke up one morning unable to walk. "I had to crawl across the floor," he said quietly. "It hurt so bad."

"I went to a medicine man in Red Rock. He said there was lots of stuff that needed to be done on me, so the thing wouldn't affect my wife and kids." The medicine man performed a rite, and suddenly Wilson could walk. "He said, 'It will go away now, but it will come back again.'" Wilson paused. "After my leg got better, my wife lost our child when she was five months pregnant."

We sat in silence around the fire, until I asked our guide how today's visit to Promontory Ruin had felt to him. It was the first cliff dwelling Wilson had ever entered. "The place jumped on me," Wilson said, choosing his words carefully. "I thought, 'Should I go up, or stay down below?' It seemed OK to go up."

"But then when you found that leg bone—" Wilson nodded at me. In the midden, or trash dump, below one of the rooms at Promontory, I had stumbled upon the thigh bone and vertebrae of a human. An ancient burial had eroded to the surface.

"When I go home," Wilson went on, "I'll change clothes, and wash everything I have before I handle my kids. And I won't tell a lot of people about the place—just a few friends. I'll keep it to myself."

Just before I had belayed him down the hand-and-toe trail, Wilson had complained of a sharp pain in his knee. He was sure it had been caused by visiting the ruin. Now, taking Ibuprofen every few hours, he kept the pain at bay.

A dyed-in-the-wool rationalist, I privately dismissed Wilson's tales as coincidence or even superstition. But there was no mistaking the man's somber mood. Later, I would have reason to rethink my skepticism.

On our fourth day in Tsegi-ho-chon, Dennis and Kelly had to hike out to attend a conference. We were sorry to see them go, with their archaeological expertise. Among their insights into the ruins we had seen was the recognition that, in terms of the dwellings' masonry style and the designs on the hundreds of potsherds we had found in the dirt, this canyon owed everything to the influence of Mesa Verde, fifty miles to the northeast. Surprisingly, the great Kayenta centers, equally near, such as Betatakin and Keet Seel, seemed to have exerted little pull on the Lukachukais.

The remaining five of us still had much to explore. On horseback, Fred and Bryan circled far to the east, up a tributary that was actually larger than the main canyon. They found four beautiful arches and windows in the sandstone, but no way to escape what amounted to another, colossal box canyon. High in one draw they came across a wild bull, gone feral like the burros many years ago. Rico and Shamrock shied and retreated in the face of this monarch of the wild.

Meanwhile, Wilson and I set out in another branch of the eastern tributary to find a way to the tableland above. We knew that Morris in both 1930 and 1931 had started his expeditions near Cove—Wilson's home town—on the far side of the Lukachukai divide. To get to Tsegi-ho-chon, they had climbed up to Cove Mesa at 7,000 feet, then looped far to the north before entering the labyrinthine canyon roughly where we had. But on one jaunt, their Navajo guide had chased a runaway horse almost all the way back to Cove, then on his return found a difficult but rideable shortcut back into Tsegi-ho-chon near our base camp.

For three miles Wilson and I pushed up the tributary. There was no break in the enclosing precipices. Then, with binoculars, I spotted a chute that seemed to split two vertical cliffs.

It took a nasty bushwhack to reach and climb the chute, but it "went." At the very top, I saw a few steps hacked out of the bedrock with picks—classic Navajo trail work. It seemed unlikely that a horse could navigate this treacherous passageway, but evidently horses had.

We sailed up onto Cove Mesa. A stiff breeze chilled us, but the views were stunning—east to the great volcanic plug of Shiprock, west all the way to the buttes and towers of Monument Valley. Hawks spiraled on thermals above us. We crossed a pair of old Navajo driftwood fences, then began to see recent prints of sheep. Wilson, homesick to be so close to his wife and children, tried to think which of his acquaintances ran herds so far up on Cove Mesa.

Pushing on south, we came in sight of a small shack. A man puttered about the yard. In true Navajo fashion, he ignored us as we approached. Later he admitted he was startled, even alarmed, to see strangers coming from the north, where no one ever appeared.

Wilson chatted with the man in Navajo. At last he invited us in and served us cups of spring water and coffee. We shared our lunch with him. His name was Jonathan Lee, out of Two Gray Hills; he was spending a month on Cove Mesa, tending a relative's herd of thirty-five sheep.

We had hired Wilson not for his familiarity with the country, which he knew no better than we, but for his take on what we saw and for his service as a liaison to the locals. We had an official hiking permit from the Navajo Nation in Window Rock, but that scrap of paper carried little value in the outback. Had I, an Anglo, arrived alone at his windy shack, Jonathan Lee might have been downright hostile. As it was, the talk between Wilson and Jonathan partook of the dark and the supernatural: about a strange, bare-chested runner with long white hair many had seen but none had talked to; about a giant snake that lived a few miles to the north on the mesa, the ground around whose den was riddled with big cistlike holes into which a man might fall.

Late that afternoon, Wilson and I forced our way back into Tsegi-ho-chon by the middle tributary. It took a blind, thrashing bushwhack and some tricky climbing—definitely not a horsepacking route. Just as I began to wonder how many humans had preceded us into this brushchoked gorge, we came to a pourover—an overhanging lip of sandstone in the valley floor that portended a dead end. But on the right, across a frighteningly steep stab, led a pecked trail of Anasazi steps.

The ancients had been everywhere.

For our last full day in Tsegi-ho-chon, I had saved my most ambitious effort. Not far from camp, we had spotted three high caves, 200 feet above the valley, 100 feet below the rim of Cove Mesa. With binoculars, I could see that the ceiling of each cave was covered with soot—a dead giveaway that the Anasazi had used them, probably as living shelters. At the mouth of one of the caves, we saw masonry and roof beams: Fred thought the half-hidden structure might be a kiva.

In all likelihood, no Anglo or Navajo had ever been to these caves—for it would obviously take a technical climb to get to the ledge that linked the three sites. After reconnoitering the base of the 200-foot cliff, I saw that there was only one conceivable approach. A steep corner in the sandstone snaked up left, then right, to the ledge. Unlike the staircase that led to Promontory Ruin, however, this corner was devoid of pounded hand-and-toe holds.

With my ropes and high-tech climbing gear, I thought I might be able to scale the corner. I tied Wilson into the other end of my lead rope, anchored him to a juniper tree, and taught him how to belay, while Bryan filmed and Ira photographed. Wilson looked apprehensive.

As soon as I left the ground, I realized the climb was going to be dangerous. There were plenty of holds, but the sandstone was so rotten, great chunks came loose in my hands. I managed twenty-five feet of ascent: because of the poor rock, what looked like easy climbing turned out to be hard and scary.

I reached a small platform from which the corner angled at seventy degrees up to the right. Here I had hoped a vertical crack would allow me to place protection. But I saw at once that the corner was seamless, without even a pencil-thin crack.

There were holds, but all it would take was for one piece of sandstone to prise off under my weight, and I would plunge all the way down to Wilson's useless belay. It was what climbers call a "death route."

The only reasonable course was to back off. In that instant, as I raised my leg, I felt a hot stab of pain shoot through my right knee. "Damn!" I yelled down. "I've pulled a ligament, or something." In the first twenty-five feet of climbing, I had made an awkward long step, shifting all my weight onto a small hold high under my right foot.

Now, as I climbed down to the ground, feeling inept and vexed, the pain grew worse. Making the awkward step, I must have pulled or twisted something in the knee.

I left my gear in a forlorn pile at the base of the cliff while we scrambled up to one last Anasazi cave—this one a "pure" Basketmaker site that, Fred thought, might well harbor burials under the drifted dust. My knee felt worse and worse.

"So how the hell did the Anasazi get up there?" I asked Fred, miffed at my failure to reach the three high caves.

"Log ladders," he answered. "That'd be my guess."

An hour later, packing up my climbing gear, I noticed an old dead tree lying at the foot of the corner. Sorting out my hardware earlier, I had stepped across the tree without even looking at it.

"My God, Fred, look!" I blurted out. "You called it!" For the dead tree was indeed an Anasazi ladder. Ancient notches in the wood, chopped with a stone axe, had served as footholds. So perishable are these ladders that in years of prowling around the Southwest, Fred and I had found only three or four apiece.

But we knew that the Anasazi had been virtuosi of dead-tree-ladder technique. Archaeologists had found these notched logs hundreds of feet off the ground, propped insecurely on some mortared platform. No doubt a series of such logs had given the Anasazi access to their three high caves. Only this, the initial log, had survived the decay of the centuries.

As I limped back to camp, I marveled at Anasazi daring. And I recognized for the first time that in one odd sense stone-axe-cut dead trees were superior to the snazziest modern rock-climbing gear. With all my nuts and friends, I still had to climb the rock itself, which here was treacherously loose. With an Anasazi ladder, bad rock didn't matter: you climbed the log, not the cliff.

In the dangerous corner that led up to the three high caves, the ancients had eschewed a hand-and-toe trail, probably because the rock was so friable. Instead they had hauled custom-made ladders into place. Even so, the daily ascent and descent must have been terrifying.

That evening, our last in Tsegi-ho-chon Canyon, the five of us huddled around the campfire, warding off the chill of a sharp wind out of the northwest. Staring at the red coals, I pondered the three high caves I had failed so utterly to reach and explore.

The obvious question such ruins provoke is—Why? Why build and live in eyries so difficult and dangerous to reach? All over the Four Corners, especially during the last century before the 1300 A.D. abandonment, the Anasazi retreated to such cliff dwellings, ones that could be entered only by hand-and-toe trails or log ladders.

The obvious explanation—that the retreat was defensive, in response to some new threat to the people's existence—seems after all to be the likely one. Yet among archaeologists, the defensive theory has spurred decades of bitter controversy.

From the discovery of Cliff Palace in 1888 on, scholars postulated that the Anasazi had holed up against raids by nomadic invaders such as Navajos, Utes, and Apaches. Yet excellent research during the last thirty years argues that none of these nomads reached the Southwest before 1400 A.D.—a century after the Anasazi abandonment. In the face of these findings, the defensive hypothesis lapsed for a while into limbo. Within the last decade, however, it has come back to the fore.

The Anasazi, we now believe, did indeed retreat into high cliff dwelling in response to a marauding enemy. But that enemy was themselves. During extended thirteenth-century droughts, the water table of the farmland dropped, and the big game were hunted into near-extinction, fragmenting the Anasazi into bands that may have raided and killed each other. There is new evidence even of cannibalism among the people.

The high caves I had tried in vain to reach had stirred me with their majestic inaccessibility. Yet I had to recognize that, whatever beauty hung about those cliff dwellings, it was a beauty born of a daily, gnawing fear.

That last night, the pain in my knee throbbed. When I had pulled up my trousers leg to look, I had discovered a splinter embedded in my kneecap. Using his Swiss Army knife tweezers, Fred had dug it out. We were both disturbed to find that the splinter had gone straight in half an inch. During my rough bushwhack with Wilson the day before, the splinter had evidently pierced my trousers and entered my knee without my feeling it.

"I wonder if you haven't got an infection," Fred mused. Two days later, in the emergency room in Cortez, Colorado, his hunch was confirmed. The splinter had been the conduit for a deep anaerobic infection. Left untreated, the doctor warned, the infection could go into the joint, and I might even lose the leg. I was put on massive doses of antibiotics, but it was three weeks before the swelling subsided and the pain went away.

Though he was kind enough to say nothing, I knew that Wilson had a different understanding of what had happened to my knee. It was no coincidence that I had felt the pain suddenly as I had started to climb to the high caves. Just as Wilson had awakened one morning in Cove, unable to walk, after he had dug up the skeleton of the fifteen-year-old Anasazi girl, so my hubris in attempting to reach the forbidden caves had everything to do with my own crippling.

That night I had to take a strong pain-killer to sleep. The wind increased to a gale, and the temperature plummeted. At 2:00 a.m. I woke hearing rain on the tent fly, but when I opened the door, a driving sleet hit me in the face.

In the morning, our snowstruck camp looked like something out of an arctic survival tale. With numb fingers, keeping our backs to the gale, we packed up the horses, cramming the panniers with frozen tents and soggy sleeping bags. Only three days before, we had hiked in T-shirts and shorts!

I could barely walk. Popping another pain-killer, I faced into the storm and started the long hobble out to civilization.

Despite the pain and the storm, I left the Lukachukais full of richly contradictory feelings. For a week we had had one of the most spectacular corners of Arizona to ourselves. Yet the place, Fred, Wilson, and I agreed, was distinctly spooky. We had not unraveled the legend of the Lost City, but in Promontory Ruin we might well have plumbed its source. (Yet there are many other canyons in the Lukachukais, and a man could spend his lifetime exploring all of them. . . .)

As for the timeless conundrum of the Anasazi achievement—we left that behind us, too, shining like a star wreathed in a cloud. What dwellings, what artifacts, what clues to lost meaning lay inside those three high alcoves, unseen by anyone since the last ancient climbed down the teetering ladders more than 700 years ago? We had pushed hard into the Lukachukais, only to halt in awe at the edge of a mystery— a mystery that had once, for the Anasazi, been as plain as daily life.

from Antisuyo: The Search for the
Lost Cities of the Amazon
by Gene Savoy

Hiram Bingham in 1911 discovered the ancient city of Machu Pichu atop a towering mesa deep in the Peruvian jungle. He proclaimed it to be the legendary Vilcabamba, capital city of the ancient Incan civilization. Gene Savoy (born 1927), self-styled explorer and self-taught archaeologist, fiercely believed that Vilcabamba lay elsewhere. He went to Peru in 1964 determined to find it.

Bright and early the next morning twelve of us set out up the Concevidayoc. The Cobos boys had told us about a stone bridge over the river and I wanted to see it. The men were in a surly mood. It had rained the night before and they blamed the expedition. Anything foreign in the valley upsets the balance of nature and brings cloudy, unruly weather—and rain at this time of the year is bad luck. Human skulls are set out along the river banks and in other appropriate places to ward off the rain. The dry season has a special significance for an agricultural people in the rain forest. It is their spring after a long, wet winter. I can't really blame them for resenting intruders who upset the balance.

The day turned out to be exhausting and pointless. The "bridge" proved to be an overhanging section of cliff that had slipped into the river at some time. Our only compensation for the grueling trip was the great quantity of wild bees' honey found in the trunk of an old tree.

Rain caught us on the trail back to the house. We returned to our

base by the old Inca road we had come over the day before and found
Ascensión waiting with three new men from Pampaconas. Santander
said the men were grumbling about the change of weather. They were
convinced that "The City of the Incas" was trying to hide itself. They
complained about having to explore the pampas. They were afraid of
the *relámpago* and the *espíritus*. Ascensión boldly proclaimed that even
the Machi, poor ignorant savages that they were, knew better than to
go into the pampas. One of the men, a barefoot, volatile fellow with a
curvo machete draped around his neck, said in Quechua that the pampas were inhabited by Purun Machu, an old devil that enchants abandoned ruins. This was the same spirit believed to have enchanted
Machu Picchu. The natives believed that men could live on the edge of
the jungle, as they did when Bingham arrived, but that no one should
dare venture into the ruins. This is why the ruins have remained
unknown for so long, though their whereabouts were known to the
local populace. Ascensión told us that by failing to perform the "proper
ceremonies" we would never succeed in penetrating the pampas without arousing the wrath of Apu Manco (Lord Manco).

I allayed the men's fears somewhat by suggesting to the Governor
that we limit each man's contract to two or three days only, and double the pay. Over the next three weeks we hired a total of seventy men
from the surrounding area, shuttling them back and forth over the
mountain trails at a rate never seen in these quiet valleys, at least not
for centuries. It was a successful game of psychology. Governor Ardilles
would dispatch written orders with his official seal requesting that the
lieutenant governors send men to Espíritu Pampa. When this failed,
we would coax, plead, bribe, flatter and hound the men, appealing to
their emotions until they agreed to hire out for a few days. We were
not able to overcome all their fears of the enchanted pampas, but at
least we got men.

Monday, July 13, Espíritu Pampa. New Discoveries
At dawn we send Ascensión down river with a can of salt, a machete
and a small axe from our stores (money has absolutely no value to

these isolated tribes) to barter with the Machiguengas. He is instructed to speak with the chief (tribal custom forbids them from giving out their names for fear of losing their souls, so he is to address the chief as Mariano) and to try to obtain information about ruins. Ascensión is told to give the items to the chief if he agrees to tell us of the whereabouts of ancient remains. This will be our only chance to make contact, we are told. Once our man enters the "Machi" camp they will fade away in the jungle and not come out.

I set out with a dozen men to explore the pampas. Packs of wild pigs, forty or fifty head each, are said to frequent the jungle plains. Vicious when disturbed, they will charge a man. If he attempts to escape by climbing a tree, they uproot it and try to tear the man apart. I have the rifle and ammunition broken out. We head for the bridge we had seen two days before, where we start cutting trails into the dense vegetation. I fan the men out and shortly one of them reports he has come to a wall, below the fountain with three spouts. It turns out to be another stone fountain with a single waterspout; but better worked than the first. Incredible! Not more than twenty feet from the other fountain and no one was aware of its existence, so thick was the tangle of jungle growth.

We find another stone wall directly behind the fountain. It proves to be a walled avenue of some kind. It is under a thorn forest so thick we would have been hours cutting through it. We give up trying to breach it and turn our attention to the other side of the bridge where one of the men has found a retaining wall of an elevated group of Inca houses. Across from this group we fall into a depression and discover we have accidentally stumbled into a sunken group of Inca buildings under a mass of twisting vines and growth. It is below street level, completely walled. An hour of exploring the colossal group reveals inner streets, stairways and eighteen independent rooms. The group measures a stupendous 297 feet long! A canal with flowing water runs on one side. Tons of dead vegetation top the old ruins. One Inca house measuring 40 feet long by 18 feet wide is graced with thirteen niches and a broken doorway. The stones are cemented with adobe, as with the Spanish

Palace. The architecture is Inca, but strangely different. Clearing the site, we discover some twenty odd circular buildings 15 to 20 feet in diameter. My men show surprise at finding these ruins.

We scramble back up to the upper wall over which we had come and find it is a walled passage 15 feet wide. We cut our way over this street for 300 feet until we reach the upper walls of the long structure observed the day before. Making our way blindly along the inner walls we come to a slab of white stone, which appears to have been some kind of altar. Outside we find an elevated platform some 150 feet long by 115 feet wide. Atop the walled structure sit two Inca buildings with three rooms, each topped by jungle. We find evidence that the wall of irregular stones had been covered with a red ceramic-like stucco or terracotta. Between this unusual find and the long building we had chanced on, we found a huge boulder weighing hundreds of tons. It is topped by a great *matapalo* tree whose bole is 12 feet in diameter and covered with layers of moss and tropical vegetation. The buttress roots of the great tree enclose the boulder in a tenacious grip like arms of an octopus. The forest is so dark and dense it takes a long time and much effort to uncover a stone platform which supports the large stone. A stone stairway and walled avenue lead to two rectangular Inca buildings below the big boulder. The building materials used in construction are rough, white limestone blocks, but the corners of the buildings are hand-hewn and well-cut. But so much of the construction is covered with vegetation and displaced by the numerous vines that have dislodged the stonework, it is difficult to determine exact dimensions (field sketches were made at a later date when the buildings were cleared and the huge tree covering the elevated boulder cut away. The latter was found to measure nearly 65 feet long and 20 feet wide and oriented north to south). The big rock is an important discovery and we would have passed by this curious stone had I not been on the lookout for one of these large white stones or Yurak-Rumis, as Father-Calancha calls them at Ñusta Hispana. The boulder suggests we are inside an important ancient Inca community; for such stones were used for oracles and called huacas by the Sun Priests. These stones also served as a kind of war idol, a mother Huancauri that inspired the Incas to victory in battle. The use of this stone as a war idol would have been most fitting for the last refuge of the Incas. Resting atop its dark platform, it has the appearance of a giant egg. Inca folk myth tells of the Sun having sent down three eggs that generated the three Inca estates.

I am greatly excited by the find of the giant boulder and cannot move ahead fast enough. The natives feel differently. If it weren't for the money, none of them would be here on the enchanted pampas. We forge ahead on the road we have been following. An excitement has taken over, an excitement that only discovery produces, an intoxicating feeling.

A hundred feet later, we come to three terraces. The outer wall is nearly 300 feet long. Together they staircase up 25 feet high. The top is gained with difficulty. We approach a wall, clear some growth away with our curvos, then take a stairway that leads to a spacious courtyard, now a wild garden of exotic tropical flowers, lianas, fern and palm trees. Seven houses, their walls in ruins, rise up in the center of the terraced citadel in an atmosphere of deathly silence (in keeping with the mood of the machetemen).

We drop back down to the road and soon come to another group of rectangular buildings built atop a terraced platform 306 by 178 feet. The men chop away some of the growth that clings to the walls of large stones and then we jump back to the floor of the jungle and resume our search for other ruins.

The road we have been following comes to a halt. Rather than retrace our steps, we decide to keep going in the same direction hoping to pick it up again. I have the men spread out. It is a half hour before we find two small Inca houses perched on a promontory overlooking a river, and another group of buildings. The stonework is of better quality than what we have seen before. It is evident that the cut white limestone blocks had once fit snugly together, although many had now been broken by feeder vines that had wormed their way between the stones and pried them apart. One of the buildings, a rectangular construction with two doorways, guards a green-lit temple; a high elevated bulwark of stone consisting of rooms with niches and fallen door lintels, inner courtyards and enclosures. It must have been very impressive when the Incas lived here. A large huaca boulder rests beside one of the walls. It looks as if it may have fallen from the top of the platform wall. A magnificent *matapalo* tree with a spreading crown some one hundred feet above our heads locks one of the walls in a grip of gnarled roots. Some of the rocks are squeezed out of place by its vice-like grip. Rattan vines hang down from its upper branches, forming a screen through which we must cut our way.

Tramping on blindly through the jumbled growth, cutting a path with our blades, we intersect a trail of dead leaves. Our circuitous route has brought us to yesterday's trail. Benjamin shouts, "The Spanish Palace is ahead!" Strange how the shallow little footpath of the day before gives the men a sense of assurance. Even I feel it. It is our mark upon the jungle, a meandering ribbon we had claimed from the unknown. It is our link with the outside world. A trail is everything in the jungle. Without it a man is unsure of himself, on unfamiliar ground.

The virgin jungle can truly be beautiful in the daytime; when one has time to enjoy it, when it isn't raining and there is space enough to see. We are on higher ground now, above the boggy swamplands caused by dammed and overspilling canals. Cedrela trees, tree ferns, cane, bamboo and palm thickets of various species: Iriartea, Euterpe, Bactris, hem us in on all sides. Lianas creep and twist over the jungle floor winding up feeder vines toward the light. The trunks of the trees are covered with mossy bryophytes, lichens and bromeliads. Even without strong sunlight, vegetation thrives in the rich alluvial soil and the heavy rains. Nowhere have I seen such vivid colors as the deep red, orange and yellow of the tropical flowers overhead. With a single blow from a machete, they cascade about our heads and shoulders by the dozens, so delicately balanced and fragile is their hold on upper vines. Flowering parasite plants and bromelia add a touch of red and yellow to the hanging garden. A cardinal finch blares its song from above, no doubt saluting the sun from its lofty perch. Other than this sound the jungle is deathly still, as if we were the only living creatures. The monkeys have moved to higher ground and won't be back until the rainy season. It would have been pleasant to hear their chattering. Of all marvels of nature, the jungle has the power to evoke both fear and wonder in man.

We return down to the lower group of white stone ruins and I put the men to work clearing so plans and a photographic record can be made. Watching the first sunlight fall upon these ancient walls after a lapse of several centuries is a memorable experience. The white granite blocks, covered by thin layers of delicate lichen, take on a ghostly appearance. An ominous quiet falls over the jungle as the axemen bite into green wood. The forest seems to shudder. The men chop at the base of a tall tree until it hangs suspended from a spiderweb of vines, like a tottering mast of a ship. Machetes glint in the sun. Vines snap. The tree falls. Leaves flutter earthward, caught in shafts of light. Thin, diamond-marked snakes coil like corkscrews and slither for cover.

For the first time I realize what we have found. We are in the heart of an ancient Inca city. Is this Manco's Vilcabamba—the lost city of the Incas? I am certain we are in parts of it. I experience an overwhelming sense of the history the ruins represent. For four hundred years they have remained in the realm of legend. Some even doubted they existed. But I always knew they were there, somewhere, awaiting discovery. To me they were the most important historical remains in Peru. Important because Manco was a glorious hero who gave dignity to Peru when all was lost. Important because so many great names had looked for them. Some would expect to find cyclopean walls covered with sheets of gold, or finely cut stone of the classic Cuzco style. Old Vilcabamba wasn't this at all. She was old and worn. The walls of her buildings were toppled, covered with thick, decaying vegetable matter; their foundations under tons of slide and ooze. She had been put to the torch by the Incas who had built her and ransacked by the Spaniards who were looking for gold. Four centuries of wild jungle had twisted that part which remained. But she had not lost her dignity. One could easily see she had been a great metropolis, a colossus of the jungle. A wave of melancholy swept over me. It would require an army to clear these ruins properly; cost a fortune to restore the buildings to their original form, and they were so far from civilization that it might never be accomplished. The city represented everything for which the Incas stood. It was a monument to their industry, their struggle with nature, their fight for freedom against overpowering odds. This was immortal Vilcabamba—that legendary city of a thousand history books. If I never succeeded in finding another city it would not matter. Legend had been turned into history.

Cahill Among the Ruins in Peru
by Tim Cahill

Tim Cahill's (born 1943) adventures generally include equal parts farce and discovery. This one is no exception. Cahill set out to find undiscovered pre-Incan ruins in the montaña between the mountains and jungle of northeastern Peru. Oily bureaucrats, superstitious locals, a know-it-all companion and the Peruvian wilderness did not daunt him—though they were kind of annoying.

In the northeastern section of Peru there is a state called Amazonas, and the capital city of six thousand is Chachapoyas. Three blocks off the Plaza de Armas, down the narrow streets between clean pastel houses, there is a high wooden door that leads into a courtyard, and just off that courtyard, under his second-story apartment, Carlos Gates, the supervisor of Archaeological Monuments for Amazonas, keeps an office. For Chachapoyas, it is a luxurious affair. The floor is poured concrete, not dirt, for one thing, and for another, there is an electric light. On the walls there are various certificates and diplomas, along with the obligatory framed painting of Christ showing the Sacred Heart glowing in His chest.

A man in his middle years, Gates, like most of the people of Chachapoyas, is short, no more than five feet two inches, and very broad in the shoulders and chest. Despite his exuberant gestures, Carlos exuded grace and dignity. He smiled often, in a kindly fashion, and gave us no help at all.

"It is very difficult for you to explore here," he said in Spanish. "You must have a permit to dig."

Laszlo Berty, who spoke the best Spanish, said, "But we do not wish to dig. Only explore." The other two members of the expedition—Tom Jackson and I—nodded our assent.

"To explore, you must have a permit. You must have a permit to go into certain areas," Gates said. He suggested we visit the known ruins: Kuélap, Congona, and others.

Laszlo explained that we would certainly want to see those ruins, for we had read of them and we understood that they were beautiful. Still, our research indicated that there were other, unexplored ruins in Amazonas, and our goal was to find some of them. Señor Gates knew more of these ruins than any man alive. Could he not give us help on our expedition?

Gates stared at his desk top in what appeared to be great sorrow. Sometimes, he said, it is not good when new ruins are discovered. Men come searching for the gold and they destroy what is left of the ruins. *Huacos*—prehistoric objects—are removed and sold to wealthy collectors, and the work of scientists is made difficult.

Laszlo explained that he intended to run commercial trips down the rivers of Amazonas and that he wanted to find ruins near the rivers where he could take his clients. Tom Jackson worked for the South American Explorers' Club and he would note our discoveries, in a scientific fashion, in that club's journal. I intended to publish the results of our expedition in an American magazine. We would not dig and we were not *huaqueros*, not grave robbers.

Gates apologized profusely. He did not mean to suggest that we were huaqueros—never. It is the men who come later, like vultures, who defile the ruins. He was referring to those men and not to us.

There was silence. We were getting nowhere. Finally Laszlo said, "It is true that we are not professors of anthropology or professors of archaeology. We are adventurers. But adventurers with an object." He fixed Gates with his most sincere stare. "In the life of a man," he said with great dignity, "it is important for adventure. What else is in life?"

I am incapable of uttering a statement like that. It would wither and die on my tongue like a snake in the sun. But it was Laszlo's genius, when dealing with Peruvians, to say the right thing at the right time. Carlos nodded sagaciously as if he agreed that, yes, it is adventure and adventure alone that is important in the life of a man.

Laszlo knew enough not to push any further at this point. We would visit Kuélap, he said, and the others. When we returned to Chachapoyas, perhaps Señor Gates would be able to help us then.

Yes, Carlos said, if he could find the time, perhaps.

There is, in northern Peru, a unique area known as the *montaña* located just east of the Andes and west of the awesome forests of the Amazon basin. It is a wet, mountainous, transitional surface between the mightiest mountains of the Americas and the largest jungle in the world.

The montaña is close to the equator; and, along rivers such as the Utcubamba, people grow tropical fruits and rice and sugar cane. But the vegetation of the surrounding mountains seems strangely inverted to those familiar with ranges in the temperate region. The lower slopes are poor and sandy—a cactus and mesquite environment similar to what we call high chaparral. Above the cactus the land becomes fertile—it is much like the American Midwest—and here people raise livestock and grow corn and potatoes and melons on small terraced farms called *chacras*. Above the chacras, one comes upon the strangest inversion. The terraced fields rise into thick, choking jungles. It is as if the tropical forests of the Amazon basin had made one last effort to claim the entire continent. These mountaintop jungles of the montaña are known as the *ceja de selva*, the eyebrow of the jungle.

From the highest points on the ridgetops, it is possible to watch clouds form, wispily, in the great river basins four thousand and five thousand feet below. They rise to the ridge, thicken into great roiling banks, drop a hard cold rain, and fall again into the valleys.

The ceja, then, is a jungle formed of clouds—a cloud forest—and one thousand years ago there was an Indian people, the Chachapoyas, who lived among the clouds, in fortresses constructed high on jungle ridgetops. It is thought that they chose the cloud forests for their cities for obvious defensive purposes, and also to avoid the malaria and other tropical diseases endemic to the river valleys.

Conquered by the Incas in 1480—who were, in turn, conquered by the Spanish in the 1530s—the Chachapoyan empire fell into obscurity and ruin. The great fortresses, the graceful stone cities, the grand plazas of the Chachapoyas were abandoned, left to the jungles. Many are known to archaeologists, but they are little studied. Other cities and fortresses—dozens of them, perhaps hundreds—lie undiscovered, undisturbed in a millennium, in seldom-visited frontier country the Peruvians describe as *silvestre* and *salvaje*, wild and savage.

During the month of July, *Outside* magazine launched an expedition into the montaña of northeastern Peru. Our objective was to locate undiscovered jungle ruins of the people of the clouds.

The expedition was the brainchild of Laszlo Berty, thirty, of Erie, Pennsylvania, the owner of Amazon Expeditions, a fledgling Peruvian river-running operation. Berty had been both a computer systems analyst and a Marine, and he managed to combine the fine attributes of both these professions into one remarkable personality.

Puns and jokes were lost on Laszlo. The English language is best suited for issuing orders so that one may achieve specifically stated goals.

"Don't do that," Laszlo would say.

"What?"

"Put that cup on the filthy ground."

Laszlo had outfitted the expedition—tent, sleeping bags, stove, cooking equipment—and it was important to him that these things be kept spotless. He didn't like me putting the sleeping bag I was using— his bag—on the filthy ground. He didn't like Peruvians to drink out of his canteen because you call never tell what strange diseases they might have. Driving along the broiling river basins, we were frequently obliged to bake in the car with the windows up because Laszlo is *allergic to dust*.

In the little cafes, Laszlo ordered the waiters to stop wiping his bottle of Amazonas Kola with their towels. The towels were invariably *sucio*, filthy. My hands were usually sucio, Tom Jackson's hands were sucio, even Laszlo's hands were sucio at times, a condition which disturbed him greatly. He'd examine his fingers and mutter, "Filthy, filthy."

It is fair to say there was tension between Laszlo and me. By the morning of the third day—no later—we had come to an unspoken agreement. At odd intervals I'd simply explode. Laszlo would regard me with injured dignity and apprehension—you call never tell what a crazy person will do—and I'd shout in his face for five or ten minutes at a crack, walk off stiff-legged and steaming, think of something else and charge back to stand inches from him, waving my arms and pointing. After one of these beserk tirades, Laszlo and I would be very polite to each other for, oh, two or three days. Then the cycle would start over.

Tom Jackson, twenty-five, the third member of the expedition, watched these outbreaks in noncommittal silence. He was a slight, handsome fellow, and a missing tooth in the front of his mouth gave him a boyish, Huck Finn look. Tom had accompanied Laszlo on a previous river trip, and I assumed that he had sided with Laszlo during that first high-volume confrontation. I was wrong.

"Naw," he told me privately, "I was hoping you'd punch his lights out."

Jackson swallowed what I interpreted as a lot of abuse from Laszlo: orders issued in bored disgust, as if Tom were some witless incompetent. Because *Outside* had funded the expedition and Laszlo had organized and outfitted it, Tom attempted to remain neutral regarding the basic unsettled question of who was to lead the party. It took him a week to break. When he finally did, he erupted, burning Laszlo with a number of acid and intolerable comments. After some time I was invited to arbitrate. Who would continue with me, who should return to Lima?

Wrong approach, I said. Stupid. Together we were a complete entity. Apart our chances of success were minimal. We were all pretty fair woodsmen, but Laszlo had a knack for getting information out of Peruvians. Tom was the most accomplished climber, the hardest working, the most adept at fixing mechanical things. I was the strongest swimmer—we would have to get our equipment across a number of rivers at the rapids—and I had done more reading on the area, more recently. Decisions, I suggested, should be a three-way affair.

In the end, my position prevailed. Still, we spent the next few weeks gnawing on one another's nerves like rats on a rope. Laszlo had to put up with incredible stupidity on my part, and at times Jackson was even dumber. Once we found ourselves halfway up a mountain just as the sun set. We were on a grassy flat and we could see several two-story wattle-and-daub huts: two feet of mud and clay packed onto a frame of branches and thin tree trunks. The huts were empty.

We had drunk all our water on the climb. We were exhausted and sweated out and my tongue was stuck to the roof of my mouth. I suggested that our first order of business should be to find water.

Laszlo could hardly believe I had said such a thing. "There's no water up here," he said. It should have been self-evident. "That's why there's no people here. They only come up in the wet season." He paused to let this sink in. "When there's water."

Still, you can't talk good sense to cretins. Tom and I decided that since there was new corn and wheat in the chacras, and since we could see horses in a pen, and since there had been a fiesta in the town below, that the people who lived in the huts were at the fiesta, that there had to be water for the crops and livestock, and that we would look for that water. Laszlo, who knew the search was fruitless, lay on his back in the grass, wisely conserving energy.

At dusk Tom found a small pool, about two feet in diameter, behind a stand of trees. Later, after dinner and over coffee, I expressed the opinion that Tom had saved our ass, finding the water.

Laszlo sighed heavily. "Of course you found water," he explained. "Water runs down the side of a hill. You guys walked across the side of the hill. *Anybody* could have found water."

This was the kind of irritating idiocy Laszlo had to put up with *every single day*.

Shortly after our second visit to Carlos Gates, we drove south from the city of Chachapoyas to Tingo, where we started the long walk to Kuélap. That fortress, discovered by Juan Crisóstomo Nieto in 1843, was the keystone of known Chachapoyan culture. It is simply massive—the largest pre-Inca construct in Peru—and the fort is set like a ship upon high, crumbly cliff walls. The battlements rise some sixty feet above the cliffs and stretch for nearly half a mile. One stands before the main gate feeling dwarfed and impotent.

Kuélap had been cleared in spots, but for the most part it belonged to the jungle. It was an easy matter to become lost *inside*, and wander about, stumbling into typical Chachapoyan circular habitations. These are round stone buildings, usually open at some point to form a door, and constructed out of what appears to be local limestone. They are five, ten, fifteen, sometimes twenty feet high. In all probability, the circular habitations (or "circle habs," as we soon began to call them) had been covered with the same kind of thatched roof we had seen on the huts below. They were now, of course, open to the sky, and countless generations of jungle plants had grown in their interiors—grown and died and provided the loam for other plants so that most of the constructs were filled with soil. Flowers and trees and thorns grew where the roofs had been.

There were more battlements, rising in concentric circles behind the main walls, and everything there built by the hand of man, even the outer walls, was curvilinear. Small trails wound among the circle habs and underground chambers and mossy walls. Off the trails, the jungle was so thick it took a good fifteen minutes of machete work to move a hundred yards.

The vegetation was thick and rank and thorny. To walk it was necessary to clear an area from head to thigh. It was impossible to see more than three feet ahead, and the odor was intense. Everywhere there was the smell of faded lilacs, a sickly sweet odor, that combined with something thick and dead and skunklike.

We camped for a night atop a tower situated at the highest point in the fort. Twenty-seven feet high with crumbling steps to the top, it had been cleared, and there was a grassy spot for our tent. We could see forever, in every direction.

As the sun set, we listened to the jungle. At twilight there was a last frantic avian burst: green parrots shrieked over the constant chatter of smaller birds and occasionally we heard a series of strange, high-pitched whoops. As darkness fell, the birds gave way to crickets and the odd frog, croaking deep and resonant, like the sound of two rocks striking together underwater. Fireflies flashed in the jungle and, this night, there was a full moon; the tops of the trees shown silver in its light. Occasionally, there was a deep-throated wail, probably a monkey, followed by about half a dozen barks or grunts.

I slept the sleep of a Chacha warrior, secure in this fort at the center of the universe.

Virtually nothing is known of the Chachapoyan people (also called Chachas) before the Incas. We have some information—about a page and a half—in a book written by Garcilaso de la Vega. Born in 1539, Garcilaso was in a unique position to record the events of the conquest of Peru by the Spanish; his mother was the granddaughter of the Inca Túpac Yupanqui, his father was a conquistador with Pizarro. Combining his own memories of the conquest and interviews with Inca court historians—the Indians had no written language, but their historians memorized a set chronology, using colored ropes in which various knots had been tied as mnemonic devices—Garcilaso wrote his massive Royal Commentaries of the Incas.

The Chacha women, he tells us, were considered especially beautiful and the men fierce fighters. They worshiped the serpent and they lived in a hard, mountainous land where travelers were routinely required to raise and lower themselves by rope. In the late 1470s, the eleventh Inca, Túpac Yupanqui, moved north from the Inca capital of Cuzco on a march of imperial conquest. In 1480, his armies conquered the Chachapoyas and subdued seven major cities. Garcilaso places these cities in a rough geographical context: one can be found on the other side of a certain snowy pass, another located atop a sloping hill so many leagues long.

In the mid-1960s, an American explorer, Gene Savoy—inspired by the exploits of Hiram Bingham, who discovered Machu Picchu in 1911—launched a series of expeditions into the montaña in search of the cities mentioned by Garcilaso. A University of Portland dropout and former newspaperman, Savoy was not a professional scientist. "I taught myself what I know about archaeology, anthropology and history from reading, study and practical field experience," Savoy states in his book, *Antisuyo.* (The name refers to that quarter of the Inca empire east of the Andes.) In his last expedition, Savoy may have discovered as many as six of the seven cities mentioned by Garcilaso.

In his travels, Savoy hoped to examine a theory first propounded by Dr. Julio C. Tello, one of the fathers of Peruvian archaeology. Having discovered one of the first full-blown Peruvian cultures—the Chavín, dated about 900 to 400 B.C.—Tello postulated that the forerunners of the Chavín may have originated in the jungle.

More accepted theories say that culture there first evolved among less sophisticated local peoples or that it was imported by Central American or Mexican peoples who migrated to northern Peru. The idea that culture in Peru might have originated in the montaña or jungle is not taken seriously by most archaeologists. The jungles of both regions, it is thought, could not have supported a high culture.

But what if a major migration had taken place along long-forgotten jungle trails? If so, it was possible that the remains of a culture earlier than the Chavín existed, undiscovered, somewhere in the tropical rain forest.

Savoy's expeditions in Amazonas did not prove, conclusively, that ancient man in Peru rose up out of the jungle. However, the dozens of cities, the hundreds of curvilinear Chachapoyan ruins Savoy found, did prove, he wrote in *Antisuyo,* that the mountaintop jungles of the ceja de selva "could support a vigorous civilization whose monumental remains are as imposing if not superior to anything found on the coast or sierra." Potsherds taken from Savoy's finds were carbon-dated and found to be between 800 and 1400 A.D. All were from superficial grave sites, and test pits undoubtedly would have yielded older specimens.

Throughout *Antisuyo* one senses an obsessiveness: "Where did the Chachapoyas originate and who were their forerunners . . . from an explorer's point of view, the work has only just begun—with three million square miles of tropical forest still to be archaeologically explored, one hardly knows where to begin. I believe that tropical Amazonas holds the vestige of ancient cultures of which we know nothing— perhaps a civilization of far greater magnitude than we suspect (the size of the Chachapoyan ruins, which surpass those of Cuzco, hint at such a possibility)." Unstated in *Antisuyo* is a glittering vision: the great mother metropolis with its massive towers and battlements and plazas, out there—somewhere—in Amazonia. The cradle of the continent's civilization. The final discovery.

When Pizarro landed in 1532, Peru was bleeding in the aftermath of a brutal civil war. Following the death of the Inca Huayna Cápac in 1525, Atahuallpa, the Inca's son by a concubine, launched a war against Huáscar, the legitimate heir. Huáscar's forces were defeated, he was imprisoned, and Atahuallpa assumed the throne.

Pizarro and less than two hundred men crossed the mountains and established themselves in the great Inca plaza at Cajamarca. Atahuallpa and an unarmed retinue of thousands entered the plaza in good faith to meet the strange white men. There, Pizarro's chaplain approached the Inca and informed him that a certain God the Father, who was actually a Trinity, had created the world and all the people in it. But, because people had sinned, God the Father had to send His Son, part of the Trinity, to earth, where He was crucified. Before that happened, the chaplain explained, the Son, whose name was Jesus Christ, had conferred His power upon an Apostle, Peter, and Peter had passed that power on, successively, to other men, called Popes, and one of these last Popes had commissioned Charles the Fifth of Spain to conquer and convert the Inca and his people. Atahuallpa's only hope of salvation, the chaplain concluded, was to swear allegiance to Jesus Christ and to acknowledge himself a tributary of Charles the Fifth.

Atahuallpa then informed the chaplain that he, the Inca, was the greatest prince on earth and that he would be the tributary of no man. This Pope, he said, must be crazy to talk of giving away countries that didn't belong to him. As for Jesus Christ Who had died, the Inca was sorry, but—and here he pointed to the sun—"my God still lives in the heavens and looks down on his children."

The conquistadores lay in wait, hiding in the massive buildings that surrounded the square. When the chaplain returned with the Inca's reply, Pizarro, his foot soldiers, and cavalry erupted into the plaza. Muskets and cannons firing, they slaughtered between two thousand and ten thousand unarmed Indians that day and took the Inca prisoner.

Atahuallpa, in captivity, spoke often with the Spanish, and he understood soon enough—all talk of Popes and Trinities notwithstanding—that it was the love of gold which brought the white men to his country. He offered Pizarro enough gold to fill a room measuring seventeen by twenty-two feet to a height of nine feet.

It would be a simple matter, Atahuallpa told his captors, for the interiors of the temples at Cuzco were literally plated with gold and all ornaments and utensils used in religious ceremonies were fashioned of gold or silver. There were immense silver vases and statues, and silver reservoirs to hold water. Even the pipes which carried water into the sacred buildings were made of silver. In the temples and royal palaces there were gardens of gold and silver: sculpture representing corn, potatoes, and other crops grew from a glittering soil of gold dust.

Before the king's ransom had been completely paid, Huáscar was murdered in his prison cell. Pizarro said Atahuallpa had issued the order, and a swift trial was followed by a swifter execution. Pizarro had seen that the Inca empire was an absolute theocracy and that without the Inca—especially in the wake of a bloody civil war—the Indians would fall into disorganization and despair.

The gold and jewels that the Spaniards took out of Peru in the following years is estimated at over $11 billion. And yet, after the conquest, the Incas themselves told the Spaniards that they had seen only a small fraction of the actual wealth of the empire. During the time of the ransom, most of the gold—tears of the sun, the Incas called it—had been hidden in the jungles or thrown into the lakes. (One treasure, mentioned in some chronicles, is a massive chain of gold, *seven hundred feet long*, fashioned in celebration of Huáscar's birth.) Many historians and treasure hunters believe that the gold of the Incas was smuggled over the Andes, into the eastern land that was called Antisuyo.

The day after our night on Kuélap, we drove south along the Utcubamba River to the town of Leimebamba. This area must have been important to the cloud people, judging by the number of ruins to be found there. Leimebamba itself consists of a paved square and about half a dozen rock-strewn mean streets where black wiry-haired pigs doze in the sun and goats root among the rocks, and the old white-haired Indian women in black robes sit cross-legged in the dust, spinning wool.

We sat at a rickety table in the Bar El Caribe, a dank, dirt-floored restaurant just off the square, and studied our maps and diagrams. The owner, a sly, hatchet-faced man with a severe crewcut, lurked about—a pace or two away—staring over our shoulders.

"You have come for the gold," he informed us. "You have a metal detector."

Laszlo told him that we were only tourists, not interested in gold, and that metal detectors are too heavy to carry up mountains in a backpack.

The man would not be taken for a fool. "There are portable metal detectors," he said.

As was usual in Amazonas, where gringos are seldom seen, we were surrounded by friendly people who simply stared for minutes on end before opening up with questions.

"You search for gold?"

"No. "

"You are huaqueros?"

"No. "

"Why have you drawn your own maps then?"

Leimebamba was rife with rumors about Gene Savoy: he had come into the area with experts, had followed the old Inca road, and had found a body of water which he called the Lake of the Condors. There he sent a scuba diver down, and when the diver came up he and Savoy had a fight about the gold. People believe that the treasure of the Incas is buried in the ruins; that it is gleaming there, beneath the waters of the Lake of the Condors.

Savoy, so the rumor goes, returned to Leimebamba alone. Later he was seen, it is said, crossing the mountains on the trail to Balsas, which is on the Marañón River. With him were two heavily laden mules. No one who tells the story doubts that those mules carried gold. Here the details get a little fuzzy. At Balsas, Savoy was arrested, or perhaps only detained. Some say he was deported as a huaquero. Others say he escaped to Ecuador.

The owner interrupted to show us a prize possession. It was a cassette tape recorder and he stroked it as if it were a favorite pet, then slipped a tape into its mouth. It was American music, country and western, and the song we heard was about a bunch of cowboys who find a fortune in gold and end up killing each other.

There are, in Amazonas, several stories of people who have entered or violated ruins and these people invariably have sickened and died, victims, it is said, of *el abuelo*—the grandfather—an unpleasant transference in which all the diseases of the gathered dead enter and infest the interloper's body.

The first person we met who actually showed fear approaching the ruins was one Manuel Anunsación Hidalgo Garcia, nineteen, but he was very cagey about it. After guiding us along an easy trail from Leimebamba to a high meadow near the mountain ruins of Congona, he simply pointed into a wall of thorny brush and left us to machete our way the remaining quarter-mile.

The odor was sharper than at Kuélap, more like licorice or anise, though still pervaded by that melancholy smell of faded lilacs. Congona was thick with a massive-trunked tree that adapts itself to the jungle canopy by sending out thick branches in grand horizontal thrusts. These branches were hung with green streamers and moss, and wherever a branch found the sun, there were large, sharp-petaled red flowers.

The first circular habitations we saw were unimpressive, but as we moved higher, they became larger and more ornate. In places, the branches of these massive trees had burst through the walls of the ruins. At the summit, we found a grassy meadow fronting a magnificent double tower with a winding stairway to the top.

Where Kuélap had been awesome, Congona was a marvel of symmetry and grace. There was an ineffable beauty to it, even in ruin. Huge yellow flowers grew around the rim of the central towers and green creepers fell along the mossy walls. There was no apparent military value in the towers and they suggested nothing so much as a place of worship, a cathedral in the jungle.

After we established camp at the top of the towers, I hacked my way, alone, through vines and creepers, the odor of licorice thick in the dying twilight. The inside of one of the less ornate circle habs I found had been cleared, and the work had been done, at a guess, two or three years previously. Moving into the ruin, I saw something wrong and bad, something that seemed palpably evil, and I felt, for a chill moment, the Thing that had caused Manuel Anunsación Hidalgo Garcia to leave us at the lip of the jungle.

There, dead center in the floor of the ruin, I saw a grave-shaped hole, five feet deep, three wide, four long. The sides of the hole were covered with thick green moss. Huaqueros—grave robbers—had been to Congona.

A few feet above the hole, four or five flat black insects, like wasps or hornets, hovered in formation. It was a simple matter, in the near darkness, to let oneself go, to feel a dread like paralysis taking hold of the arms and legs. I could imagine the golden priests atop the central towers and the people of the clouds strolling among the most graceful achievements of their culture. Momentarily, in that mood and in the presence of a defilement, I tried to believe that we were wrong to be there, that these ruins were best left to time and the jungle.

In the morning, that shivery sense of blasphemy seemed a conceit, a romance. Early that afternoon we returned to Leimebamba, walking three abreast and filling the narrow streets. There were scratches on our arms and faces and our machetes swung by our sides. We were giants, taller and heavier than the biggest men in town. The old women gathered up the children and shooed them indoors as we passed. We had come from Congona, and something in the eyes of the people begged us to swagger. We were brave men, foolish men. Soldiers of fortune. Huaqueros.

When the owner of the Bar El Caribe delivered our drinks and asked if we had found gold, we smiled and gave noncommittal answers.

There is no such thing as a good map of Amazonas, and we have Ecuador to thank for that. In July of 1941, that country, claiming the land from its border south to the Marañón River, launched an undeclared war against Peru. At the battle of Zarumilla, Peruvian forces won a stunning victory and Peru retained control of 120,000 square miles of land. There are Ecuadorians who object to this state of affairs and, in the hinterlands of Amazonas, one still hears of sporadic border clashes.

Good, detailed contour maps of the state, then, have a military significance and they are impossible to obtain. Additionally, the Guardia Civil, a national police force, maintains control points along the only road into the jungle; there foreigners must show their passports and explain what they are doing in that area of Peru.

Hotels are required to obtain the same information, as is the PIP (pronounced "peep"), the Peruvian Investigative Police, an FBI analog. Officers of the PIP—we called them pipsqueaks—wear plain clothes and strut around looking significant. My favorite was the chief—El Jefe—of the Chachapoyas division. One night at the Bar Chacha, four pipsqueaks surrounded our table and told us there was some problem with our papers and that we must go with them to headquarters. We were shown into a large room where El Jefe, a fat man of middle years, pretended not to notice us. His flowing black hair gleamed under the electric light and smelled strongly of rose water. He wore blue-tinted aviator glasses, an iridescent blue raincoat, and a blue-and-white polka-dot ascot. On one side of his desk there was a neat pile of official documents without stamps. On the other side was a smaller pile of official documents that had been stamped. In the middle of the desk, just behind the nameplate that read "Miguel Zamora," there were half a dozen different stamps. Miguel took his time with a couple of documents, looked up with an oleaginous smile, and asked, "What can I do for you gentlemen?"

"Can you walk like a duck?" is the only appropriate response to that question; but, of course, we didn't say that. There were many things we didn't say to police officers during our stay.

Carlos Gates, the supervisor of archaeological monuments, was actually beginning to like us. We were well read, well prepared, and we were persistent. Between trips to the known ruins we visited him a total of four times, and missed him on three other passes. Finally, Señor Gates stopped talking about permits and broke out the gin in the middle of one of our visits. We were getting somewhere.

Because our Spanish was not the best, Gates spoke slowly and distinctly, and tended to shout a bit, as if we were also hard of hearing. He helped us out with gestures and expressions. If something was large or interesting or beautiful, Carlos would widen his eyes as if awestruck. If something was difficult or dangerous, he would snap into a serious expression and pretend to brush lint off his shirt front with his right hand.

Yes, Gates said, he was the man mentioned in Savoy's book, and no, he didn't believe for a moment the rumors we had heard in Leimebamba. People in Amazonas, he said, are jealous of their history and they delight in its mystery. He knew Savoy wasn't a huaquero because he had worked with him, had helped the American plan his expeditions.

And now he was willing to help us. We knew, of course, that most of the known Chacha ruins were located on high forested peaks near the Utcubamba River. This was clear. Many of the ruins were fortified cities: a fortress at the highest point surrounded by circle habs. There were a dozen or more of these the Utcubamba basin and the main doors of the forts always faced Kuélap. Gates drew a simplified sketch.

The known ruins lay in a rough semicircle, east of Kuélap. The area west of Kuélap had yet to be explored. Gates drew a second diagram.

On this diagram Gates indicated that there would be ruins in the area west of Kuélap. It was his theory that the Chachas would have had cities or fortresses there for reasons of defense and symmetry. If we were willing to share our findings with him, Carlos said, he would introduce us to Don Gregorio Tuesta, a landowner in the area, who could find us a guide who knew the trails there.

We looked at our map. There were no trails marked in the area, and only one pueblo. "What's the land like there?" Laszlo asked.

Carlos said he'd never been there, but from what he'd heard, it was (here Señor Gates popped his eyes for us), but also (he brushed lint off his shirt).

One cool, misty morning I found myself just outside of a seven-hut pueblo called Choctamal, a four-hour walk west of Kuélap. Not far away, on a heavily forested ridge, there was a fortress known as Llaucan, the last known Chacha ruin west of the Utcubamba. This day we were to push on: climb the mountains separating the Utcubamba River basin from the Marañón River basin. There would be, we fervently hoped, unknown ruins ahead. In a sense, it was the start of our expedition.

I was squatting in the bushes with the last of the confetti they call toilet paper in Peru. The local pigs had just demonstrated to me, in the most concrete manner, that they would eat *anything*. Not only that, but they seemed to prefer it directly from the horse's mouth, as it were. For this reason, I was clutching a long sturdy stick, the better to crack the porcine bastards as they made their move. So they milled about, just out of range, squealing and grunting and fixing me in their beady little hungry pink eyes. Not an auspicious start for an expedition of discovery.

Don Gregorio Tuesta, fifty-five, the man whom we had met through

Carlos Cates, was big, five feet ten inches and 175 pounds—a giant of a man for Amazonas. He had eleven children, was a rich man, and walked a lot like John Wayne, only faster. Carlos Cruz, twenty-two, a local potato farmer and hunter, tended the mule carrying our supplies. Carlos was a little over five feet tall, dark of skin, and poor. He and Tuesta chewed coca leaves together in a friendly fashion.

"You need coca to make you strong to climb to the ruins," Tuesta said. Strictly in the interests of good journalism, I chewed about a pound of primo coca. Taken along with a taste of quicklime, called *cal*, it tended to depress the appetite, deaden the tongue, and overcome fatigue. The rush was minor and somewhat disappointing: about what you'd expect from a chocolate bar eaten late in the afternoon of a particularly hectic day.

"What's the trail like ahead?" we'd ask Tuesta.

"*Muy fácil*," very easy, he would lie. We came to calibrate the difficulty ahead by a system I called the coefficient of coca. If Carlos and the Don plunged on with only a single mouthful, it would be a bearable climb; three or more mouthfuls meant we were in for hell on a hill.

At ten thousand feet we came on some small circle habs. There were three of them, in very poor condition. It was not an impressive set of ruins, but it was unknown to scientists and explorers.

It was there, at our first discovery, that I was treated to an example of Carlos's humor. In a steep clearing, the loose forest loam turned muddy and I slid a fast dozen yards down the slope on my back. Dirt poured into my pants, and, when I finally managed to turn over and pull myself to a halt by grabbing handfuls of ground cover, I saw Carlos laughing like a lunatic at a parade.

"Don Timoteo," he said, "*ichunga*."

Ichunga, I found to my discomfort some moments later, is a small prickery plant that imparts a painful chemical sting that lasts for half an hour. The palms of my hands were on fire and the dirt in my pants was full of ichunga. Carlos could hardly stand it. He kept muttering "Don Timoteo" and chuckling to himself for minutes at a stretch. I was convinced that he had the brain of a hamster.

An hour above the first circle habs, we explored a sparse, almost dry jungle where we came upon a series of high, natural rock walls. Where these walls met the forest floor there were a number of overhangs, some of which contained small caves. In a rock pile under one of the overhangs, Don Gregorio spotted a human jawbone. Tom crawled back into a cave and came out with three complete skulls, two of which were bleached pure white and one was a pale muddy brown.

We found nearly a dozen skulls in all. The beige pottery fragments scattered among the skulls had a red line around the inside lip, just above a contiguous series of broad red spirals. The fragments were similar in size, shape, color, and design to a bowl I had seen in Lima at the National Museum of Anthropology and Archaeology. That bowl had been taken from Kuélap and was dated at 1000 A.D.

These bones had lain in place perhaps a thousand years or more. They were not, as I had expected, brittle, but were, instead, very flexible. Perhaps it was the dampness or the acid in the sod, but you could squeeze these skulls at the temple and they would give several inches. Then, slowly, they would settle back into shape. The urge was strong to squeeze each skull.

A heavy cloud rolled up from the Río Tingo below and cast everything in a pale, leaden light so that the dry moss on the trees hung gray and lifeless. What had earlier been a slight breeze became a chill wind and, at odd intervals, we heard the caw of an unseen bird. It was a harsh, mechanical sound and it contrasted eerily with another animal noise, a soft mournful cooing that seemed to be very near.

Don Gregorio anointed our fingers with a fragrant oil; protection, he said, against the *antimonia*, a supposed disease caused by breathing the dust of archaeological excavations. A person suffering from the antimonia, it is said, will die coughing up the entire volume of his body's blood.

The mountains that form the watershed between the Utcubamba and Marañón rivers rise to 12,000 feet and higher. Above 10,400 feet or so, the jungle gives way to *puna*, cold, wind-whipped grasslands. At night the temperature drops well below freezing and cold stars howl in the sky.

There was a pass, Abra Asomada, behind us, and we were making our way through a region of intermontane passes that seldom dropped below eleven thousand feet. (Don Gregorio had returned to Chachapoyas, and now Carlos led, forging the trail with uncanny skill.) The ground looked like easy walking but it was treacherous. High green-brown grasses hid impassable marshes and there were sinkholes deep enough to drop a man from the face of the earth.

Coming out of the marshes, we followed a ridge toward a high stone outcropping. Nearing the outcropping, we came upon a round grassy indentation. It was, unmistakably, a circular habitation. The hill above was pockmarked with circle habs, twenty-five to thirty of them scattered like a skirt before the rock above. To the north, over a gentle ridge, there were twenty more.

And the rock outcropping itself: where there were gaps in the natural stone, we saw high limestone walls. It was a fort, and we hurried to climb our way to the top. At 11,720 feet, the highest point in the fort proper, there was a small tower, similar in shape to the one we had seen at Kuélap.

To my knowledge, this miniature Kuélap was the first Chachapoyan fort to be found *above* the cloud forests. Located as it was, on a commanding position over a natural Marañón-to-Utcubamba route, I imagined the fort was Kuélap's defense early warning point. The vision goes like this:

The tower lookout spots suspicious movement from the Marañón side. A staggered series of runners is dispatched to Kuélap. A drum sounds, and those in the circle habs, warriors all, march out to meet the invading army. Repulsed by superior numbers, they retreat to the fort, which they can hold indefinitely. The invaders, anxious to claim richer prizes below, march off toward the Utcubamba.

Where the warriors of Kuélap are lying in ambush.

I don't know why this should be, but finding a fort, a military installation, is more thrilling than coming upon the remains of an ancient but apparently peaceful community. It has an effect on the ego and, I suspect, this is especially true of rank amateurs like myself who enter into expeditions not really convinced there is anything out there to find. We become Explorers, with a capital E, and that gives us the right to call things by any name we choose.

Never mind the handful of local hunters who know of the place and call it something or other in some goddamn foreign language. Just because a sheer accident of birth and geography put them there first, just because we are talking about their country and their ancestors, these arrogant bozos think they have the right to go around slapping names on things willy-nilly. The hell with them, I say.

It's up to us Explorers to name these places. We rush into print, the better to screw our expeditionary friends. It gives us near orgasmic pleasure to consider the other fellow—Laszlo Berty, let's say—reading our report in a mounting fury. We like to think that now—at this very moment—the color is rising in his face, making it all red and mottled, like a slice of raw liver. We chuckle over our typewriters. We are Explorers. We get to name things.

Okay?

Okay.

Henceforth, let the fort above Abra Asomada be known as Fort Big Tim Cahill. This is a good name, and I think it sings.

The passes and the puna formed a natural boundary line, like a river, and I imagined that Fort Cahill would be the last Chacha construct we would find west of the Utcubamba. I was wrong. We swept down out of the cold grasslands onto a forested ridge with three prominent peaks. There were dozens of circle habs on each peak and, inexplicably, there was no evidence of fortification. In case of attack, the people of Three Peaks must have retreated back over the puna—which seemed unlikely because of the distance and the cold—or they massed at some yet-undiscovered fort, another Kuélap perhaps, on the Marañón side.

Dropping from 10,500 feet at Three Peaks to 9,250 feet at a grassy area called Laguna Seca, we chose a steep ridge-running trail. At 9,300 feet, we came upon a score of circle habs just off the trail and, rising with the ridge, we found dozens more. This was one of the wetter jungles we had seen and the walls of the ruins were badly crumbled. In places we would come upon a high, unnaturally round mound of earth. A machete sank two feet into soft loam before striking solid stone. We attempted to clear one of these buried circle habs, but it was painstaking work. Wrist-thick roots had burrowed through the stone, and it was difficult to remove them without damaging the structure.

There were perhaps a hundred circle habs on the ridge, and still we found no evidence of fortification. At one point, we came upon three rectangular buildings, each thirty feet long, sixteen across, separated by alleys six feet wide. Rectangular construction was characteristic of the Incas, and a good guess would be that these had been built sometime in the 1480s, just after Túpac Yupanqui conquered the Chachas.

Following the ridge from about 9,500 feet to 8,300 feet, we found over a hundred more circle habs and about twenty-five rectangles among them.

Below the ridge, the jungle opened into bright green broadleaf plants, and the trees were hung with brilliant red and yellow and green creepers, so that it was rather like walking through a continuous bead curtain. Dozens of large black butterflies with white Rorschach patterns on their wings rested on the broadleafs and darted among the creepers.

On my map of the area, I found one pueblo, Pisuquia, and the trail brought us there early one steamy afternoon. The pueblo consisted of four or five stone and mudpack houses, a few huts, one haggard young man, a suety señora, two bony pigs, a flock of decrepit chickens, and half a dozen of the dirtiest, most sullen children in the universe. There were, the young man told us, ruins on that ridge—he pointed south— and that one—east—and that one—west. Not to mention the two hundred and some ruins we found on the ridge that brought us into Pisuquia.

The people of Pisuquia farmed with wooden plows and lived in dirt-floored huts that crumble in about twenty years. It was boggling to

think that a thousand years ago there were not only *more* people living
in the area, but that they were certainly more accomplished builders,
and probably better potters, jewelers, and farmers than the present
locals. The Chachas of prehistoric Peru were, by all objective standards,
more civilized than the people of Pisuquia.

Three hours beyond Pisuquia, there is a pueblo called Tribulón, and
Carlos directed us to a large house where some of his relatives lived.
Half a dozen men sat on a low bench in front of the house and in front
of them there was a dented metal can that might once have held
kerosene. Occasionally one of the men would rise unsteadily and dip
their only cup, a cracked wooden bowl, into the can. He would then
shout *"jugo do caña"* and down the pale liquid in a rush that left half
the contents streaming down his shirt front. The men had a glazed and
sanguine look about the eyes and their lips were green from the coca
they chewed.

It was the eve of the feast of the Virgin of Carmen, reason enough to
drink, and the men greeted us warmly. We were offered bowls of jugo
de caña, which is fermented sugar-cane juice. Tom took a few polite
sips, but Laszlo and I downed several bowls. It had a thin, sugar-water
taste, rather like super economy orange Kool Aid, and the alcoholic
content seemed small. It tasted good after a long, hot walk and Laszlo
and I drank quite a lot of it.

An hour or two after sunset, when things started getting blurry, we
were ushered into a dark, smoky dirt-floored room some eight feet
wide and thirty long. We sat with the men at a low table with benches
a foot or two off the ground and ate corn soup with what I took to be
bits of grilled pork floating on top. There were eight or nine women
who didn't eat, but who sat opposite us, on the floor, talking quietly
among themselves. In the far corner, one of the women tended a small
wood fire and she hurried to pour more soup when the men called for
it. The only other light in the room was a small candle set high on a
wooden ledge above the women. There were bits of stringy-looking
meat hanging out to dry on the underside of the ledge.

Between bowls of jugo de caña and sips of soup, I watched the guinea pigs, called *cuy*, scurrying about in the corners of the room. The small ones made high keening sounds and hid under the women's skirts. Larger ones, snow white and the size of small rabbits, moved across the room in a stately waddle. Cuy have been a source of protein in Peru since prehistory. I glanced up at the meat hanging under the ledge, watched one of the big guinea pigs relieve itself near my foot, and examined the little piece of gray meat on my spoon.

"Más jugo de caña," I said. Every time I drank, I seemed to lose half the bowl down my shirt front. Laszlo was developing the same problem.

Tom noted that Carlos had turned out to be a terrific guide: he knew the jungles and trails as if by instinct. I drank to that. Then I drank a couple of bowls in celebration of Carlos's rotten sense of humor.

Laszlo said that he noticed that *"caramba"* was the strongest word Carlos ever used. Caramba translates to something like "Great Scott." Laszlo said he really liked Carlos and was going to teach him some great American swear words and how they could be used in potent combination. He started with the word "fuckload" to indicate a great amount. Carlos seemed acutely embarrassed by this information.

Sometime later, after more bowls of jugo de caña, I found myself in another room where Tom was playing "Oh! Susanna" on his harmonica and I was dancing with Carlos's brother-in-law, who was sweating profusely and whose lips were green. The thing to do, it seemed, was hop around on one foot or the other, machete flopping by our side, with the right hand raised in a fist high above your head and the left held steady behind the back, like a fencer. Faces swam up out of the crowd and most of them seemed to be laughing hysterically.

About midnight we were allowed to spread our bags out in a room on the second floor. Laszlo held forth for some time about all the things he had to do and about how he was going to get up at 3:00 a.m. in order to accomplish them all. There was no doubt about this. He would be up at three. Absolutely. He could do it. He didn't see how all the Peruvians could have gotten so drunk on jugo de caña since he had drunk more than anybody and didn't feel a thing. I was stricken with sudden unconsciousness just after that last statement.

About 6:30 the next morning, I woke to a very imperfect world. Laszlo was still there and I would have said he was dead except that he was snoring painfully. Though seriously ill, I made one of those superhuman efforts you read about—a young mother lifts an auto off her child, that sort of thing—and worked up a passably bright and alert tone.

"LaszIo, Laszlo," I shouted, alarmed and concerned, "it's after three. You have things to do, places to go, people to meet."

He opened one eye. The lid came up slowly, as if it were operated by several tiny men straining away at some heavy internal crank.

"Shut up," he croaked.

Laszlo lurched to his feet several hours later and, despite the fact that he hadn't been drunk, even though he drank more than anybody, his bladder had failed in the night. He had to hang his bag up to dry. It was absolutely filthy. Sucio. Laszlo would have to sleep in that stained and stale bag for the remainder of the expedition. You can imagine how I felt.

In a remote valley called Santa Rosa there is a town called Pueblo Nuevo, and just above the town there are two wattle-and-daub huts belonging to Marino Tuesta, the brother of Don Gregorio Tuesta. We had a letter of introduction.

Marino took us above his farm to a forest where most things—tree trunks, rocks, the ground itself—were covered with a soft ferny moss called musco. Everything felt fuzzy and gentle, even the circle habs we found there. Somewhat below the highest point, we came to a gently sloping area where the sun burst through the jungle canopy in oblique golden pillars, highlighting a high, sharp-cornered wall. Probably Inca. I cleared away the foliage while Tom paced off the wall for his map of the city. This is an inexact process because you must walk on broken ground and over fallen trees, hacking your way through where the jungle is thick.

Twenty-five minutes later I caught sight of Tom. *He was coming the other way*. It had taken him nearly half an hour to pace off the building. It was immense—150 feet by 150 feet—and I saw on Tom's face a glazed and incredulous expression. His map indicated that this, the largest single ruin we had found, was the central plaza of a symmetrical jungle city. The arrangement recalled governmental plazas seen in many modern American cities, and something about that realization set the mind diving into chilly waters. There is, in us all, an idiot pride which argues that our age alone possesses civilization. Standing in the midst of indisputable proof to the contrary can be terrifying, like a sudden premonition of death.

The city of the great plaza had been discovered by Miguel Tuesta, the father of Gregorio and Marino. He called it Pueblo Alto, the high city, and Marino said we were the only other people he knew who had ever seen it. He considered the ruins beautiful and went up there often, to think.

On another day, we walked across the Santa Rosa Valley to explore a mountain visible from Marino's front door. There, in a jungle thick with *bejuco*—moss-covered hanging vines the size of a man's wrist—we came on another city. The grand plaza here was larger than the one at Pueblo Alto—270 feet by 261 feet—and it was apparent that the two cities would be visible to each other when the jungle was cleared. We called this place Pueblo Alto South.

On a rise above the plaza we found three very large, very well-preserved circle habs. One had a bisecting wall inside as well as a number of small niches set at about chest level. In the niches we found five hibernating bats. Carlos plucked them from the niches, threw them in a heap on the ground, and, before we could stop him, stomped them all to death with a satisfied smile. They were, he said, vampire bats, and they preyed on the local livestock.

Within minutes, we were engulfed in a heavy downpour during which I reflected on the *relámpago*. This is a belief, common in Amazonas, that those who venture too close to the ruins will hear the thunder roll before they are incinerated by a bolt of lightning. As it was, we only got a little wet. None of us ever spat up any blood, so the antimonia didn't get us; and we didn't have any problems with el abuelo, unless all those dead Chachas suffered from chronic loose bowels. I like to think that our expedition succeeded and that we escaped retribution because we took nothing from the ruins, because we weren't huaqueros. I'm pretty sure it wasn't because we were pure of heart and lived in harmony with one another.

Back in Lima, we took our notebooks to Dr. Ruth Shady of the National Museum of Anthropology and Archaeology. We told her about the burial site and the fort above Abra Asomada, about the city on Three Peaks, about the hundreds of ruins on Pisuquia's ridge, about Pueblo Alto and Pueblo Alto South. Dr. Shady took a few sketchy notes and excused herself. The new American ambassador to Peru was visiting and she didn't have time to listen to a lot of excited talk and speculation about the Chachapoyans, none of whom had ever paid a cent to visit the museum.

So I am forced to draw my own conclusions. We proved that the Chacha culture existed west of Kuélap and extended, in force, into the Marañón River basin. I think there may be a Kuélap-like fort somewhere near the area we explored. We found no evidence of fortification past Fort Cahill, although the Chachas of the Marañón must have had at least one strong defensive position. I think our findings tend to support Savoy's hypothesis: the jungles of the montaña could and did support a vigorous culture. That culture was probably larger and more far-flung than most archaeologists now believe. It is, then, all the more possible that part of the great migration south from Mexico and Central America took place overland, through the jungles. The mother metropolis could be there still, somewhere in the vast rain forest of the Amazon basin.

In the end, I am pleased with the lack of response from the museum and Dr. Shady. It means that vast areas of our world are going to remain unexplored and unstudied. Mystery is a resource, like coal or gold, and its preservation is a fine thing.

There were many ruins our expedition didn't reach for simple lack of time. There are said to be circular habitations above Pisuquia, and in the mountains surrounding Pueblo Alto and Pueblo Alto South. One valley over from Santa Rosa, people talk of finding perfectly pre-served mummies. On a mountain across from Fort Cahill we saw a series of ancient terraces, obviously man-made, and their size suggested impressive ruins to be found there. In a place called Chilchos there are said to be mountaintop fortresses. An ancient pre-Inca road leads out of Chilchos into the jungle. No one knows where it goes.

I keep thinking about that road. It leads out of Chilchos. Into the jungle. And no one knows where it goes.

from Farthest North

by Fridtjof Nansen

Norwegian explorer Fridtjof Nansen (1861–

1930) in 1893 sailed north in hopes that the

ice would trap his ship, the Fram, *and carry it to*

the North Pole. When the ice didn't cooperate,

Nansen and crew member Hjalmar Johansen

left the ship to head for the Pole by dogsled and

kayak. Forced by conditions to abandon their

attempt, the pair made for home. They sighted

land five months after quitting the Fram—*but*

their ordeal was far from over.

W EDNESDAY, July 24th. At last the marvel has come to pass—land, land! and after we had almost given up our belief in it! After nearly two years, we again see something rising above that never-ending white line on the horizon yonder—a white line which for millennium after millennium has stretched over this sea, and which for millenniums to come shall stretch in the same way. We are leaving it, and leaving no trace behind us; for the track of our little caravan across the endless plains has long ago disappeared. A new life is beginning for us; for the ice it is ever the same.

"It has long haunted our dreams, this land, and now it comes like a vision, like fairly-land. Drift-white, it arches above the horizon like distant clouds, which one is afraid will disappear every minute. The most wonderful thing is that we have seen this land all the time without knowing it. I examined it several times with the telescope from 'Longing Camp' in the belief that it might be snow-fields, but always came to the conclusion that it was only clouds, as I could never discover any dark point. Then, too, it seemed to change form, which, I suppose, must be attributed to the mist which always lay over it; but it always came back again at the same place with its remarkable regular curves. I now remember that dark crag we saw east of us at the camp, and which I took to be an iceberg. It must certainly have been a little islet of some kind.

"The ice was worse and more broken than ever yesterday; it was, indeed, a labor to force one's way over pressure-ridges like veritable mountains, with valleys and clefts in between; but on we went in good spirits, and made some progress. At lanes where a crossing was difficult to find we did not hesitate to launch kayaks and sledges, and were soon over in this manner. Sometimes after a very bad bit we would come across some flat ice for a short distance, and over this we would go like wildfire, splashing through ponds and puddles. While I was on ahead at one time yesterday morning, Johansen went up on to a hummock to look at the ice, and remarked a curious black stripe over the horizon; but he supposed it to be only a cloud, he said, and I thought no more about the matter. When, some while later, I also ascended a hummock to look at the ice, I became aware of the same black stripe; it ran obliquely from the horizon up into what I supposed to be a white bank of clouds. The longer I looked at this bank and stripe the more unusual I thought them, until I was constrained to fetch the glass. No sooner had I fixed it on the black part than it struck me at once that this must be land, and that not far off. There was a large snow-field out of which black rocks projected. It was not long before Johansen had the glass to his eye, and convinced himself that we really had land before us. We both of us naturally became in the highest spirits. I then saw a similar white arching outline a little farther east; but it was for the most part covered with white mist, from which it could hardly be distinguished, and, moreover, was continually changing form. It soon, however, came out entirely, and was considerably larger and higher than the former, but there was not a black speck to be seen on it. So this was what land looked like, now that we had come to it! I had imagined it in many forms, with high peaks and glittering glaciers, but never like this. There was nothing kindly about this, but it was indeed no less welcome; and on the whole we could not expect it to be otherwise than snow-covered, with all the snow which falls here.

"So then we pitched the tent and had a feast suited to the occasion: lobscouse made of potatoes (for the last time but one; we had saved them long for this occasion), pemmican, dried bear's and seal's flesh, and bear tongues, chopped up together. After this was a second course, consisting of bread-crumbs fried in bear's grease, also vril-food and butter, and a piece of chocolate to wind up."

We thought this land so near that it could not possibly take long to reach it, certainly not longer than till next evening. Johansen was even certain that we should do it the same day, but nevertheless thirteen days were to elapse, occupied in the same monotonous drudgery over the drift-ice.

On July 25th I write: "When we stopped in the fog yesterday evening we had a feeling that we must have come well under land. This morning, when we turned out, the first thing Johansen did when he went to fetch some water for me to cook with was, of course, to climb up on the nearest hummock and look at the land. There it lay, considerably nearer than before, and he is quite certain that we shall reach it before night." I also discovered a new land to our west (S. 60° W. magnetic) that day; a regular, shield-like, arched outline, similar to the other land; and it was low above the horizon, and appeared to be a long way off.

We went on our way as fast as we could across lanes and rough ice, but did not get far in the day, and the land did not seem to be much nearer. In reality there was no difference to be seen, although we tried to imagine that it was steadily growing higher. On Saturday, July 27th, I seem to have a suspicion that in point of fact we were drifting away from land, I write: "The wind began to blow from the S.S.W. (magnetic) just as we were getting off yesterday, and increased as the day went on. It was easy to perceive by the atmosphere that the wind was driving the ice off the land, and land-lanes formed particularly on the east side of it. When I was up on a hummock yesterday evening I observed a black stripe on the horizon under land; I examined it with the glass, and, as I had surmised, there was an ice-edge or glacier stretching far in a westerly direction; and there was plainly a broad lane in front of it, to judge by the dark bank of mist which lay there. It seems to me that land cannot be far off, and if the ice is tolerably passable we may reach it to-day. The wind continued last night, but it has quieted down now, and there is sunshine outside. We try by every means in our power to get a comfortable night's rest in our new bag of blankets. We have tried lying on the bare ice, on the 'ski,' and tonight on the bare ice again; but it must be confessed that it is hard and never will be very comfortable; a little chilly, too, when one is wet; but we shall appreciate a good warm bed all the more when we get it.

"Tuesday, July 30th. We make incredibly slow progress; but we are pushing our way nearer land all the same. Every kind of hinderance seems to beset us: now I am suffering so much from my back (lumbago?) that yesterday it was only by exerting all my strength of will that I could drag myself along. In difficult places Johansen had to help me with my sledge. It began yesterday, and at the end of our march he had to go first and find the way. Yesterday I was much worse, and how I am to-day I do not know before I begin to walk; but I ought to be thankful that I can drag myself along at all, though it is with endless pain. We had to halt and camp on account of rain yesterday morning at three, after only having gone nine hours. The rain succeeded in making us wet before we had found a suitable place for the tent. Here we have been a whole day while it has been pouring down, and we have hardly become drier. There are puddles under us and the bag is soaked on the under-side. The wind has gone round to the west just now, and it has stopped raining, so we made some porridge for breakfast and think of going on again; but if it should begin to rain again we must stop, as it will not do to get wet through when we have no change of clothes. It is anything but pleasant as it is to lie with wet legs and feet that are like icicles, and not have a dry thread to put on. Full-grown Ross's gulls were seen singly four times to-day, and when Johansen was out to fetch water this morning he saw two.

"Wednesday, July 31st. The ice is as disintegrated and impracticable as can well be conceived. The continual friction and packing of the floes against each other grind up the ice so that the water is full of brash and small pieces; to ferry over this in the kayaks is impossible, and the search is long before we eventually find a hazardous crossing. Sometimes we have to form one by pushing small floes together, or must ferry the sledges over on a little floe. We spend much time and labor on each single lane, and progress becomes slow in this way. My back still painful, Johansen had to go ahead yesterday also; and evening and morning he is obliged to take off my boots and socks, for I am unable to do it myself. He is touchingly unselfish, and takes care of me as if I were a child: everything he thinks can ease me he does quietly, without my knowing it. Poor fellow, he has to work doubly hard now, and does not know how this will end. I feel very much better to-day, however, and it is to be hoped shall soon be all right.

"Thursday, August 1st. Ice with more obstacles than here—is it to be found, I wonder? But we are working slowly on, and, that being the case, we ought, perhaps, to be satisfied. We have also had a change—a brilliantly fine day; but it seems to me the south wind we have had, and which opened the lanes, has put us a good way farther off land again. We have also drifted a long distance to the east, and no longer see the most westerly land with the black rocks, which we remarked at first. It would seem as if the Ross's gulls keep to land here; we see them daily.

One thing, however, I am rejoicing over; my back is almost well, so that I shall not delay our progress any more. I have some idea now what it would be like if one of us became seriously ill. Our fate would then be sealed, I think.

"Friday, August 2d. It seems as if everything conspired to delay us, and that we shall never get away from this drift-ice. My back is well again now; the ice was more passable yesterday than before, so that we nearly made a good day's march; but in return wind and current set us from shore, and we are farther away again. Against these two enemies all fighting is in vain, I am afraid. We have drifted far off to the south-east, have got the north point of the land about due west of us, and we

are now in about 81° 36′ N. My only hope now is that this drift east-
ward, away from land, may stop or alter its course, and thus bring us
nearer land. It is unfortunate that the lanes are covered with young ice,
which it would be disastrous to put the kayaks through. If this gets
worse, things will look very bad. Meanwhile we have nothing to do but
go on as fast as we can. If we are going to drift back into the ice again,
then—then—

"Saturday, August 3d. Inconceivable toil. We never could go on with
it were it not for the fact that we *must*. We have made wretchedly little
progress, even if we have made any at all. We have had no food for the
dogs the last few days except the ivory-gulls and fulmars we have been
able to shoot, and that has been a couple a day. Yesterday the dogs only
had a little bit of blubber each.

"Sunday, August 4th. These lanes are desperate work and tax one's
strength. We often have to go several hundred yards on mere brash, or
from block to block, dragging the sledges after us, and in constant fear
of their capsizing into the water. Johansen was very nearly in yesterday,
but, as always hitherto, he managed to save himself. The dogs fall in
and get a bath continually.

"Monday, August 5th. We have never had worse ice than yesterday,
but we managed to force our way on a little, nevertheless, and two
happy incidents marked the day: the first was that Johansen was not
eaten up by a bear, and the second, that we saw open water under the
glacier edge ashore.

"We set off about 7 o'clock yesterday morning and got on to ice as
bad it as could be. It was as if some giant had hurled down enormous
blocks pell-mell, and had strewn wet snow in between them with water
underneath; and into this we sank above our knees. There were also
numbers of deep pools in between the blocks. It was like toiling over
hill and dale, up and down over block after block and ridge after ridge,
with deep clefts in between; not a clear space big enough to pitch a tent
on even, and thus it went on the whole time. To put a coping-stone to
our misery, there was such a mist that we could not see a hundred yards
in front of us. After an exhausting march we at last reached a lane

where we had to ferry over in the kayaks. After having cleared the side of the lane from young ice and brash, I drew my sledge to the end of the ice, and was holding it to prevent it slipping in, when I heard a scuffle behind me, and Johansen, who had just turned round to pull his sledge flush with mine, cried, 'Take the gun!' I turned round and saw an enormous bear throwing itself on him, and Johansen on his back. I tried to seize my gun, which was in its case on the fore-deck, but at the same moment the kayak slipped into the water. My first thought was to throw myself into the water over the kayak and fire from there, but I recognized how risky it would be. I began to pull the kayak, with its heavy cargo, on to the high edge of the ice again as quickly as I could, and was on my knees pulling and tugging to get at my gun. I had no time to look round and see what was going on behind me, when I heard Johansen quietly say, 'You must look sharp if you want to be in time!'

"Look sharp? I should think so! At last I got hold of the butt-end, dragged the gun out, turned round in a sitting posture, and cocked the shot-barrel. The bear was standing not two yards off, ready to make an end to my dog, 'Kaifas.' There was no time to lose in cocking the other barrel, so I gave it a charge of shot behind the ear, and it fell down dead between us.

"The bear must have followed our track like a cat, and, covered by the ice-blocks, have slunk up while we were clearing the ice from the lane and had our backs to him. We could see by the trail how it had crept over a small ridge just behind us under cover of a mound by Johansen's kayak. While the latter, without suspecting anything or looking round, went back and stooped down to pick up the hauling-rope, he suddenly caught sight of an animal crouched up at the end of the kayak, but thought it was 'Suggen'; and before he had time to realize that it was so big he received a cuff on the ear which made him see fireworks, and then, as I mentioned before, over he went on his back. He tried to defend himself as best he could with his fists. With one hand he seized the throat of the animal, and held fast, clinching it with all his might. It was just as the bear was about to bite Johansen in the head that he uttered the memorable words, 'Look sharp!' The bear kept glancing at me continually, speculating, no doubt, as to what I was going to do; but then caught sight of the dog and turned towards it Johansen let go as quick as thought, and wriggled himself away, while the bear gave 'Suggen' a cuff which made him howl lustily, just as he does when we thrash him. Then 'Kaifas' got a slap on the nose. Meanwhile Johansen had struggled to his legs, and when I fired had got his gun, which was sticking out of the kayak hole. The only harm done was that the bear had scraped some grime off Johansen's right cheek, so that he has a white stripe on it, and had given him a slight wound in one hand; 'Kaifas' had also got a scratch on his nose.

"Hardly had the bear fallen before we saw two more peeping over a hummock a little way off—cubs, who naturally wanted to see the result of the maternal chase. They were two large cubs. I thought it was not worth while to sacrifice a cartridge on them, but Johansen expressed his opinion that young bear's flesh was much more delicate in flavor than old. He would only shoot one, he said, and started off. However, the cubs took to their heels, although they came back a little while later, and we could hear them at a long distance growling after their mother.

"Johansen sent one of them a ball, but the range was too long, and he only wounded it. With some terrific growls it started off again, and Johansen after it; but he gave up the chase soon, as he saw it promised to be a long one. While we were cutting up the she-bear the cubs came back on the other side of the lane, and the whole time we were there we had them walking round us. When we had fed the dogs well, and had eaten some of the raw meat ourselves, and had furthermore stowed away in the kayaks the meat we had cut off the legs, we at last ferried over the lane and went on our way.

"The ice was not good; and, to make bad worse, we immediately came on some terrible lanes, full of nothing but tightly packed lumps of ice. In some places there were whole seas of it, and it was enough to make one despair. Among all this loose ice we came on an unusually thick old floe, with high mounds on it and pools in between. It was from one of these mounds that I observed through the glass the open water at the foot of the glacier, and now we cannot have far to go. But the ice looks very bad on ahead, and each piece when it is like this may take a long time to travel over.

As we went along we heard the wounded bear lowing ceaselessly behind us; it filled the whole of this silent world of ice with its bitter plaint over the cruelty of man. It was miserable to hear it; and if we had had time we should undoubtedly have gone back and sacrificed a cartridge on it. We saw the cubs go off to the place where the mother was lying, and thought to ourselves that we had got rid of them, but heard them soon afterwards, and even when we had camped they were not far off.

"Wednesday, August 7th. At last we are under land; at last the drift-ice lies behind us, and before us is open water—open, it is to be hoped, to the end. Yesterday was the day. When we came out of the tent the evening of the day before yesterday we both thought we must be nearer the edge of the glacier than ever, and with fresh courage, and in the faint hope of reaching land that day, we started on our journey. Yet we dared not think our life on the drift-ice was so nearly at an end. After wandering about on it for five months and suffering so many disappointments, we were only too well prepared for a new defeat. We thought, however, that the ice looked more promising farther on, though before we had gone far we came to broad lanes full of slush and foul, uneven ice, with hills and dales, and deep snow and water, into which we sank up to our thighs. After a couple of lanes of this kind, matters improved a little, and we got on to some flat ice. After having gone over this for a while, it became apparent how much nearer we were to the edge of the glacier. It could not possibly be far off now. We eagerly harnessed ourselves to the sledges again, put on a spurt, and away we went through snow and water, over mounds and ridges. We went as hard as we could, and what did we care if we sank into water till far above our fur leggings, so that both they and our 'komager' filled and gurgled like a pump? What did it matter to us now, so long as we got on?

"We soon reached plains, and over them we went quicker and quicker. We waded through ponds where the spray flew up on all sides. Nearer and nearer we came, and by the dark water-sky before us, which continually rose higher, we could see how we were drawing near to open water. We did not even notice bears now. There seemed to be plenty about, tracks, both old and new, crossing and recrossing; one had even inspected the tent while we were asleep, and by the fresh trail we could see how it had come down wind in lee of us. We had no use for a bear now; we had food enough. We were soon able to see the open water under the wall of the glacier, and our steps lengthened even more. As I was striding along I thought of the march of the Ten Thousand through Asia, when Xenophon's soldiers, after a year's war against superior forces, at last saw the sea from a mountain and cried, 'Thalatta! thalatta!' Maybe this sea was just as welcome to us after our months in the endless white drift-ice.

"At last, at last, I stood by the edge of the ice. Before me lay the dark surface of the sea, with floating white floes; far away the glacier wall rose abruptly from the water; over the whole lay a sombre, foggy light. Joy welled up in our hearts at this sight, and we could not give it expression in words. Behind us lay all our troubles, before us the waterway home. I waved my hat to Johansen, who was a little way behind, and he waved his in answer and shouted 'Hurrah!' Such an event had to be celebrated in some way, and we did it by having a piece of chocolate each.

"While we were standing there looking at the water the large head of a seal came up, and then disappeared silently; but soon more appeared. It is very reassuring to know that we can procure food at any minute we like.

"Now came the rigging of the kayaks for the voyage. Of course, the better way would have been to paddle singly, but, with the long, big sledges on the deck, this was not easy, and leave them behind I dared not; we might have good use for them yet. For the time being, therefore, there was nothing else to be done but to lash the two kayaks together side by side in our usual manner, stiffen them out with snowshoes under the straps, and place the sledges athwart them, one before and one behind.

"It was sad to think we could not take our two last dogs with us, but we should probably have no further use for them, and it would not have done to take them with us on the decks of our kayaks. We were sorry to part with them; we had become very fond of these two survivors. Faithful and enduring, they had followed us the whole journey through; and, now that better times had come, they must say farewell to life. Destroy them in the same way as the others we could not; we sacrificed a cartridge on each of them. I shot Johansen's, and he shot mine.

"So then we were ready to set off. It was a real pleasure to let the kayaks dance over the water and hear the little waves plashing against the sides. For two years we had not seen such a surface of water before us. We had not gone far before we found that the wind was so good that we ought to make use of it, and so we rigged up a sail on our fleet. We glided easily before the wind in towards the land we had so longed for all these many months. What a change, after having forced one's way inch by inch and foot by foot on ice! The mist had hidden the land from us for a while, but now it parted, and we saw the glacier rising straight in front of us. At the same moment the sun burst forth, and a more beautiful morning I can hardly remember. We were soon underneath the glacier, and had to lower our sail and paddle westward along the wall of ice, which was from 50 to 60 feet in height, and on which a landing was impossible. It seemed as if there must be little movement in this glacier; the water had eaten its way deep underneath it at the foot, and there was no noise of falling fragments or the cracking of crevasses to be heard, as there generally is with large glaciers. It was also quite even on the top, and no crevasses were to be seen. Up the entire height of the wall there was stratification, which was unusually marked. We soon discovered that a tidal current was running westward along the wall of the glacier with great rapidity, and took advantage of it to make good progress. To find a camping-ground, however, was not easy, and at last we were reduced to taking up our abode on a drifting floe. It was glorious, though, to go to rest in the certainty that we should not wake to drudgery in the drift-ice.

"When we turned out to-day we found that the ice had packed around us, and I do not know yet how we shall get out of it, though there is open water not far off to our west.

"Thursday, August 8th. After hauling our *impedimenta* over some floes we got into open water yesterday without much difficulty. When we had reached the edge of the water we made a paddle each from our snow-shoe-staffs, to which we bound blades made of broken-off snow-shoes. They were a great improvement on the somewhat clumsy paddles, with canvas blades lashed to bamboo sticks. I was very much inclined to chop off our sledges, so that they would only be half as long as before; by so doing we could carry them on the after-deck of the kayaks, and could thus each paddle alone, and our advance would be much quicker than by paddling the twin kayaks. However, I thought, perhaps, it was unadvisable. The water looked promising enough on ahead, but there was mist, and we could not see far; we knew nothing of the country or the coast we had come to, and might yet have good use for the sledges. We therefore set off in our double kayak, as before, with the sledges athwart the deck fore and aft.

"The mist soon rose a little. It was then a dead calm; the surface of the water lay like a great mirror before us, with bits of ice and an occasional floe drifting on it. It was a marvellously beautiful sight, and it was indeed glorious to sit there in our light vessels and glide over the surface without any exertion. Suddenly a seal rose in front of us, and over us flew continually ivory-gulls and fulmars and kittiwakes. Little auks we also saw, and some Ross's gulls, and a couple of terns. There was no want of animal life here, nor of food when we should require it.

"We found open water, broader and broader, as we paddled on our way beside the wall of ice; but it would not clear so that we could see something of our surroundings. The mist still hung obstinately over it.

"Our course at first lay west to north (magnetic); but the land always trended more and more to the west and southwest; the expanse of water grew greater, and soon it widened out to a large sea, stretching in a southwesterly direction. A breeze sprang up from the north-north-east, and there was considerable motion, which was not pleasant, as in our double craft the seas continually washed up between the two and wetted us. We put in towards evening and pitched the tent on the shore-ice, and just as we did so it began to rain, so that it was high time to be under a roof.

"Friday, August 9th. Yesterday morning we had again to drag the sledges with the kayaks over some ice which had drifted in front of our camping-ground, and during this operation I managed to fall into the water and get wet. It was with difficulty we finally got through and out into open water. After a while we again found our way closed, and were obliged to take to hauling over some floes, but after this we had good open water the whole day. It was a northeasterly wind which had set the ice towards the land, and it was lucky we had got so far, as behind us, to judge by the atmosphere, the sea was much blocked. The mist hung over the land so that we saw little of it. According as we advanced we were able to hold a more southerly course, and, the wind being nearly on the quarter, we set sail about 1 o'clock, and continued sailing all day till we stopped yesterday evening. Our sail, however, was interrupted once when it was necessary to paddle round an ice-point north of where we are now; the contrary current was so strong that it was as much as we could do to make way against it, and it was only after considerable exertion that we succeeded in doubling the point. We have seen little of the land we are skirting up to this, on account of the mist; but as far as I can make out it consists of islands. First there was a large island covered with an ice-sheet; then west of it a smaller one, on which are the two crags of rock which first made us aware of the vicinity of land; next came a long fjord or sound, with massive shore-ice in it; and then a small, low headland, or rather an island, south of which we are now encamped. This shore-ice lying along the land is very remarkable. It is unusually massive and uneven; it seems to be composed of huge blocks welded together, which in a great measure, at any rate, must proceed from the ice-sheet. There has also, perhaps, been violent pressure against the land, which has heaved the sea-ice up together with pieces of ice from the calving of the glacier, and the whole has frozen together into a conglomerate mass. A medium-sized iceberg lay off the headland north of us, where the current was so strong. Where we are now lying, however, there is flat fjord-ice between the low island here and a larger one farther south.

"This land grows more of a problem, and I am more than ever at a loss to know where we are. It is very remarkable to me that the coast continually trends to the south instead of to the west. I could explain it all best by supposing ourselves to be on the west coast of the archipelago of Franz Josef Land, were it not that the variation, I think, is too great, and also for the number of Ross's gulls there still are. Not one has with certainty been seen in Spitzbergen, and if my supposition is right, this should not be far off. Yesterday we saw a number of them again; they are quite as common here as the other species of gull.

"Saturday, August 10th. We went up on to the little islet we had camped by. It was covered by a glacier, which curved over it in the shape of a shield; there were slopes to all sides; but so slight was the gradient that our snow-shoes would not even run of themselves on the crust of snow. From the ridge we had a fair view, and, as the mist lifted just then, we saw the land about us tolerably well. We now perceived plainly that what we had been skirting along was only islands. The first one was the biggest. The other land, with the two rocky crags, had, as we could see, a strip of bare land along the shore on the northwest side. Was it there, perhaps, the Ross's gulls congregated and had their breeding-grounds? The island to our south also looked large; it appeared to be entirely covered by a glacier. Between the islands, and as far as we could perceive southeast and east, the sea was covered by perfectly flat fjord-ice, but no land was to be discerned in that direction. There were no icebergs here, though we saw some later in the day on the south side of the island lying to the south of us.

"The glacier covering the little island on which we stood joined the fjord-ice almost imperceptibly; only a few small fissures along the shore indicated where it probably began. There could not be any great rise and fall in the ice here, consequent on the tide, as the fissures would then, as a matter of course, have been considerably larger. This seemed remarkable, as the tidal current ran swift as a river here. On the west side of the island there lay in front of the glacier a rampart of ice and snow, which was probably formed of pieces of glacier-ice and sea-ice welded together. It had the same character as the massive shore-ice which we had seen previously running along the land. This rampart went over imperceptibly with an even slope into the glacier within it.

"About three in the afternoon we finally set off in open water and sailed till eight or so in the evening; the water was then closed, and we were compelled to haul the fleet over flat ice to open water on the other side. But here, too, our progress seemed blocked, and as the current was against us we pitched the tent."

On August 10th we were "compelled partly to haul our sledges over the ice, partly to row in open water in a southwesterly direction. When we reached navigable waters again, we passed a flock of walruses lying on a floe. It was a pleasure to see so much food collected at one spot, but we did not take any notice of them, as, for the time being, we have meat and blubber enough. After dinner we managed, in the mist, to wander down a long, bay into the shore-ice, where there was no outlet; we had to turn back, and this delayed us considerably. We now kept a more westerly course, following the often massive and uneven edge of the ice; but the current was dead against us, and, in addition, young ice had been forming all day as we rowed along; the weather had been cold and still, with falling snow, and this began to be so thick that we could not make way against it any longer. We therefore went ashore on the ice, and hauled until ten in the evening.

"Bear-tracks, old and new, in all directions—both the single ones of old bachelors and those of she-bears with cubs. It looks as if they had had a general rendezvous, or as if a flock of them had roamed backward and forward. I have never seen so many bear-tracks in one place in my life.

"We have certainly done 14 or 25 miles to-day; but still I think our progress is too slow if we are to reach Spitzbergen this year, and I am always wondering if we ought not to cut the ends off our sledges, so that each can paddle his own kayak. This young ice, however, which grows steadily worse, and the eleven degrees below freezing we now have, make me hold my hand. Perhaps winter is upon us, and then the sledges may be very necessary.

"It is a curious sensation to paddle in the mist, as we are doing, without being able to see a mile in front of us. The land we found we have left behind us. We are always in hopes of clear weather, in order to see where the land lies in front of us—for land there must be. This flat, unbroken ice must be attached to land of some kind; but clear weather we are not to have, it appears. Mist without ceasing; we must push on as it is."

After having hauled some distance farther over the ice we came to open water again the following day (August 11th) and paddled for four or five hours. While I was on a hummock inspecting the waters ahead, a huge monster of a walrus came up quite near us. It lay puffing and glaring at us on the surface of the water, but we took no notice of it, got into our kayaks, and went on. Suddenly it came up again by the side of us, raised itself high out of the water, snorted so that the air shook, and threatened to thrust its tusks into our frail craft. We seized our guns, but at the same moment it disappeared, and came up immediately afterwards on the other side, by Johansen's kayak, where it repeated the same manœuvre. I said to him that if the animal showed signs of attacking us we must spend a cartridge on it. It came up several times and disappeared again; we could see it down in the water, passing rapidly on its side under our vessels, and, afraid lest it should make a hole in the bottom with its tusks, we thrust our paddles down into the water and frightened it away; but suddenly it came up again right by Johansen's kayak, and more savage than ever. He sent it a charge straight in the eyes, it uttered a terrific bellow, rolled over, and disappeared, leaving a trail of blood on the water behind it. We paddled on as hard as we could, knowing that the shot might have dangerous consequences, but we were relieved when we heard the walrus come up far behind us at the place where it had disappeared.

We had paddled quietly on, and had long forgotten all about the walrus, when I suddenly saw Johansen jump into the air and felt his kayak receive a violent shock. I had no idea what it was, and looked round to see if some block of floating ice had capsized and struck the bottom of his kayak; but suddenly I saw another walrus rise up in the water beside us. I seized my gun, and as the animal would not turn its head so that I could aim at a spot behind the ear, where it is more easily wounded, I was constrained to put a ball in the middle of its forehead; there was no time to be lost. Happily this was enough, and it lay there dead and floating on the water. With great difficulty we managed to make a hole in the thick skin, and after cutting ourselves some strips of blubber and meat from the back we went on our way again.

At seven in the evening the tidal current turned and the channel closed. There was no more water to be found. Instead of taking to hauling over the ice, we determined to wait for the opening of the channel when the tide should turn next day, and meanwhile to cut off the ends of our sledges, as I had so long been thinking of doing, and make ourselves some good double paddles, so that we could put on greater pace, and, in our single kayaks, make the most of the channel during the time it was open. While we were occupied in doing this the mist cleared off at last, and there lay land stretched out in front of us, extending a long way south and west from S.E. right up to N.N.W. It appeared to be a chain of islands with sounds between them. They were chiefly covered with glaciers, only here and there were perpendicular black mountain-walls to be seen. It was a sight to make one rejoice to see so much land at one time. But where were we? This seemed a more difficult question to answer than ever. Could we, after all, have arrived at the cast side of Franz Josef Land? It seemed very reasonable to suppose this to be the case. But then we must be very far east, and must expect a long voyage before we could reach Cape Fligely, on Crown Prince Rudolf Land. Meanwhile we worked hard to get the sledges ready; but as the mist gradually lifted and it became clearer and clearer, we could not help continually leaving them, to climb up on to the hummock beside us to look at the country, and speculate on this insoluble problem. We did not get to bed till seven in the morning of August 12th.

"Tuesday, August 13th. After having slept a few hours, we turned out of the bag again, for the current had turned, and there was a wide channel. In our single kayaks we made good headway, but after going about five miles the channel closed, and we had to clamber on to the ice. We thought it advisable to wait until the tidal current turned, and see if there were not a channel running farther. If not, we must lash proper grips of wood to our curtailed sledges, and commence hauling towards a sound running through the land, which I see about W.N.W. (true), and which, according to Payer's chart, I take to be Rawlinson's Sound."

But the crack did not open, and when it came to the point we had to continue on our way hauling.

"Wednesday, August 14th. We dragged our sledges and loads over a number of floes and ferried across lanes, arriving finally at a lane which ran westward, in which we could paddle; but it soon packed together again, and we were stopped. The ivory-gulls are very bold, and last night stole a piece of blubber lying close by the tent wall."

The following day we had to make our way as well as we could by paddling short distances in the lanes or hauling our loads over floes smaller or larger, as the case might be. The current, which was running like a mill-race, ground them together in its career. Our progress with our short, stumpy sledges was nothing very great, and of water suitable for paddling in we found less and less. We stopped several times and waited for the ice to open at the turn of the tide, but it did not do so, and on the morning of August 15th we gave it up, turned inward, and took to the shore-ice for good. We set our course westward towards the sound we had seen for several days now, and had struggled so to reach. The surface of the ice was tolerably even and we got over the ground well. On the way we passed a frozen-in iceberg, which was the highest we saw in these parts—some 50 to 60 feet, I should say. I wished to go up it to get a better view of our environment, but it was too steep, and we did not get higher than a third part up the side.

"In the evening we at last reached the islands we had been steering for the last few days, and for the first time for two years had bare land under foot. The delight of the feeling of being able to jump from block to block of granite is indescribable, and the delight was not lessened when in a little sheltered corner among the stones we found moss and flowers, beautiful poppies (*Papaver nudicaule*) *Saxifraga nivalis*, and a *Stellaria* (*sp.?*). It goes without saying that the Norwegian flag had to wave over this our first bare land, and a banquet was prepared. Our petroleum, meanwhile, had given out several days previously, and we had to contrive another lamp in which train-oil could be used. The

smoking hot lobscouse, made of pemmican and the last of our potatoes, was delicious, and we sat inside the tent and kicked the bare grit
under us to our heart's content. . . .

"Saturday, August 17th. Yesterday was a good day. We are in open
water on the west coast of Franz Josef Land, as far as I can make out,
and may again hope to get home this year. About noon yesterday we
walked across the ice from our moraine-islet to the higher island west
of us. As I was ready before Johansen, I went on first to examine the
island a little. As he was following me he caught sight of a bear on the
level ice to leeward. It came jogging up against the wind straight
towards him. He had his gun ready, but when a little nearer the bear
stopped, reconsidered the situation, suddenly turned tail, and was
soon out of sight.

"This island (Torup's Island) we came to seemed to me to be one of
the most lovely spots on the face of the earth. A beautiful flat beach, an
old strand-line with shells strewn about, a narrow belt of clear water
along the shore, where snails and sea-urchins (*Echinus*) were visible at
the bottom and amphipoda were swimming about. In the cliffs overhead
were hundreds of screaming little auks, and beside us the snowbuntings
fluttered from stone to stone with their cheerful twitter. Suddenly the sun
burst forth through the light fleecy clouds, and the day seemed to be all
sunshine. Here were life and bare land; we were no longer on the eternal
drift-ice! At the bottom of the sea just beyond the beach I could see
whole forests of seaweed (*Laminaria* and *Fucus*). Under the cliffs here and
there were drifts of beautiful rose-colored snow.

"On the north side of the island we found the breeding-place of
numbers of black-backed gulls; they were sitting with their young in
ledges of the cliffs. Of course we had to climb up and secure a photograph of this unusual scene of family life, and as we stood there high
up on the cliff's side we could see the drift-ice whence we had come. It
lay beneath us like a white plain, and disappeared far away on the hori-

zon. Beyond this it was we had journeyed, and farther away still the *Fram* and our comrades were drifting yet.

"I had thought of going to the top of this island to get a better view, and perhaps come nearer solving the problem of our whereabouts. But when we were on the west side of it the mist came back and settled on the top; we had to content ourselves with only going a little way up the slope to look at our future course westward. Some way out we saw open water; it looked like the sea itself, but before one could get to it there was a good deal of ice. We came down again and started off. Along the land there was a channel running some distance farther, and we tried it, but it was covered everywhere with a thin layer of new ice, which we did not dare to break through in our kayaks, and risk cutting a hole in them; so, finally, a little way farther south we put in to drag up the kayaks and take to the ice again. While we were doing this one huge bearded seal after another stuck its head up by the side of the ice and gazed wonderingly at us with its great eyes; then, with a violent header, and splashing the water in all directions, it would disappear, to come up again soon afterwards on the other side. They kept playing around us, blowing, diving, reappearing, and throwing themselves over so that the water foamed round them. It would have been easy enough to capture one had we required it.

"At last, after a good deal of exertion, we stood at the margin of the ice; the blue expanse of water lay before us as far as the eye could reach, and we thought that for the future we had to do with it alone. To the north there was land, the steep, black, basalt cliffs of which fell perpendicularly into the sea. We saw headland after headland standing out northward, and farthest off of all we could descry a bluish glacier. The interior was everywhere covered with an ice-sheet. Below the clouds, and over the land, was a strip of ruddy night sky, which was reflected in the melancholy, rocking sea.

"So we paddled on along the side of the glacier which covered the whole country south of us. We became more and more excited as we approached the headland to the west. Would the coast trend south here, and was there no more land westward? It was this we expected to decide our fate—decide whether we should reach home that year or be compelled to winter somewhere on land. Nearer and nearer we came to it along the edge of the perpendicular wall of ice. At last we reached the headland, and our hearts bounded with joy to see so much water— only water—westward, and the coast trending southwest. We also saw a bare mountain projecting from the ice-sheet a little way farther on; it was a curious high ridge, as sharp as a knife-blade. It was as steep and sharp as anything I have seen; it was all of dark, columnar basalt, and so jagged and peaked that it looked like a comb. In the middle of the mountain there was a gap or couloir, and there we crept up to inspect the sea-way southward. The wall of rock was anything but broad there, and fell away on the south side in a perpendicular drop of several hundred feet. A cutting wind was blowing in the couloir. While we were lying there, I suddenly heard a noise behind me, and on looking around I saw two foxes fighting over a little auk which they had just caught. They clawed and tugged and bit as hard as they could on the very edge of the chasm; then they suddenly caught sight of us, not twenty feet away from them. They stopped fighting, looked up wonderingly, and began to run around and peep at us, first from one side, then from the other. Over us myriads of little auks flew backward and forward, screaming shrilly from the ledges in the mountain-side. So far as we could make out, there appeared to be open sea, along the land to the westward. The wind was favorable, and although we were tired we decided to take advantage of the opportunity, have something to eat, rig up mast and sail on our canoes, and get afloat. We sailed till the morning, when the wind went down, and then we landed on the shore-ice again and camped.

"I am as happy as a child in the thought that we are now at last really on the west coast of Franz Josef Land, with open water before us, and independent of ice and currents.

"Wednesday, August 24th. The vicissitudes of this life will never come to an end. When I wrote last I was full of hope and courage; and here we are stopped by stress of weather for four days and three nights, with the ice packed as tight as it can be against the coast. We see nothing but piled-up ridges, hummocks, and broken ice in all directions. Courage is still here, but hope—the hope of soon being home—that was relinquished a long time ago, and before us lies the certainty of a long, dark winter in these surroundings.

from Snow on the Equator
by H. W. Tilman

H. W. Tilman (1898–1977) and his frequent traveling companion Eric Shipton were among the great explorers of the 20th century. They pioneered a new style of mountaineering—fast and light—which became the standard for expeditions. Their tactics were in evidence in 1932, when the two men explored and climbed in East Africa's Ruwenzori mountain range for the sheer pleasure of seeing it.

We left Turbo by car on the morning of January 9th and, leaving the squat bulk of Mount Elgon on our right, headed for the high granite obelisk seen in the distance marking the position of Tororo, on the Uganda border. The Uganda roads have a well-deserved reputation, so that we sped rapidly along, dropping gradually until Jinja was reached about tea-time.

Jinja is a little town on the shores of Lake Victoria close to the Ripon Falls, where the Nile issues from the lake to begin its long journey to the sea. The falls were discovered by Speke in 1862, who thus solved the problem of the position of one of the Nile sources. They are only about 20 feet high, but even without the romantic associations of the river it is an impressive sight to see the great volume of water sweeping over the falls to run through a gorge and disappear round a wooded bend a mile lower down. Above the falls are pools and shallows in which crocodiles and hippos laze, while immediately below, the water seems to be alive with big Nile perch,

30 lbs. to 40 lbs. in weight, trying ceaselessly but vainly to jump up the falls.

In addition to its romantic situation, Jinja is celebrated for a nine-hole golf-course lying close to the lake shore, the grass of which is kept short by the hippos which emerge nightly from the lake to graze. There is a local rule about hippo foot-marks, which are treated in the same way as rabbit scrapes at home, where the ball can be lifted without penalty. One of these hippos was such a regular visitor that he was known to the people of Jinja, indeed of Uganda and even further, as Horace. A usual way of entertaining visitors was to drive down to the links in the evening to watch Horace enjoying his supper. There was a story current when we were there that one party, which had dined not wisely but too well, went down with the avowed intention of pulling Horace's tail. One of the 'pot valiant,' boldly leaving the car, advanced towards the hippo, but Horace, also feeling playful, came for the man and chased him back to the car, taking a large piece out of something more than the slack of his breeches *en route*. The party were too happy to notice much amiss until someone discovered the presence of quantities of blood, and, after returning hastily to the town, they spent a long time in persuading a doctor that he was not being made the victim of a drunken leg-pull. The upshot was that the would-be humorist spent a month or so in hospital.

Until 1928 the Uganda Railway, so called, perhaps, because it never entered Uganda, stopped at Kisumu, on the east shore of the lake. Now, the main line enters Uganda to the north, crosses the Nile by a bridge just below the Rippon Falls, and terminates at Kampala, 80 miles away. The bridge also carries a road, but before that was built travellers by road were obliged to cross an arm of the lake by a rather cranky ferry running at very infrequent intervals. Thanks to the bridge, no time had to be wasted by us on the ferry, and we pushed on that evening, reaching Kampala at seven after a run of 250 miles.

We were ready for an early start next day in order to cover the remaining 200 miles to Fort Portal in good time, but we were delayed until seven waiting for a mechanic who we had agreed to take out to a car stranded 75 miles out. It was a case of assisting a damsel in distress, so the delay was suffered gladly by one of us, and by the other without impatience.

At four we reached Fort Portal, where we put up at a small hotel. It is the centre of the Toro district of Uganda, a district more favoured by spoil and climate than the rest of the Protectorate. The altitude is about 5,000 feet, the rainfall well distributed, and the soil a fertile, volcanic ash. Coffee is the main European crop, but bananas, citrus fruits, maize, wheat, potatoes and other vegetables, all flourish. To live in this garden is pleasant and simple, but to earn money from it is a different matter, for its remoteness is a severe handicap. To export anything involves 200 miles of road haulage and 800 miles of rail before one starts paying for sea carriage, so that only high-priced crops can justify themselves, and coffee, unfortunately, can no longer be put in that category.

Outside the township, on a neighbouring eminence, are the houses which comprise the palace of the King of Toro, or the Kabaka, who rules his country with the assistance of a Prime Minister and a Council of Elders, advised when necessary by the District Commissioner, who lives in Fort Portal. The thatching of the houses of the palace and the neat reed fences surrounding them are evidently the work of real craftsmen.

Fort Portal lies at the northern end of the Ruwenzori range, and only two miles north-west is the brink of the steep escarpment which plunges down 2,000 feet to the floor of the Western Rift Valley, through which the Semliki River winds. It is called the Semliki, but it is in reality the head waters of the White Nile. Across the bare, brown, sun-scorched plain at the bottom, broken only by the silver coils of the river, is the steep opposing wall of the Rift, crowned on top with the outer fringes of the Congo forest and forming the Congo-Nile divide, the watershed of Africa.

We spent a busy morning buying blankets, cooking-pots, and cigarettes for the porters, and interviewing the District Commissioner, from whom we got a letter to a native chief, who lived at the entrance to the Mobuku Valley, invoking his aid. Which things done, we drove south for 45 miles, reaching the Mobuku River at midday.

We hoped to find our chief somewhere in the neighborhood, but the task promised to be difficult, for, to our surprise, the whole of the native population of Uganda seemed to be gathered there. We learnt that a bridge across the Mobuku was being built; an operation that had been in progress for the past two years. Several times it had almost reached completion, only to be washed away by the river coming down in flood. That day H.E. the Government of Uganda, who was on tour, had come in person to inspect progress; hence the assembled multitude.

Contrary to all expectations, we did find the needle in the haystack of humanity and gave the chief the D.C.'s letter, but that was all, for under the circumstances we could not expect to receive much attention.

We had another stroke of luck when we found amongst the crowd at the bridge a local settler, or, since he was the only one, *the* local settler. He lived a few miles up the Mobuku Valley, and he it was who had been Dr. Humphrey's companion in 1926. We were invited to make his house our headquarters and offered every assistance.

The farm was seven miles away, whither we at once proceeded along a very narrow and tortuous farm track. Driving away from the vicinity of the bridge when it was apparently the duty of everyone to be present, we had the guilty feeling of playing truant, while even the car registered a protest by puncturing a tyre. While we were perspiringly jacking it up to effect a change, two very smart and impressively large cars came round a bend, the leading one flying a small Union Jack. By pulling off the road a little they could have squeezed past, but we realised that this was hardly to be expected, so, fearful of delaying the ceremony at the bridge and feeling like the blundering hero of some Bateman drawing—the bluejacket who spat on the quarter-deck—we hastily kicked the jack away to manhandle the car off the road into the bush. It was a good car, but we blushed for its dingy paint and battered wings festooned with kit, and as the gubernatorial procession filed past in slow and shining solemnity it seemed to us that the bush was the only place for it.

Rather shaken by this little incident, we finished changing the wheel, and pushed on, only abandoning the car where the road came to an abrupt end below a steep hill. On top of this hill were some thatched huts belonging to the farm, and, having procured some boys to assist with the baggage, we toiled up to them.

The D.C.'s letter bore fruit. Very early next morning there arrived at the huts a great crowd of volunteers eager to accompany us, indeed, we had difficulty in persuading them that we wanted only a few. After much haranguing on both sides we picked out fourteen of the toughest-looking and finally got away about midday. Thirteen of the men carried 50-lb. loads, while the duty of the other was to go ahead with a panga (a heavy bush knife) to open up the overgrown track.

Some of these natives, Bakonjo, living on the lower slopes of the mountain knew what lay ahead, as they had been up to about 13,000 feet, with previous parties. They were a cheerful, willing lot, as tough as they looked, and well suited to carrying 50-lb. loads over the difficult country we presently reached. They had little equipment and less clothing, and were delighted to receive the blanket and vest issued to them out of the expedition's slender resources. Their most treasured personal possessions, chief of which was a pipe and tobacco, were carried in a little fur pouch slung from the neck. Another very important item of equipment carried by many was a cigar-shaped package of leaves closely wrapped and bound up against the weather. Inside was a sort of moss or lichen, which seemed to have the faculty of smouldering away happily without any air for days on end. When a light was wanted, the package was unwrapped and a few breaths soon blew the smouldering tinder to life.

The day was fine and hot as we marched through banana groves by the river before ascending a steep and narrow spur to a camping-ground called Bihunga. This was a small level spot on top of the spur at an altitude of about 7,000 feet.

Here cultivation ceases, and 1,000 feet higher thick forest is reached. Before burying ourselves in this, we stopped for a last look at the outside world to see beyond the green foothills a wide, flat expanse of light brown, almost yellow, country, a monotony of colour only relieved by the pale blue of a distant lake. The whole was bounded by the gentle, rounded summits of the Ankole Highlands. The sun still shone, but on entering the forest we were unaware of it, nor were we to see it again for many days. We climbed steeply to a pleasant little forest clearing called Nakitawa, where we camped. It was only one o'clock, but nothing, not even bribes, would induce the porters to go a step further. We realised there were also disadvantages in having men who had been up before, for they knew the time-honoured camping-grounds and used them in undeviating ritual, at whatever time they were reached.

From this point it was a matter of fighting one's way rather than marching, and every day the work became more severe. The track—or rather the line we followed, for track there was none—plunged headlong into deep valleys, only to climb the opposing slope with uncompromising abruptness. The Mobuku was already behind us, and now we crossed its greater tributary the Bujuku, up the valley of which our route lay.

Overhead, tall trees wrapped about with a tangle of creepers formed a dense canopy which shut out the light; underfoot was a matted carpet of undergrowth—ferns, brambles, fallen bamboos, giant nettles (said to be capable of making even an elephant sit up), and dead trees—over which we sometimes crawled, sometimes crept beneath on all fours, and sometimes had to cut a way through with the panga. The pace was painfully slow, but it was something that the porters could advance at all, balancing their loads on their heads, walking barefoot along the green and slimy trunk of some fallen giant many feet above the ground, or lowering themselves down steep and slippery cliffs of earth; torn by thorns, snatched at and caught by creepers, stung by nettles, plastered with mud, and everlastingly wet.

Through a window in the living green wall of our prison we saw for a brief moment the ice peaks of Stanley and Speke, filling the head of the valley, before they vanished once more in wreathing cloud. From now on 'Ruwenzori weather' prevailed, so that, but for one other occasion, this was the only time the peaks revealed themselves to us between dawn and sunset.

We camped that night under a dripping, overhanging cliff at about

9,500 feet at almost the upper limit of the forest zone. As forest it compared ill with the clean, straight-growing cedar and the podocarpus giants of the Mau or the forested slopes of Mount Kenya, for a few indifferent prodocarpus were the only trees that looked as if they would make timber. The forest zone is succeeded in turn by a short but dense belt of bamboo, and then, above 10,000 feet, by a forest of tree heaths. This is a thick stand of leafless trees of a uniform height of 20 to 30 feet, made grotesque by waving beards of lichen hanging from every branch, and by the mossy growths covering the trunks.

The going, however, was very much better in this forest of tree heaths. The gradient was slight, with little to hinder progress except the soft and spongy ground, so that the camping-place of Kigo was reached by midday. We were welcomed by a cold drizzle, which made the porters the more resolute to stop where they were in spite of our protests at the shortness of the march.

Beyond the tree heaths we found an even stranger country, where solid earth disappeared altogether under an overburden of moss or fallen and rotting giant groundsel (senecio). Thick groves of these grow on every hand; they are from 12 to 20 feet high, and thick in proportion, but can easily be pushed over with one hand, so that in the groves themselves there are many more trees lying than standing. So rotten are these fallen trunks that they will not support the weight of a man, with the result that forcing a path through the labyrinth presented by senecio forest, growing as it does out of a morass, is laborious to the point of exhaustion.

By way of variety one can make a less slimy but perhaps more strenuous way through the suggestively named 'helichrysum' bushes; this is a pink and white flowered 'everlasting', growing nearly as high as a man. It·is stiff, tough, wiry, trying to both clothes and temper. Its pretty flowers, like coloured paper, which do a little to brighten a drab landscape, make insufficient amends for a harsh, stubborn, unyielding nature. Over all a clammy mist hangs like a pall, and a deep silence broods. Even the innumerable brooks and rivulets are hushed as they flow deep below ground level in a narrow trench of moss—

moss that seems to breed wherever the mist touches, on tree, plant, earth, or rock.

Such was the nightmare landscape across which we toiled on our fifth day, and such is the nature of all the high valleys below the snow-line, giving to Ruwenzori a mystery and strange beauty that has not its likeness in any other land. A country that only the language of Lewis Carroll could paint, the natural habitat of Snarks and Jabberwoks and jub-jub birds. A slough, but not a Slough of Despond, for were not the Delectable Mountains at hand?

We camped in a damp but welcome cave at about 13,000 feet, hard by the Bujuku Lake, a mournful, shallow mere which, with its fœtid mud-lined shores, was in harmony with the desolate landscape surrounding it. But from the cave our eyes lingered, not on this, but on the grim precipices across the valley below the snows of Mount Baker, on the serrated ridge of the Scott Elliott Pass, and the peaks and glaciers of Mount Stanley. This, however, was a view which was seldom, if ever, seen in whole except for a minute or so at dawn or dusk, so that we were usually compelled to trust to fleeting glimpses of rock and ice, peak and ridge, seen through the writhing mists, and in imagination link the whole together.

Our first plan had been to carry all our own food and kit to an advance base near the Scott Elliott Pass—a pass lying between Mount Stanley and Mount Baker which we hoped would give us access to both mountains. It was some time before the mist cleared sufficiently for us to identify the pass, and from that distance it looked as though the approach to it might prove too much for our porters. We had already sent eight of these down, retaining six with us in the cave. They were comfortable enough and moderately content, but were so daunted by the appearance of things higher up that it seemed advisable to leave them out of our calculations and shift for ourselves. On account, there-fore, of this alteration in our plans the afternoon of our arrival at the cave was a busy one, sorting out food and kit for ourselves for five days, and making it up into two loads of 40 lbs. We intended to establish our camp on the Stanley plateau, from there climb Margherita and Alexandra, move our bivouac nearer to Mount Baker and climb that before returning to the cave to refit. We had yet to discover that as the hare must first be caught, so, on Ruwenzori, the peak must first be found.

We left camp at eight on the morning of the 17th, with two men carrying our loads. Skirting the lake-shore, we climbed through senecios, reached the rocks, and at about 15,000 feet came upon the site of a former bivouac. It was now eleven o'clock, and, as snow was beginning to fall, we sent the men back to the cave, shouldered our 40-lb. packs, and climbed slowly upwards. About one o'clock we reached the foot of the Elena Glacier, and, climbing now on snow at an easy angle, we presently reached the yet flatter slopes of the Stanley Plateau. The weather was thick, so that our sole guides were infrequent glimpses of the rocks of the Elena and Moebin Peaks close on our left. By three o'clock we were completely at a loss as to our whereabouts, so we pitched our little tent in what we imagined was a sheltered spot, and prayed for the mist to lift. At sunset the longed-for clearing came, showing, to our amazement, our camp pitched almost on the divide. A few hundred steps up a snow-slope, and we were brought to a stand as much by a view which held us spellbound as by the sudden falling away of the ground at our feet. Far to the west and below us, through a rift in the driving clouds, we could see the dark green, almost black, carpet of the Congo Forest, upon whose sombre background was traced a silvery design by the winding Semliki River. To the south showed a lighter patch, where the waters of Lake Edward reflected the last light of day; but in a moment sinking sun and rising mist merged all but the snow at our feet in a once more impenetrable gloom.

Of more practical value to us than this wonderful sight was the exposure for a brief minute of a snow ridge to the north leading up to a peak which we knew must be Alexandra. In spite of the conditions, we had pitched camp in a position well placed for an attempt on this peak, and we turned in with unjustified complacence, for it was more by good luck than good management. It snowed all night and was still snowing at dawn, so that the clearing from which we had hoped to refresh our memories never came. When we started at 7.30 to try to 'hit off' the ridge which we had seen the previous evening, visibility was limited to about ten yards, and, after wandering perplexedly for two hours amongst a maze of crevasses, we returned to camp. Caution was needed, as tracks were obliterated by fresh snow almost as soon as they were made.

The persistent snow soon found the weak spots in our little tent, which was not well adapted either for sheltering two men or for use on snow. Pools of water soon accumulated on the floor, limiting the area at our disposal, an area already made small by an inconvenient centre pole, so that it became increasingly difficult to keep our sleeping-bags dry. In the evening another clearing in the mist caused us to dash out, but we only got as far as the foot of the ridge before gathering darkness compelled us to return.

On the third day it was still misty but the snow had stopped falling. Assisted by our tracks of the previous night, which in places were still visible, we reached the ridge and began climbing. Except for one awkward cornice and the uncertain quality of the snow, the climb was not difficult, the summit (16,740 feet) being reached by midday. There was a patch of rock on top where we found a cairn in which were records left by the Duke of the Abruzzi in 1906 and Dr. Humphreys in 1926. We sat there till 2.30 p.m., but caught only passing glimpses of the neighbouring summit of Margherita. Camp was reached at 4 p.m., when a brief clearing enabled us to wring out our sleeping-bags and bale the tent. Our success on Alexandra, combined at sunset with another remarkable view of the Congo and a sight of the Margherita ridge, sent us to bed in a more or less contented frame of mind.

More snow fell in the night, but we turned out at 7.30 a.m. and were rewarded by seeing Margherita clearly for five minutes. By the time we had got under way, the mist had re-gathered, so that in a short time our ideas as to position and direction became as nebulous and woolly as the mist itself. The crevasses seemed more numerous and the mist thicker than on our first attempt, but, after groping about for some hours, we saw looming before us what was undoubtedly a ridge. At the foot of it was a steep rock buttress, which we managed to turn on the right, traversing back above it to the left. Hopes ran high as we reached the crest of the ridge and began to follow it, but next moment we stood dumbfounded, staring, Crusoe-like, at footprints in the snow. Such was our bewilderment that wild and impossible conjectures of another party on the mountain flashed across our minds before we realised the unflattering, truth that these were our tracks of the previous day, and that we were climbing Alexandra for the second time.

We crept back to camp with our tails well down, to pass a rather miserable night, depressed as much by our failure as by the state of the tent, whose contents, including our sleeping-bags were now sopping wet. By now our food was almost finished, but before our forced descent on the morrow we determined to make one more attempt to reach the summit of Margherita.

By three in the morning we were so cold in our wet sleeping-bags that we gave up trying to sleep, brewed some tea, and prayed for dawn. Camp was struck, the sodden loads packed, and at six we moved off down the glacier, dumping the loads near the foot of the Stanley Plateau. Then, in a last desperate resolve to find the Margherita ridge, we turned north again. The usual mist prevailed, while the width and frequency of unbridged crevasses made vain any attempt at following a compass course, which in any case could only have been an approximation.

These repeated changes of direction enforced on us by the crevasses tried our tempers severely; every change gave rise to heated argument, during which each of us would fall to drawing little maps in the snow with ice-axes to illustrate our respective theories.

Once more a rock buttress loomed up. It was viewed with suspicion and tackled without enthusiasm, while every moment we expected to come once again upon our old tracks. In this we were delighted to be disappointed, and at eleven o'clock we reached the summit of an undoubted peak, but which we could not tell. It was snow-covered, so there could be no records to find; all to be done was to wait for the mist to clear. This we did, sitting in a hollow scraped in the snow.

The climb had been an interesting one but not difficult. The ridge and the summit were draped with cornices of a strangely beautiful feathery appearance. Very little melting appears to take place at these heights, so it is possible that this formation is due to wind rather than rapid alterations in temperature. On the other hand, the presence of numbers of large ice stalactites under the cornices suggests a considerable range of temperature.

Unless another night without food was to be spent on the glacier, our departure had to be timed for 3 p.m. A searching wind began to lessen our interest as to what peak we were on, threatening to drive us off its summit with our knowledge unsatisfied. Time after time the swirling mists seemed to be thinning. Repeatedly we would take off our snow-glasses in the hope of finding a tangible clue in the sea of fog, only to be baulked by fresh clouds rolling up from some apparently inexhaustible supply. Repeatedly we were disappointed, but at last a clearing came. It lasted hardly a minute, but it was long enough for us to see and recognise the familiar summit of Alexandra, and to realise from its relative position that we must be on Margherita (16,815 feet).

It was sheer luck to have hit off the ridge on such a day, so that we were almost jubilant as we started down. Helped by our outgoing tracks, we reached our rucksacks at 4.30 p.m., and, stopping only to swallow a mouthful of raw pemmican, we hit out for the cave. In spite of mist and gathering gloom we found the route, quitted the snow for the rocks, slid and slithered down moss-grown slabs, and soon were fighting our way through the senecios above the lake. Burdened as we were with water-logged packs and exhausted by our previous efforts, our condition was such that our progress was governed more by the impulse of gravity than by our legs. So with one mind we steered straight for the mud of the lake-shore, knowing that it would be soft, but doubting whether a quicksand itself could be worse than the senecio toils in which we were struggling.

It was not a quicksand, but a very fair imitation, and, withal, very evil-smelling; 'Here, therefore, they wallowed for a time, being very grievously bedaubed with dirt; a Christian, because of the burden that was on his back, began to sink into the mire.' Frying-pan and fire, devil and deep sea, Scylla and Charybdis, all seemed weak comparisons for the horns of our dilemma. Finally we took once more to the senecio forest—perhaps because it did not smell—and by nightfall reached the cave and the welcome warmth of a roaring fire.

Although, on the march, no words could be bad enough for the senecio, or giant groundsel, in camp we sang a different tune. To all appearances it looks as likely to burn as cabbage-stalk, but, dead or alive, wet or dry, it burns almost as well as birchwood. Without it life in the high valleys of Ruwenzori, where the sun is hardly ever seen and where to move a yard from camp is to be soaked, would be almost unbearable; at any rate to natives, to whom sitting over a fire, or even in the smoke of a fire, is meat and drink.

After devoting a day to food and rest, and the drying of clothes and sleeping-bags, we set out for Mount Speke in thick weather on January 23rd. As it lies to the north of the Bujuku Lake, our line of march lay up the valley towards the Stuhlmann Pass at its head. In an attempt to cut short the struggle with vegetation and morass we tried to break out of the valley by climbing the cliffs of its eastern flank, but we were repulsed by the moss-covered slabs. After several great strips of moss had peeled away, almost taking us with them, we continued up the valley, at last reaching the snow above the pass. We roped up, more from ingrained orthodoxy than necessity, and climbed an easy snow slope to Vittorio Emmanuele (16,080 feet), gaining its summit at half past ten. From this vantage-point, almost the centre of the range, we should have seen, but for the mist, most of the snow peaks and their glaciers. For three hours we sat there waiting patiently for a clearing. At half past one the mist did lift a little, giving us a glimpse of a summit along the ridge to the north, which appeared to be higher than ours. Whether it was or not, it gave us an excuse for getting warm, so we raced off along the ridge, climbed three small intervening hillocks, and reached the top of the fourth unnamed peak. Dr. Humphreys was of the opinion that this summit was higher than Vittorio, which is officially the highest, an opinion with which we were inclined to agree. The point is only of academic interest, however, for not one of the four is worthy of the name of 'peak'.

We started back at half past two in a curious mixture of thunder and snow, reaching camp in two hours. We tried more short cuts on the way, and at least had the melancholy satisfaction of proving once again that if mossy slabs are not ideal for ascents, they are excellent for descents, if effortless speed is the main consideration.

Our six porters, who were in a fair way to becoming troglodytes, began to hope that the madness which had driven us to these inhospitable wastes had now spent itself, and that with a return to sanity there would be a return to a warmer climate. Whether man could be eternally happy in the heaven, paradise, or nirvana offered by the several religions has always seemed to me doubtful (for, after all, bliss is only appreciated after spells of misery), and here were these natives, enjoying what I imagine to be a native's idea of heaven, with nothing to do but eat, drink, sleep, and draw their pay, and yet counting the days until they could return to work, women, and taxation. Since the only obligation they were under was to remain passive, and desertion would involve being active, it was not difficult to persuade them to wait a little longer, as we were able to assure them that one more day would suffice to exorcise the devil which possessed us.

That day, January 24th, we proposed to devote to the climbing of Mount Baker direct from our base camp—a much more formidable task than the climbing of Speke although it was the lower of the two, being only 15,986 feet. Our original plan had been to attempt it by the ridge, leading up from the Scott Elliott Pass, but the shattered, ice-glazed rocks of that ridge presented a very forbidding appearance. The alternative was to climb it by the north face from a point in the Bujuku Valley lower than our camp site. We started very early to see what we could do.

'Reculer pour mieux sauter' may sometimes be sound strategically, but it calls for high morale in those called upon to practise it, and there is no more trying a way of starting an ascent than by a descent. Our route began with a descent of the valley for a good half-mile. It was not as though we could just run down. On the contrary, every foot of it had to be fought for in the depressing knowledge that every foot so gained was a foot lost on the mountain, so that it was with mingled feelings of relief and dismay that we at last found ourselves at the foot of the lower cliffs of Baker, which bound the south side of the valley, faced by a climb of what was now more than 3,000 feet. The lower part of the cliffs were, of course, sheathed in moss, a fact which, after our experiences of yesterday, caused us to approach them with misgivings and climb them with caution, the more so because we knew it was seldom possible to safeguard the party with a rope belay. As we slowly gained height, the moss gave place to less treacherous but more difficult ice-glazed rock, while the mist clinging to the face made it impossible for us to choose the best line of ascent. Just below the crest of the east ridge of Baker the rocks steepened. Several attempts were made before we finally overcame these, and, after four hours of continuous climbing, hoisted ourselves on to the snow-covered ridge.

Turning westwards, we followed the ridge at an easy angle over three lesser summits, reaching Semper Peak (15,843 feet) at about one o'clock. Here we found a cairn containing the records of the all-too-thorough Italian party, but we derived some satisfaction from having made a new route. To the south, a quarter of a mile away, was the top, Edward Peak (15,986 feet), and almost as we reached it we enjoyed the novel and pleasing experience of the mists melting away in the middle of the day. Looking across to the Stanley Plateau, where we had played at Blind Man's Buff for four days with Alexandra and Margherita, we found it difficult to imagine that anyone could have had any trouble in finding them. The whole scene stood revealed, and took on a fresh aspect in this almost unnatural sunlight. As dawn dispels the weird shapes and half-seen horrors of the night, so the Mubuku Valley became a smooth and smiling pleasance; the vile tangle of its spongy floor became a firm green lawn, the dark and desolate waters of the mere sparkled gaily, the slimy mud of its shores looked like hard yellow sand. The snow peaks themselves took on a milder aspect, and with the clouds filling and blotting out the lower valleys, which might have destroyed the illusion by their emptiness, we might have been amongst one of the homely lesser ranges of the Alps, instead of the mysterious Mountains of the Moon.

Encouraged by this fair scene, and momentarily forgetful, perhaps, of what the smiling faces of the valleys concealed, we planned an ambitious return journey by a complete traverse of Mount Baker, with a descent towards the Freshfield col which divides Mount Baker from Luigi di Savoia, the southernmost peak. From the col we would drop down into the unnamed valley between Mount Baker and Mount Stanley, on the south side of the Scott Elliott Pass, returning to the Bujuku Valley and our camp over this last-named pass. It meant a long day, and was rather a shot in the dark, but it took us into fresh country, and, in spite of the prudent adage, we preferred the unknown to the known evils of the mossy slabs up which we had come.

After half an hour's rest on the summit we began the descent of the south ridge towards Freshfield col at about two o'clock. Realising too well that every step south was taking us further from home and lengthening our forthcoming struggle in the valley, we decided to cut matters short by descending from the ridge into the valley before reaching the col. The steeper snow below the ridge lay insecurely on top of ice and needed care, but we were soon off the glacier, encountering the less obvious but greater perils of steep rock covered with a type of moss new to our experience, which was almost imperceptible. The rock itself looked bare, and seemed reasonably trustworthy, until a sudden skid provoked closer inspection and revealed the presence of the new enemy.

The slope which fell away at our feet was steep and convex, so that we could not see what lay between us and the valley floor. In the nature of things some sort of steep wall was to be expected near the bottom, and so it was found. It was so steep that but for the assistance of the hated helichrysum which grew out of it we could never have tackled it, and must have returned to the ridge to descend by the much longer way of the Freshfield col. The helichrysum grew in profusion on the face of the cliff, clinging there with all the toughness and tenacity that we knew so well and had so often cursed—a toughness we now had occasion to bless. It was at once an enemy and friend; one moment we were reviling it as heartily as ever for holding us back, and the next giv-

ing thanks as we used it for a 'Thank-God-handhold' in the descent of
some steep rock wall. But for its aid many such places would have
defeated us, while the only toll it exacted for me the loss of a wrist-
watch and for S. a sprained shoulder.

Once we were down on the valley floor there began what we had
expected and feared—a long fight against the giant groundsel, helichrysum, chaotic boulders, and the approach of night. The valley was closely
shut in between the high containing walls of the lower cliffs of Mount
Baker and Mount Stanley. Debris falling from the slopes of these mountains filled the valley, and in one place had dammed it to form two lifeless tarns which deepened the melancholy aspect of this grim defile.

Approaching the foot of the Scott Elliott Pass, the impeding vegetation gave way to scree, but we had to summon all our flagging energies
in an effort to reach the col quickly, to see something of our way down
the other side before darkness descended and left us benighted. We
pressed on, and, as we topped the ridge, there was just light enough to
see the Bujuku Lake below, and at our feet a narrow gully which
seemed to offer a practicable route.

Hurrying down this as fast as safety permitted, we joined battle once
more with senecio forest and helichrysum, in which I suffered the
additional loss of my camera and the irreplaceable exposed film which
it contained. We reached the lake-shore in a darkness which, though
'hellish', did not 'smell of cheese', like the cupboard which the half-
drunk James Pigg thrust his head into in mistake for the window. It
smelt instead like a sewer as we began floundering along the margin of
the lake, sinking to our knees in the noisome mud at every step. On
this occasion we preferred it to the senecio, and resigned ourselves,
more or less happily, to long wallowing in the slough, because with the
water to guide us we were sure of our direction. Presently a boy who
had heard our shouts met us with a lamp, and in a short time we were
sitting by the fire discussing food and the day's adventures.

In the morning we packed up and bade farewell to the friendly cave
which we had come to look upon as home, so warm was its welcome
on our belated returns from long, wet days. By promising the porters

extra baksheesh we persuaded them to double march all the way, for our road lay downhill and the trail was already broken. They were eager to get back certainly, but it needed a pretty strong incentive to goad them into this fierce activity.

Their labours finished, these six worthies received, besides the blankets and clothes, eleven shillings each, with which they were well pleased. A full month's work on farm or road would not have brought them in as much as this, the fruits of only sixteen days' absence. Now they could return in affluence to their villages, willing and able to astonish the stay-at-homes with tales of hardship and peril amidst the mysterious snows.

The boy we had deputed to keep an eye on the car, left by the roadside, met us with the news that all was well. This was a great relief because it was quite on the cards that some elephant had stepped on it or that it had been destroyed by a bush fire. Not only was all well with it, but, according to the boy, rather better than well, because a swarm of bees had settled in the boxbody. He was surprised when we told him that we did not want them, that we did not even want the car so long as the bees were in possession, but that we would come along again as soon as the present tenants had left. I had experienced swarms of bees in cars before, and I have yet to own a car that will go fast enough in these circumstances.

We were not there to see what wiles he employed to eject them, but when we got down later the swarm had gone but for a few bewildered stragglers. Most natives, if not exactly bee-keepers, encourage bees by hanging up hives made from hollowed logs in trees near their huts; while in the forest, they have an extraordinary keen nose for the honey which is often found in hollow trees and crannies in the rocks. Naked as they are, their boldness and indifference to stings when dealing with the rightful owners would startle the gloved and netted apiarist. Before loading up we held a snake inspection, for it has already been recorded how on another occasion a puff adder, one of the deadliest snakes, was found dozing peacefully on the cylinder head.

In spite of the long exposure to sun, rain, and curious natives, the car consented to start, and we bowled along cheerfully to Kampala and home, giving thanks for the twin blessings of snow mountains on the equator and the means of getting to them. It is interesting to recall that the Abruzzi expedition, as recently as 1906, spent more time in getting from Kampala to the foot than we did on the mountains—thanks to a road and a car. Even to such light-hearted coffee-planters as ourselves, the time involved without such transport could not have been spent away from the farm without some twinges of conscience, to say nothing of the extra cost a caravan of porters would have entailed. Delightful though the slow-moving porter safari may be, giving opportunities of seeing the country, the natives, and the game which no traveller by car ever has, it is but a means to an end, and the loss of these things is compensated for by the more memorable days spent in high places, among the solitudes of ice and snow.

from In Trouble Again
by Redmond O'Hanlon

Explorer and naturalist Redmond O'Hanlon (born 1947) is known for witty and gorgeously erudite accounts of his journeys to horribly dangerous and uncomfortable places. Here members of the feared Yanomami tribe guide O'Hanlon and his companions to their less outgoing tribe members, deep in the South American rain forest.

W e nodded and smiled at the Yanomami, and the Yanomami, sitting with us on logs in a ring round the fire, nodded and smiled at us.

'We'll leave tomorrow,' I said.

'We'll be the first people to reach the end of the Emoni river', said Chimo, looking Buddha-like in the firelight, 'just like I always said. You can trust Chimo. But first we must feed the Yanomami. They're not allowed to have what they kill—not until all their wives and children have eaten. And one báquiro is not enough for all those people. So they've cheated and come here!'

Galvis piled our spare mess-tins with cubes of meat and pieces of heart and liver and Jarivanau, Wakamane and Kadure, adding fistfuls of manioc, ate with speed and concentration, in silence. By the time we had finished they were on their fourth helpings, their stomachs distended. After their fifth, Jarivanau grinned and laid his tin aside. Wakamane and Kadure climbed into their bongo and, without looking round, set off into the darkness.

The temperature fell, the frogs and cicadas stopped their noise. A wind bent the trees above us and we heard the dull hiss of an approaching storm. Culimacaré picked up Jarivanau's hammock and made as if to tie it in the space between his and Pablo's, beneath the communal tarpaulin, but Jarivanau, shaking his head, took a machete, cut down, trimmed and sharpened two saplings and drove them into the ground, about five feet apart, leaning away from each other, and right beside the fire. Culimacaré fetched our small surplus polythene sheet from the dugout and, with parachute cord, rigged it between the posts like a tent top.

Jarivanau piled sticks on the fire, slung his hammock and placed his bag of possessions beneath it. I dug out my last Oxford pipe and my last tin of Balkan Sobranie from the bottom of my bergen and presented them to him. He took the gifts without a word, wrenched open the tin, stuffed the pipe with tobacco, lit it expertly with a burning twig, and got into his hammock. It looked as uncomfortable as any hammock could be: he was bunched up, almost in a semicircle, the lengths of vine (there were no cross-pieces) cutting lines into the flesh of his back.

The rain arrived. It blasted down through the trees like pig-shot, and we retreated beneath the big tarpaulin. Jarivanau, naked but for Gabriel's trousers, his pipe alight and upside-down in his mouth, his thumb over the bowl, his bow and arrows leaning against his hammock post, lay back in obvious delight, his stomach full, and his thoughts apparently wholly comprised of admiration for his new plastic roof.

It was still raining when we tied the dugouts together and left at dawn.

Jarivanau crept beneath the big tarpaulin at our backs, next to the sack of rice; his head formed an unmoving hump in the canvas, his knees supported a small lake which overflowed in two cataracts over the top of his thighs and splashed down onto the duckboards. Only his right foot stuck out—it was short but remarkably high, the skin sloping sharply down from the bottom front of his ankle to the top back of his toes, a boot of muscle. It was thickly callused at the base, with no discernible instep, cross-hatched with the scars of small cuts, and pock-marked with the purplish roundels of healed ulcers. The skin around each toenail was slightly inflamed and the nails themselves were buckled into ridges and half-eaten away by chiggers. Staring at such a record of jungle strolls I fervently hoped that my own last pair of boots would hold together.

At midday the rain eased slightly, and shortly afterwards we turned into the Emoni. Chimo, his pipe in his mouth but his tobacco too wet to burn, was so dispirited that he forgot to stand up and anoint the new river. The country was low and flooded, the tall manaca palms had disappeared.

Worryingly late in the evening we found a small island of bank, made camp in the rain, changed into dry clothes, finished the peccary soup and went to sleep.

In the morning the mist was thick and cold, but rising; and after we had travelled for several hours, it began to clear. We were emerging, too, from the flooded mouth of the river; the banks became continuous, the trees grew tall again and, for the first time since Neblina, between swathes of mist and the slow swirl of black cloud, we could make out the low shapes of forest-covered hills.

A watery sun appeared. Jarivanau came out of hiding and lay on top of the tarpaulin, our clothes began to steam a little, and a flock of Black-headed parrots sang *toot-toot-toot* from the trees beside us.

I took the lens flaps off my binoculars, pulled Schauensee out of its canvas bag, and began to feel that life still had a lot to offer.

'Juan, I just have a feeling—I think this is going to be the most beautiful river we have ever been up.'

Juan scrutinised me, like a scientist.

'The real Yanomami wait at the end of it,' said Juan, and then: 'Are you *very* happy?' he asked.

'Yes, yes I suppose I am,' I said.

'Then you have a fever,' said Juan decisively, squeezing water out of his beard and turning away.

Cuvier's toucans yapped unseen in the trees all around us and occasionally flew across the river with desperate, fast wing-beats. Flocks of Great egrets, hunched on their perches halfway up the taller trees, ruffled and preened their feathers after the rain and, as we approached, took to the air on their wide, rounded wings; trailing their long black legs, they flew in loose, stately, linear flocks of ten to twenty birds in front of the dugout for a hundred yards or so, and then, rising above the trees, white against the remnant of dark clouds, they would double back to safety. Giant herons, awkward and unsure in comparison, always alone, would flap from one low perch to a higher one upstream, and then labour, with a deep squawk, up over the forest canopy and out of sight.

The river was obviously undisturbed, unvisited; the pairs of Green ibis hardly bothered to fly from us; the big blue-and-white Ringed kingfishers buzzed our boats, at half-speed, to take a closer look. The birds were as tame as the very few species we had seen on the swampy channels of the overgrown Baria, but here in the open and the sunlight, on a white-water river with firm banks and tall palms and great leguminous trees and purple-flowering vines, they were absurdly various and plentiful.

For the first time we could compare all four green kingfishers, their backs an iridescent, dark, oily green which somehow caught the light even as they hid in the deep shadow of the overhanging foliage. The biggest, the Amazon kingfisher, would grip a twig higher up than the others and furthest from the bank, *cack-cack-cack*-ing as we drew level and he streaked downstream. The Green-and-rufous (which I only saw once), the next size down, skulked further back behind the leaves. The Green kingfisher, smaller still, was bolder but perched lower, and both birds, when flushed, made a noise like our stonechat, a gritty *tick-tick*. And lastly, the Pygmy kingfisher, which was difficult to spot, turned out to be quite common if you peered low into the darkest recesses near the bank for several travelling hours. It would flit away, never coming into the open, and *peep-peep*-ing to itself as it went. Apart from their size the kingfishers varied only in the different proportions of white and rufous and green on their throats and chests, an obvious case of one species evolving into four, a simple adaptation to different niches, to hunt different sizes of fish. It was all very satisfying, a flicker of easily comprehensible, natural logic in the impossibly complicated thrust and tangle of trees and bushes and lianas, of epiphytic orchids and bromeliads and ferns, an overarching presence of thousands upon thousands of different species most of whose names even Juan found it impossible to guess.

Rounding a bend on the narrowing river, the engine throttled back, we put a Cattle-egret-sized yellow heron to flight from its fishing-place, and, with mounting excitement, I failed to find it in Schauensee. Perhaps it was just too rare to earn a place? The unrecorded Emoni yellow snake-eating heron, *Snakonoshicus redmondius*? But no—a sharp little note informed me that the Capped heron 'becomes buffy in breeding season': they just go yellow with desire. I turned and waved my binoculars at Chimo in an onrush of pleasure; and was rewarded with the toothless grandfather of all grins.

About fifteen bends further on I was leaning back against the rice sack, admiring a flight of eight pairs of Blue-and-yellow macaws, their long, pointed tails streaming, their bare-skinned faces turned down to look at us, their dirty-old-crone laughter, their terminal, General Paralysis of the Insane, syphilitic shrieks filling the air, when Chimo suddenly swung the dugouts right round and headed back downstream, pointing at the opposite bank. Galvis, sitting opposite me in the other boat, looked up in alarm from his interminable study of the ancient copy of the *Reader's Digest*.

Something was arranged in sagging loops along a fallen tree-trunk at the water's edge, half-obscured by the lower leaves of upstanding lateral shoots. It was big and brown and coiled and glistening in the sun; it was an anaconda.

Chimo shut off the engine and we drifted down towards it in the current. It had rough star-shaped black rings set on a yellow background down the middle of its bulky flanks; overall it was a light brown, its head, resting in the middle of its circling body, a duller brown and surprisingly small—mostly mouth. I leaned closer over the side of the canoe, to get a decent portrait with my inadequate, fixed wide-angle lens and, from three feet away, found myself looking into its tiny, brown, impassive, piggy eyes. Galvis, unable to bear the tension any longer, yelped. The head reared an inch or two and flicked backwards; the coils seemed to lash only once; and the snake, with unnerving speed, disappeared into the watery undergrowth.

'It's a baby,' said Juan, as Chimo re-started the engine and turned the dugouts round again, 'it's the smallest I've ever seen. It's about nine feet.'

'They may be three feet long when they're born,' I said, annoyed, 'but then they're only an inch thick. So it wasn't *that* young.'

'When they go old,' said Juan, 'they go blue.'

'He came to see us,' said Chimo, 'because we talked about him. It is not good to talk too much.'

About an hour later Chimo pointed to a small snake's head, upright in the water, crossing the river from right to left.

'Bejuquilla,' he announced, grinning, swinging the two pole-linked dugouts towards it.

The snake, finding its way momentarily barred by the side of the dugout, simply lifted itself up and came aboard, exactly where Chimo had intended. Its narrow little head had been misleading; a full six foot of thin, green-backed, yellow-flanked, white-bellied, red-tongued snake looped down in front of Galvis.

Galvis, his imagination presumably still scaly with anacondas, began to yell as if he meant it, a long cry that began low and rose rapidly in pitch; he stood up on his plank seat and threw his copy of the *Reader's Digest* overboard.

The snake, unappeased, reared towards his crutch. Galvis, with equal decisiveness, jumped. Arms flung forward and long legs trailing, like a gibbon, he flew easily across the gap between the boats, over the front edge of our covered cargo, and into the arms of Culimacaré in the bow. Chimo, howling with laughter, zig-zagged the canoes. The snake drew itself up, spanned the gap between the dugouts and came for me as I took its long green blur of a portrait. It undulated a couple of half-cartwheels under my elbow, thrashed onto the top of the tarpaulin, and—across my spare pair of trousers, which I had spread to dry—it made for Jarivanau. Jarivanau backed towards Chimo, grabbed the trousers and flicked the snake into the water. His new pipe, which he had laid in pride of place in front of him, went with it.

Pablo gave a whoop, threw his right gumboot into the air and caught it; Culimacaré spluttered in Curipaco, jigging his arm up and down; even Valentine looked happy.

'It's a Green vine snake,' said Juan, 'it's only poisonous a little.'

Galvis climbed sheepishly back to his plank.

'Never mind,' he said, 'I have two more books. I have the story of the life of Marie Antoinette and the story of the life of Mahatma Gandhi.'

'That bejuquilla was after your arse,' said Chimo, wiping his old eyes.

In the late afternoon we made camp beside a small creek. Chimo and Pablo fished for piranhas, Culimacaré took the gun and set off into the forest to try and shoot a curassow, and I went for a swim fully clothed. The creek, half-dammed back by the river, smelt of rotting leaves and slack pools and undulating weeds—it smelt, suddenly, of childhood, of the patch of stream beneath the great willow at the bottom of the Vicarage garden, of my ten-year-old imaginings, of bubbles from sunken empty orange-squash bottles baited with bread and full of silver-bellied minnows, of sticklebacks and Miller's thumbs and water beetles, of the breathing of the crayfish and the stick-encrusted larva of the caddisfly, of the fishy hatching of a million eggs. And, that night, safe in my hammock, full of curassow soup and piranha soup, I dreamt that I was back with my 16-bore (blue cartridges) hiding behind a scraggy hedge on the high ground of Ferguson's farm, waiting for woodpigeons that never appeared, waiting for the largest flock of *Columba palumbus palumbus* ever recorded by the British Trust for Ornithology which might well be on its way towards me in numbers that would darken the sky, and which, at the last moment, would be forced by contrary winds to fly very slowly, one at a time, on a straight and steady course over my head. I looked out at a hare crouched in the stubble field in front of me; at the great sweep of downland behind; at the beech clumps and the Neolithic earthworks on the high points of the horizon; at the white chalk track which wound up and grew small on its way to the dewpond on Tan Hill; and at the group of hunters in wolfskins who grew large as they loped down it towards me, clacking their long bows and arrows above their heads.

Dawn erupted with an all-enveloping roar, a great bronchitic intake of breath in the trees above us; the ends of branches shook in the canopy; I could just make out the odd patch of red fur against the light. Before I could stop him, Culimacaré grabbed Chimo's gun and fired up to the left. A bundle disentangled itself from the high leaves and fell loosely to the ground. The roaring ceased; the trees emptied away from us.

'Juan, tell them not to do that again,' I said, annoyed.

'Redmon, we need food. But you are right. When you shoot a monkey and it falls to the ground with a wound and you go to hit it with a stick—it covers its head with its hands.'

'It's better to starve.'

'It is never better to starve,' said Juan.

The Howler lay on a clump of roots, shot in the chest, dead. He was about the size of a cocker spaniel, his thick fur buff-coloured along his back and a deep red-brown along his sides and stomach. His face was small and black, his ears blackish, his eyes brown and open, and his genitals skin-white. His hands and fingers were long and black (with nails like ours) and the inside last six-inches of his tail was lined with black skin like his hands. Culimacaré picked him up under his armpits, as you would a child, and placed him in our dugout.

We finished the piranha soup, disconnected the canoes, and set off up the narrowing river with both engines throttled down to save petrol. There were small, untropical-looking white clouds in the narrow band of azure sky above us and, but for the height of the trees and the looped curtain of lianas tumbling down and trailing in the water beside us, the whirr of cicadas and the constant, mournful, double wolf-whistle of the Screaming piha, we might have been travelling up a waterway in an English wood. As we rounded a bend, there were fifty English Peregrine falcons criss-crossing the air beneath the underbelly of a cloud. Except that there were forty-nine too many of them, and their wing-beats were all wrong; their flight was graceful, delicate, buoyant; they aroused no Peregrine-like suspicion that they had just fired themselves from cross-bows.

'Gavilán plomizo,' said Chimo, lifting his pipe in salute to them.

Schauensee translated for me: they were Plumbeous kites; and, once I had found them in the sixty-six black-and-white illustrations of birds of prey in flight, I could make out the three white bands across their dark tails. There were three Swallow-tailed kites soaring with them, and through the binoculars I could see that the whole flock was feeding on a swarm of large, heavy-bodied insects—probably flying ants, in which case, I thought, considered in the long term, they had not been feeding hard enough.

The banks grew taller and the river faster flowing; forest-covered hills surrounded us, seeming to block the way ahead and, once we had passed, to shut off all retreat. In our own immediate world, beneath an overhang of large-leaved, fleshy plants on the right bank, we disturbed a bird so distinctive that I recognised it at once: a sungrebe—small, long-bodied, olive-brown, skulking—it fluttered a little distance in front of us and then splashed back into the water, its head jerking, the black and white stripes on its neck flicking back and forth as it swam. We drew level and it repeated the process until we reached the invisible edge of its little kingdom, when it flew back past the boat to safety, its legs dangling: 'Builds nest of sticks in bushes above the water,' said Schauensee, 'transports its chicks in cavities on its side; swims and flies perfectly carrying its young until they fledge.'

Further upstream, three howlers ran on all fours for cover along the wide branches of a vast ceiba tree as we approached; and an hour or two later we slid by a hundred feet beneath a pair of Spider monkeys in some kind of legume tree, who just paused in their aerial walk and looked at us, black eyes in black faces, their bodies black-furred and slender, holding on with their hands and feet, their long tails S-shaped above their backs. Jarivanau stood up, mimed loosing an arrow, and gave a high-pitched Yanomami cry. The monkeys jumped twenty feet down into a smaller tree and swung away by their arms, ape-like.

It was obviously one of those rare, rich days when everyone had come out to look at us. I lay back on the tarpaulin. Large anxieties seemed to brachiate off into the forest like Spider monkeys, small ones skulked out of my stomach like sungrebes, and, despite myself, I fell asleep.

Juan woke me with a yell. I opened my eyes—and focused them straight into the green-brown pupils of the mightiest eagle in the world. The black and white rounded wings, a good six feet across, seemed to hang above the boat for ever, the grey hood and enormous hooked black bill were turned down towards us; the wrist-thick legs and the massive talons, a startling bright yellow, were held straight back towards the long barred tail.

'Jesus!' I said.

'Harpy eagle,' said Juan.

A bird that lives by ripping monkeys and sloths out of trees, it plainly intended to amuse itself by plucking Juan and me out of the dugout, one in each foot. But then, thinking better of it, with one leisurely beat of the great wings it rose over the canopy and out of sight.

'How's that?' said Chimo, immensely proud, half-raising his fist in the air and shaking it back and forth in self-congratulation. 'Only Chimo could show you such a bird.'

We cut steps up the high muddy bank and made camp. Chimo and Pablo spread palm fronds on the ground and began to prepare the Howler monkey, scalding it with boiling water and scraping off the fur. Its skin turned white, like a baby's.

That night, when Pablo had jointed the body and Galvis boiled it, Chimo handed me a suspiciously full mess tin. As I spooned out the soup the monkey's skull came into view, thinly covered in its red meat, the eyes still in their sockets.

'We gave it to you specially,' said Chimo with great seriousness, sitting on a log beside me, taking another fistful of manioc from the tin and adding it to his own bowl. 'It's an honour in our country. If you eat the eyes we will have good luck.'

The skull bared its broken teeth at me. I picked it up, put my lips to the rim of each socket in turn, and sucked. The eyes came away from their soft stalks and slid down my throat.

Chimo put his bowl down, folded his hands on his paunch, and roared with laughter.

'You savage!' he shouted. 'You horrible naked savage! Don't you think it looks like a man? Eh? How *could* you do a disgusting thing like that?'

In the morning, while Jarivanau and Culimacaré went hunting and Juan and the others dug for carbon a little way off in the forest, I retrieved the rest of the howler skull from the communal pot. The lower jaw was wide and deep at its rear angle, and a bony box which I found bobbing in the soup exactly fitted in the space beneath it. It was a parchment-thick hanging sac, the resonating chamber which amplifies the deep and breathy roar that marks out the howler group's territory. The back teeth were evenly worn down, almost to the gums, by a lifetime's eating of leaves and buds, flowers and fruit and nuts. I picked out the brains with a small stick and the tweezers from my Swiss Army knife, peeled away the scraps of flesh and rubbed salt into my trophy to preserve it.

A small bird, robin-like, came to watch from a bush on my right. It regarded me, unafraid, cocking its head first one way and then the other, its tail stumpy as a wren's, its breast white with black spots and its back brown with white spots. I drew Schauensee out of the front pocket of my bergen and found the likeliest plate—it was a Dot-backed antbird, whose habits, Phelps and Schauensee thought, were 'probably similar to Spot-backed antbird', which, in turn, 'probably follows army ants'. So we had reached a place where the habits of some of the most common-seeming birds (birds that came and sat beside you and introduced themselves) were unknown, their nests undescribed, their eggs unseen.

Jarivanau and Culimacaré came back from hunting with a curassow apiece, and the antbird flitted off through the undergrowth. I went to our canoe, wrapped the howler skull in a torn shirt and placed it in the top of a kit-bag. Juan joined me, clutching his new carbon samples in two small sealable plastic wallets. He stowed them in his waterproof box, and then he turned to me suddenly, a barely controlled ferocity in his quick movements, a half-mocking smile on his face.

'You will never reach to the real Yanomami.'

'What do you mean?'

'Redmon, there are many things you do not know. Until now I am keeping them from you. Galvis has made trouble. The Indians they want to turn back.'

'Nonsense.'

'They told me when we dug for carbon. Galvis says there is not much manioc. And only one tank of gasoline. They say they need one tank for the Siapa. No man could paddle through those clouds of blackfly.'

'I've got plenty of insect repellent. We'll share out some more. There's nothing to worry about.'

'There is everything to worry about,' said Juan. 'You must take a decision.'

A humming-bird buzzed between us and hovered for a moment. It was a Long-tailed hermit, a tiny blur of mad intensity between its bronze green head and its long white tail which hung straight down, motionless for a small part of a second.

'Not now,' I said. 'Not yet. Today we go upriver.'

Late that morning we passed beneath a great brown granite hill, massy above the trees, its upper slopes bare and rounded.

'Toucan mountain,' announced Chimo.

The river grew still narrower and faster-flowing, the banks higher. We disturbed otters who scrambled up to safety in the forest, water droplets scattering from their fur; we swung round bends between small, sandy cliffs in which kingfishers had tunnelled their nests; we annoyed a pair of Red-throated caracaras, black, buzzard-sized birds with white bellies, red-skinned throats and faces, and with bills like chickens, who just stayed perched at the top of their tree and swore at us with extraordinary volume and vehemence.

'*Ca-ca-ca-ca-cacao*,' they screamed, with no self-control whatever, until a bend in the river shut them away behind us.

And then we saw something shocking, out of place. A bridge spanned the river ahead.

'Whoooo! Whoooo!' sang Jarivanau, delighted, stretching himself.

Everyone else looked uneasily at the close banks, at the dark spaces under the leaves.

'It's okay,' said Chimo, 'it's old.'

Two long poles had been thrust into the river bed at an angle just out from the left bank and lashed where they intersected; more poles, tied together, laid in the fork of the upright, and further suspended by lianas commandeered as cables and pulled out over the water from the surrounding trees, formed a fragile walkway to similar crossed uprights on the opposite bank. But it did look reassuringly abandoned; the whole structure had been half-pushed over by the current.

'Juan,' I said, 'you must brush your teeth especially well tonight.'

'How so?'

'Because then they'll look *their very best* in a necklace!'

'If I take a sample,' said Juan, jerkily brushing a large green Leaf insect off his arm, 'I find that one in ten of your jokes is a funny, and that unit only in five percent of content.'

Chimo motored slowly, looking ahead with excessive attention, silent. I half expected to see Conrad's 'sticks, little sticks' from *Heart of Darkness* 'flying about . . . whizzing before my nose, dropping below me, striking behind me'. Maybe Galvis would suddenly 'look at me over his shoulder in an extraordinary, profound, familiar manner' and fall across his penny life of Gandhi while 'what appeared to be a long cane', stuck to his back, would clatter round and knock against our remaining petrol drum.

But the sunlight sparked white along the ridge of our little bow wave in the usual way; it fell undisturbed among the tops of the giant trees on the tierra ferme banks, picking out the moss and lichens and bromeliads high on an exposed stretch of branch; it lit the bright red of a limp cluster of new young leaves; it dropped into steep caverns of vegetation and disappeared.

And, as I watched through my binoculars, it caught the red beak of a Black nunbird, dark, contemplative, chubby, perched at the top of a lone palm tree. It was the first member of the puffbird family (large-headed, thick-necked, kingfisher-like birds) that I had seen, and I recognised it simply because its representative also sat on a very special plate in Schauensee and Phelps, one of only two illustrations (the other of humming-birds) which were painted by Phelps's wife Kathleen. Around a male Cock-of-the-rock she had also arranged a Blue-crowned motmot; an Amazonian umbrella bird (large, black, its head thatched with blue and its lower throat sporting a matching wattle, and which, according to Snow, moos like a calf and growls like a distant chain saw); a Red-ruffed fruitcrow (which 'emits a deep, booming hollow sound resembling the bellowing of a bull'); a capuchinbird (which 'bellows like an ox'); a Guianan red-cotinga (a finch-size mix of silky crimson, dusky maroon and rosy carmine with a penchant for figs); and an oilbird flat on its stomach at the base of the page (a whiskered, nightjar-like brown bird which screams, snarls, snores, echo-locates by clicks in its roosting caves, and feeds at night on fruit that is plucked in flight and swallowed whole).

Lost in comforting admiration of plate 25, I was wondering how many years I would have to live in the jungle before I saw the Amazonian umbrellabird, and what a good idea a fixed umbrella would be, and whether Toucan mountain or the highlands ahead would prove to be the previously unrecorded home of the most exotic of them all, the White bellbird, when Juan shouted, 'Macaw!'

A shiny, bright little bird, chaffinch-sized, with a crimson head, white belly and black wings flew low over the water and up into a dead branch projecting from the shore. It was a Red-capped cardinal.

Juan laughed. Chimo sat unmoved. I put Schauensee away. There was a snag ahead. A great tree lay across the river about two feet above the surface, supported on its branches.

Culimacaré stood up in the bow, grasping the axe, but Chimo shook his head and brought the dugout into the bank. There was an ominous sound of crashing water, of rapids ahead. The tree showed dull red where branches had been ripped away in its fall. It was obviously a species of hardwood, half-a-day's cutting if the Indians worked in relays. Leafcutter ants processed along its top all the way to the other side of the stream. We dug muddy steps up the bank, cleared a patch of ground and began to make camp. Chimo laid his gun in the curiara, eased the little boat beneath the tree and paddled off upriver.

Jarivanau, relaxed with us now, pleased with the machete I had given him and dressed in a pair of Culimacaré's bright green shorts, rubbed his taut stomach and gestured at a big palm, a ceje. The fruit hung in grape-like bunches, high up under the crown of fronds, dark against the light; and the trunk of the tree was ringed, all the way up, with long black spines. The problem looked insoluble. Culimacaré had never offered to climb a ceje. It was plainly a barbed-wire, broken-glass, festering-ulcer-per-spike palm.

Forgetting whose country it was, I shook my head at Jarivanau. Jarivanau grinned and shook his own, beaten-up head at me. He ran a hand over his stubby scalp and looked about at the surrounding saplings; he then cut down four, trimmed them, and laid the poles in two X-shapes with their top Vs against the base of the palm, their ends projecting on the far side. He tugged down a coil of mamure vine from a neighbouring tree, cut it into lengths, and bound his poles loosely at their divergent points beyond the trunk, tightly where they crossed each other hard against the palm on the side nearest him. He then raised the top frame to chest height, lodged it at an incline towards him, grabbed hold, hooked his muscled toes around the bottom frame's sides and, slowly but rhythmically, edged his way into the air, three feet out from the thorns, his machete in his teeth. We clapped.

Jarivanau steeplejacked upwards, his back brown and scarred like the bark of the tree behind him, his muscles alternately bunching and flattening beneath their lichen of blood spots. The frail platform, bending horribly, rose into the crown; Jarivanau reached forward and, with tremendous swipes, severed the stem. The heavy clusters thudded to the ground. Jarivanau descended, his teeth re-clamped on the blade of his precious machete. Culimacaré and Pablo picked the hard, purple-red, plum-sized fruits from their stalks and Valentine pounded them in the big pot, like manaca. Juan and Galvis set about building a fire. Jarivanau and I sat down on the top of a big surface root and began to pluck the curassows; he pulled out each black, white-tipped tail feather, smoothed it between his fingers and gently poked it tip-first into a patch of mud beside him: spare fletches for his arrows. I mimed some-one walking and pointed in the vague direction of the highlands.

'Cuántas días?' I asked. 'How many days to the Yanomami?'

Jarivanau put down the half-naked bird, swivelled round on the root, brought his arm back behind his head and then shot it straight out five times towards the west, repeating the gesture he had used that night in his communal hut. Its very emphasis suggested an insane effort. Five days' walking for a Yanomami, I thought; maybe eight days' for us.

From the landing-stage there came the kind of wet snort a bull gives when inspecting a cow on heat, a bucket-sized gob; a fart from a siege mortar. Chimo had returned. He clambered up to the camp carrying a small cayman by the front legs and dumped it in front of Galvis.

'Reymono,' he said, wiping his mouth quickly with the back of his hand, 'we will never get past the rapids. If we *walk* into the Chori lands, anything could happen. We are not welcome here. It is not our coun-try. We must turn back.'

So this was it—the moment I had feared more than any other, a moment for which I thought I had prepared myself. In my imagination I was always calm, forceful, measured, persuasive. But it was not like that; it caught me from behind, silently; I needed a piss; I was tired; it was all over. I began to shake.

Chimo took his helmet off and hung it on the hammock-post beside him. He rubbed both hands over his face, as if clearing sleep from his eyes.

'I'm going on with Jarivanau,' I said, feeling ridiculous even as the words formed themselves. 'So who's coming with me?'

I stood up. Nobody moved; Galvis looked away and poked at his fire with a stick. Juan was right; they really did mean to desert. On a leaf by my right boot a large red ant was waving its antennae about; I felt suddenly disconnected from everything, cut off from myself. I tried to smile, but failed; it was as though I had ceased to inhabit my own face. Through the gap we had cleared in the bushes I could see the desolate brown river eddying past. A Screaming piha called.

Chimo looked up; he put his helmet back on his head and he began to sing softly. He was absurd in his army shorts, his yellow gum boots. 'I'm by far the biggest girl in town,' he sang, 'but, just for you, I'll take my knickers down.' And he came and stood beside me.

Shamed, Culimacaré and Pablo picked up their machetes and joined us.

'Then that's settled,' said Chimo, 'my old friend Valentine can have a rest at last; and the girl Galvis can cook for himself and guard the boats. But we'll mark the trail well, Galvis, so that when the Yanomami have killed us they will walk here—and kill you, too; you won't hear a thing—and believe me, those arrows can lift a man right off the ground and stick him on a tree.'

Valentine, looking much older than he had that morning, silent, unsmiling, his movements querulous, set about building a smoking rack for the cayman. Galvis, on the other hand, temporarily released from his great fear of the Yanomami, re-found his usual talkative and cheerful self, opened his personal medicine box (which consisted entirely of different-coloured soaps and shampoos), hummed one of his pop songs, and shuffle-danced himself down to the river for a wash.

Juan and I began to cut up the cayman, and Jarivanau, Chimo, Pablo and Culimacaré wandered off into the forest.

'I am worried,' said Juan *sotto voce*, his face close to mine. 'Redmon, I am worried that I am not strong enough. It will be like the peccary hunt, but it will go on for days and days. We will have to keep up with Jarivanau. I will not be able to walk so far and so fast.'

'Nonsense,' I said, secretly hoping that he might be diabetic; or possess only one lung; or suffer from congenital crutch decay—anything to slow down the pace. And as if in answer to my wish, he stood up, undid his belt with extreme awkwardness, and dropped his trousers.

'Look!' said Juan. 'It hurts me a lot. It even hurts at night.'

Two red patches, slightly scaly at the edges, spread widening up his inner thighs and disappeared under his pants. The fungus had got him.

'Why didn't you tell me? Why didn't you ask for some cream?'

'I thought you made a fuss about nothing. I thought you were ridiculous.'

'I am ridiculous,' I said triumphantly, feeling like a veteran, going to my pack, taking a spare tube of Canesten from a side-pocket and handing it to him with a flourish, 'but you've only lived in research stations; when you're in the jungle all the time every man's crutch should be a Venus bug-trap.'

Juan dabbed the white goo onto his raw skin. 'And last night I caught two brown ticks feeding on my balls: they must have come from the howler. It's how you get yellow fever.'

'Not here,' I said firmly, assuming more knowledge which I didn't possess. 'There's no yellow fever here.'

Jarivanau and the others returned bearing long bundles of green palm fronds. They squatted on the ground and, watching Culimacaré who was obviously the expert, they began to plait the leaves together. In ten minutes they had made Curipaco bergens, sixty-pound-capacity palm-leaf backpacks. Chimo then selected the right tree, a medium-sized sapling, made a machete-cut at the top of his reach and tugged off long strips of bark, about six-inches wide, which he wove into the rims and sides of the baskets to make head-bands and shoulder straps.

'Catumaré's,' said Chimo, pleased with himself, testing one by trying to stretch its fretwork of leaves and stems. 'Now we can walk till our pingas drop off.'

As the tree frogs quacked and piped and trilled above and around us we parcelled out the stores—all the remaining plastic bags of beads, fish hooks, fishing line, mirrors and combs; medicines; a machete each; and half our remaining supply of all the food we had left—salt, sugar, coffee, cornflour and lentils. On top of my share of the common cargo I packed the Polaroid and our last one hundred exposures; Simon's Minolta and all the film we possessed; my spare pair of spectacles and my gym shoes, my last reserve footwear. I decided against D'Abrera's *Butterflies of South America* and my copies of Chagnon and Lizot, but for Schauensee. There would barely be room, at the top of the bergen, for the outsize, wet, heavy, Colombian hammock: for the first time I regretted leaving the compact, light, canvas SAS version in San Carlos. I wrapped my precious notebooks in two plastic bags and stowed them uneasily in Galvis's medicine box.

'300 extra bolivares,' I announced, 'to everyone who comes with me—if we find the Yanomami.' And, after supper, as we washed our mess-tins free of cayman grease in the river, '300 bolivares extra to you, too, and to old Valentine,' I whispered in Galvis's lemon-shampoo-scented ear, 'if you guard my notebooks.'

'What use is that to me,' said Galvis, 'if you don't come back?'

Chimo, stoking up the fire, whistling, talking to himself, woke us well before dawn; we packed our hammocks and mosquito nets, and Pablo and Culimacaré bound one of our smaller canvas shelter-tops apiece on top of their loads. Jarivanau simply wound his split-vine sleeping-net into a ball and stuffed it into his catumaré, beneath half the smoked tail of the cayman, wrapped in leaves.

I went down to the dugout, my torchlight diffusing into the heavy mist, to fetch a potent talisman which James Fenton had given me in Oxford. With great care, I took it out of its plastic wallet in the number one kit-bag. The prize of one of his contemplative journeys round the city's antique shops, it was the Fenton award for great bravery in Borneo in the face of no discernible danger whatever. I admired it afresh before slipping it into my pocket. One side was embossed with a profiled head of a respectable gentleman in glasses like mine: '50 JAHR PAUL LEWY HEISS ICH. 26.XII. 1926,' ran the inscription: 'MY NAME IS PAUL LEWY AND I'VE LIVED FOR FIFTY YEARS;' and, on the other side, equally boldly, were cast his buttocks: 'WAS AUCH WAR TÄGLICH SCHEISS ICH,' they announced: 'AND, WHAT'S MORE, I'VE HAD A SHIT EVERYDAY.'

Exactly at first light persons unknown began cutting wood with two circular saws. It was unnerving, insistent: a frantic reverberation of screaming and whining and rasping.

'Viudita carrablanca!' shouted Chimo, hoisting his catumaré onto his shoulders.

'It is the White-faced saki,' said Juan. 'He is very rare and we have luck to hear him. He is small and black and his wife is brown—and for a long time they were thought to be two different species. He lives with his wife and the children in the middle layer of the trees and they eat fruit and seeds. He is little known. This is the first time I hear him.'

There were two more bursts of sound, then silence.

I swung the corpse-like weight of my bergen onto my back, shook hands with Galvis, and waved to Valentine who was standing apart, leaning on a tree by the steps to the boats. The old man came up to me and took both my hands in his. He seemed smaller, as if he had withered slightly in the night. He studied me with his profoundly sad, watery, inefficient eyes.

'Thank you,' he said, 'for the pipe you gave me.'

I formed up behind our new leader, Jarivanau. Barefoot, he had his face forced down to his shoulders by the weight of his palm-leaf pack pulling on the strap across the top front third of his head; the scars on the other two-thirds were red with pressure and excitement; he grasped his new machete with one hand and held the shotgun tight round the barrel with the other; he grinned uncontrollably, horribly eager to start.

Juan stood behind me, tense; Culimacaré and Pablo waited behind him and Chimo, still whistling, wandered up from the rear. Jarivanau bounded off like a peccary.

Four foot six inches tall, brutally fit, he slipped under lianas that caught me round the waist. He swung his catumaré to his side and stooped beneath the branches of fallen tree trunks which forced me to take off my bergen and crawl through on all fours, dragging it after me.

His bare boot-feet propelled him through the small creeks and up their soft, dark, rotted banks without a change in his half-loping rhythm, while I slid in and floundered out. But, most impressive of all, I could see, through the sweat and mist on my glasses, that he was constantly alert: despite the weight hanging from his head which made the tendons in his neck stand out like chicken legs, he kept scanning the underside of the canopy for palms in fruit, for bees' nests, for the unwary guan, for the movement of leaves that might betray a Howler or a Spider monkey.

After an hour or so of such a pace my sole preoccupation became judging the moment, in the short stretches between the sluggish streams and deep, full gulleys, when it might be possible to unbutton the flap on one of my SAS water-bottle holsters, pull out the aluminum bottle without losing sight of Jarivanau's ever-receding back, unscrew the black rubber top, take a desperate swig and replace it.

Mindless with fatigue, I had just completed such a manoeuvre and even re-filled a bottle from a ditch we were crossing, when Jarivanau, jumping over a tree trunk, suddenly spun round and pointed at the rotted bark. I moved closer and stooped down to peer at the place he indicated: I could see nothing unusual, just ridges of dark brown lichen and straggles of fungus. Jarivanau yelled, waving me back. Juan, catching up from behind, grabbed my arm.

'Mapanaré!' he shouted.

Culimacaré caught up with us and took hold of my shirt.

And then I just made out a short length of brown, brushed velvet, dropped along a slight hollow in the wood. It was, I realised dimly, a snake; its head was triangular, the sides of its body shaded into black.

Jarivanau darted forward, hit it with his machete, impaled it behind the head and tossed it into the undergrowth. Its belly flashed yellow as it turned in the air.

'Mapanaré! Barba amarillo!' shouted Juan, still excited, letting go of my arm. 'You nearly died! You nearly make your last stupid! Why do you want to kiss a snake?'

'I didn't see it,' I said, weakly. 'I had no idea.'

And anyway, I thought, it was difficult to believe that anything so fundamentally peaceful, so well camouflaged, could actually rouse itself and kill you.

Culimacaré, looking anxious and protective, jigged his arm up and down, still holding my shirt, and then let me go.

'You call it the fer-de-lance,' said Juan, 'and it is very common here. A lot of people die when they clear the ground for their conucos. Every female has sixty or eighty young, all born alive, and with all their poisonous equipment ready from the day one.'

I stepped over the tree trunk. The now-machete-scarred surface was on a level with my upper thighs. The fer-de-lance was about eighteen inches long. My own equipment retracted, sharply.

Culimacaré pushed past me without a word and fell into step behind Jarivanau, marking the trail as he went, cutting a plant stem or a twig with his machete every twenty yards or so. The pace eased, the country grew even flatter, and there was time to look about; the soils were obviously poor, big trees were rare and dwarf species common—miniature palms, no more than ten feet tall, and small trees with tufts of enormous leaves sprouting from their tops grew among the saplings. Yet even in the lowered, more broken canopy formed by the middle-sized trees, bromeliads clustered in every fork of the branches, their leaves half-furled together at their bases, funnelling upwards and outwards, and the water trapped in them, I knew, would be a seethe of mosquito larvae: a marsh still stretched endlessly away in all directions above our heads.

Several hours later we came to our first deep river, about thirty yards across. Jarivanau took off his catumaré, laid down his gun and, after careful inspection of its bark and crown, he selected a tree which looked like any other. I slipped off my bergen and, as my legs gave way, sat on it. There would be at least half an hour's rest, I thought: I could undo a water-bottle as slowly as I liked; I could clean my glasses; maybe there would even be time to suck on a smoked cayman chew bar.

Jarivanau hit his tree at chest height with a flurry of machete blows;

grinning all the while, he stood for a minute in a shell-burst of white wood fragments. The tree creaked forward, split above the cut and toppled across the river, let down slowly by a tangle of stretched lianas; it was obviously the softest tree in the forest, there would be no rest for anyone.

Pablo emerged from the trail, looking fresh; and a few moments later Chimo appeared, carrying his paunch in front and his pack behind and whistling as if he took such a walk every day of his life.

Jarivanau set off along his Yanomami bridge, his feet like gecko's suction pads, lopping off branches and vines as he went, clearing a passage. Culimacaré cut us each a sapling and then, fully laden, using the pole like a tight-rope walker, he crossed to the far bank in one untroubled saunter. The others followed suit. In fact it looked so easy, and I was so tired, that I forgot the advice of the SAS Major in Hereford: 'Whatever you do, lad, never cross a river with a bergen on your back.'

My ruptured boots gave me no purchase on the slimy bark. The pole took on a life of its own, parrying the blows of invisible assailants to left and right; the river tilted up to look at me one side, lay flat, and then repeated the process with an increase in tempo. I felt like a pilot in a dragonfly, and then I fell, it seemed, from the highest point, with the maximum force. The world went black and gurgled; something closed on my leg and something else bore down on my shoulders, holding me under. This time it really is an anaconda, I thought, trying to raise my head—I have fallen into one of Colonel Fawcett's sixty-foot-long anacondas. And then there was a push on my chest; I was gulping air; and, through the water streaming down from my hat, still held in place by the chin strap, I looked into Culimacaré's slightly hooded, dark brown eyes. He was treading water, roaring with laughter, displaying his gums, and easing my arms out of the bergen which he anchored on a broken branch of the tree. As I struggled to free my foot, he submerged beside me, and forced it out of the snag.

When I climbed out on the far bank, Jarivanau, Pablo and Chimo were howling with laughter, too.

'Reymono!' spluttered Chimo, clapping me on the back. 'You'll *never* make a monkey.'

But Juan was unsmiling, anxious.

'I do not understand,' he said, folding his arms tight across his chest. 'What will you do? What will you do if they kill Jarivanau? What will you do if *we have to run from the Yanomami*?'

For the next three rivers (or perhaps they were loops of the same one) I gave my bergen to Culimacaré to carry in front of him over Jarivanau's felled trees, and swam across. The all-in soakings made little difference; everything was already as wet as it could be.

As the afternoon sweated on, Jarivanau seemed less eager to push ahead; we all walked in sight of each other. The ground became firmer, the intersecting gulleys less frequent, the trees much bigger. And then, from a near-hypnotic state, a trance induced by the slop-slop of my broken boots on the wet leaves, the rhythmic shifting of weight in my pack, I awoke, sharply, to full consciousness.

Jarivanau and Culimacaré had stopped in front of me. We had come out into an open space. The crowns of the giant trees met overhead, the understorey was intact around the perimeter, but the area before us had been cleared. Some thirty little leaf-shelters were spaced out on it, looking as if they had grown where they stood. Their triangular roofs of saplings and palm-leaves were supported by a single six-foot pole at the front and two four-foot poles linked with a cross-piece at the back, some of them still had split-vine hammocks inside, slung to the uprights front and rear. The leaves were brown and withered, the hammocks decayed, the trodden earth bare of recent footprints. Yet we all fell silent: a lot of people had been here; this was not our place and we should not be in it.

Jarivanau took off his catumaré, and walked purposefully across the clearing. I followed at once—perhaps he was looking for some ritual sign, some formal message always left in Yanomami camps? He flitted from tree to tree at the far edge of the clearing, looking embarrassed, secretive, gesturing at me to stay away. He became more emphatic, shooing at me with both hands. I became even more intrigued; I was about to make some small but crucial anthropological discovery.

Finally, exasperated, he retreated between two plank buttresses, turned his back on me, dropped the green shorts that Culimacaré had given him, and took a shit. Jarivanau had diarrhoea.

'We must camp soon,' said Chimo gloomily, leading the way. 'And well off the path. We must be close to the Choris. They may be only one day's walk away—and we must light no fires, Reymono. I would rather risk a jaguar in the night than a visit by these people.'

Half an hour further, on a small headland formed by a tight bend in a stream, Chimo stopped and unloaded. It was an exceptional place: huge trees, clearish water, and, beneath the overhang of bank, there was even a narrow stretch of muddy sand. I cleaned my glasses, washed my face, filled my water bottles, and tried not to think about the unmapped territory around us.

Pablo and Culimacaré put up the two tarpaulins over a rectangle of cut saplings and we slung our hammocks. Chimo fussed about, his great buttocks in the air, pursuing shiny, black, inch-long veintecuatros across the jungle floor and flattening them with his machete, a task altogether too serious to permit of whistling.

'Thanks to the Holy Mother,' he said, finding their nest at last, a small clear hole by the roots of the giant tree. He went to his catumaré, took out a plastic bottle of kerosene, poured half of it down the opening and dropped in a match. There was a brief spurt of blue flame.

'That's a waste of cooking fuel,' said Juan.

'They can knock a man unconscious,' said Chimo, aggrieved.

We chewed strips of smoked cayman, said very little, changed into dry clothes and collapsed into our hammocks. Darkness fell.

Fireflies, with two green lights apiece, cruised back and forth beneath the trees; the ground around us glowed with phosphorescent fungi and lichens—a pale yellow light, brighter than I had ever seen before.

'Quack! Quack! Quack!' said something, like a duck being squeezed.

'It's a duck,' I said.

'It's an agouti,' grunted Chimo. 'We must be camped near his burrow. He's annoyed with us.'

Then, very loud, came the hooting of an owl.

'It's an owl,' I said.

'Zambullidor de sol,' said Chimo.

'So *that's* what a sungrebe sounds like,' I thought, getting excited, pleased with myself.

Something else joined in, a long burbling call.

'It's a Green ibis,' I said.

'It's Jesus Christ' said Chimo, heaving himself over in his hammock so that we shook all down the line. 'Go to sleep.'

A reverberating cackle, followed by a long, loud groan, very close, woke me in the dark. Chimo was already up, rootling about in his catumaré.

'What's that?' I said.

'Pájaro vaco,' said Chimo. 'It's *all* the Pájaro vaco. But why ask me? Don't they tell you everything in those books of yours? Eh?'

Even Chimo, I realised, was getting tense. My stomach turned slightly at the thought.

I switched on my torch and took out Schauensee, always the best therapy: Pájaro vaco, he said, was the Rufescent tiger-heron, big, black and brown, with chestnut head and shoulders: 'Usually solitary, not shy. Active at night. Remains motionless when alarmed. Feeds on fishes, insects.' There was no word as to his speech-patterns; no advice as to whether or not he was given to imitating ducks and owls and girls on broomsticks.

We broke camp, chewed some more cayman, and set off the moment we could see the undergrowth.

Around midday I noticed a party of small birds flitting about us on twigs and on the ground; and a pace or two later we were walking over a mass of medium-sized black ants, a chaotic, hyperactive crowd of insects running in all directions and even streaming, for two or three yards, up the stems of ferns, the trunks of trees—they were, I assumed, one of Henry Walter Bates's species of army ants (he found ten kinds, eight of them new to science); but Jarivanau was too far ahead for me to shout and stop him; in five minutes we had passed across the column; and I just paused briefly to brush a few particularly brave individuals off my trousers.

Jarivanau paused, too. We had come to a path. There was no doubt about it this time: we had come to a well-trodden, four-foot-wide path which intersected our route at right angles. We waited for Chimo, who laboured up, stopped, took his pipe out of one pocket and his plastic tobacco pouch out of another, filled his pipe, replaced his pouch, firmed down the full bowl with his thumb, stuck the pipe in his gums, lit up, and smiled.

'How's that?' he said, as if he had found the way himself.

He gave me a leathery wink.

'Now we can all die together,' he said. 'Just to please Reymono. Just to see what it's like.'

The path led to a plantation, a large, long-established conuco of plantains. The sunlight bore down on us, stark and hard and open.

We clambered over the well-scuffed horizontal trunks of old, half-burnt trees, down to a small stream, and up into a belt of uncleared forest. There we stopped to piss as if by agreement, our bladders water-pistolled by fear.

On the other side of the hill we halted again. A young plantation sloped down in front of us; a wooded mountain filled the horizon behind. In the hollow stood a massive, enclosed, oval construction of palm-leaf thatch, yellowed with age, its back to us; the skeletal tops of poles, facing inwards, stuck into the air along its upper edges. Eight Cattle egrets sat hunched in a tree to our left.

'Redmon,' said Juan, setting down his pack and unwrapping his camera, his movements suddenly as exaggerated, as jerky as when we first met, 'will you please take my picture with Chimo and the others? For my wife?'

It was a bizarre idea. I thought I knew what he was thinking: one day, maybe, some anthropologist or missionary will come here and find a rusty, unopened camera—and then the small mystery of our disappearance will be explained.

Despite myself, I handed him my Nikonos, too, and we photographed each other: lined up against the forest edge with Pablo and Culimacaré in their Neblina boots; Chimo with his machete in his hand and his pipe in his mouth; and Jarivanau, clutching the shotgun to his chest.

As I handed Juan his camera back, Jarivanau, unable to bear the delay of his homecoming a moment longer, took off down the path. I chased him in earnest, the bergen bumping up and down on my back, my camera and binoculars swinging across my chest.

Half-way there he paused, put the gun to his shoulder and raised the barrel towards the sun.

'No! No!' I yelled. 'Don't do that! Not here!'

The explosion, unmuffled by trees, seemed extraordinarily loud; it reverberated round the hills. The egrets shattered into the air. And then, from inside the shabono, a long, undulating, sustained scream rose into the sky.

Jarivanau beckoned to me and ran, crouching low towards the curving wall. He threw down a small panel of thatch, stooped through, and disappeared. I followed, forced by the bulk of the bergen to crawl through on all fours.

I looked up from the dry ground—straight at the shafts of a pair of six-foot-long arrows. They were fitted, I noticed, with notched, syringe-sharp, curare-blackened monkey-tips. The two young men stood, their great bows fully drawn, their backs arched, their faces expressionless. Their penises were held flat up against their stomachs by the foreskin, hooked under the waistband of bark string. They had small, neat tufts of black pubic hair.

'Real Yanomami! Chagnon's Yanomami!' I thought in a rush of pleasure and relief and adrenalin. 'Doing exactly what they're meant to do!' And then, 'Jesus Christ,' I thought, *'they're going to kill me.'*

'Whooo-hooo-hooo!' whooped Jarivanau, pulling off my hat.

The young men lowered their bows and smiled. Jarivanau jammed my hat back on my head and helped me, shaky, to my feet. More men were running towards us across the huge oval expanse, waving their arms in the air.

'Whooo-hooo-hooo!' they shouted.

An old man put his emaciated arms around Jarivanau and then stood beside him, rubbing a hand fondly back and forth across his quarter-inch crew-cut and damaged skull.

Juan and Culimacaré, Pablo and Chimo appeared behind me. We stood in a group, staring stupidly at the press of people about us. The women wore red or ochre loincloths, and pudding-basin haircuts, like the men. Almost all of them had a baby or a toddler at the hip, its buttocks firmly supported by a red sash from the mother's opposite shoulder. Sticks pierced their nasal septums and projected horizontally to the edge of either cheek, three shorter sticks, spokes of a semicircle, stuck out from holes just beneath the centre and corners of their lower lips. Larger wooden plugs were lodged through their earlobes and some were further embroidered with small bunches of leaves. Casual kissing, I thought, was obviously not an option, it would be like diving into a thorn bush.

I raised my arms in the air, waved them about, yelled like the men— and was immediately mobbed, touched, it seemed, by a hundred hands. An old woman elbowed everyone aside and stood in front of me. She had spindly legs, a big belly, enormous hanging triangles of breast, and bunches of withered leaves in her ears which she had obviously forgotten to change for a week or two. I looked into her kind, weak, grandmotherly eyes. She bent down slowly—and fetched me two resounding slaps across the knees. I was too surprised to move and she hesitated—before clouting me across the thighs. It was like being bashed with carpet beaters. 'I'm going to lose the lot,' I thought, as she paused again, and I held both hands in front of my trouser zip. At this point, I was vaguely aware, the Yanomami doubled up with laughter, *en masse*. She hit me across the sides of my stomach, my arms, my shoulders, and then, not quite so hard, she slapped my face. My glasses, until then safely anchored by the top of the ear pieces under my sweatband, propelled themselves off my noise and landed on the ground between us. I bent down and picked them up, half-expecting her to shuffle round and kick me up the bum. Instead she grabbed my beard in both hands and pulled it, hard.

The Yanomami in my restored field of vision were laughing, jumping up and down, showing full sets of protein-fed teeth, miming extreme horror and holding both hands over their balls. Chimo was choking and gobbing and generally betraying me.

The old woman smiled, took out a slimy wad of tobacco from between her bottom lip and gums, readjusted it to her satisfaction with a squeeze or two here and there, acknowledged the laughter of the crowd with a coy little wave, and wandered off without a backward glance.

In the shade cast by a part of the great roof I took off my pack and sat on it, rubbing my cheeks. Old women, I remembered ruefully, were very rare and very privileged. If a group was lucky enough to have one, according to Chagnon, they treated her well: old women were the only ambassadors who were allowed to collect your dead warriors from an enemy; they were the only messengers whom you could send to a hostile shabono without their being gang-raped on the way and then cut in half when they arrived.

'That was very interesting,' said Juan, taking his own pack off and sitting beside me. 'That was a greeting ceremony.'

I forbore to reply.

Children came and sat in the dust around us; one bright-eyed girl, perhaps eight years old, with a very long stick through her nose (not quite centrally balanced in the hole in her septum, so that it tilted at a rakish angle) bolder than the others, picked the burrs off my trousers and socks, poked her fingers through the holes in my boots, ran her hands over my stinking shirt, stroked the hairs on my scratched and bitten arms, and was plainly fascinated by my beard. Her own skin was pale brown, very clean, and entirely free from blackfly bites.

The two warriors who had greeted us with their drawn bows squatted down on either side of me. They were unarmed, and had changed into small red loincloths. They spoke with extraordinary emphasis and vehemence, jabbing their thick forefingers within an inch of my eyes to mark important turns in the argument. They punched my bergen and indicated that I should get off it, stand up. Their aggression, their taut faces close to mine, made them seem huge men, not to be gainsaid, and it was a surprise to find that when we all got to our feet they were even smaller than Jarivanau and reached no higher than my chest.

Chimo, Pablo and Culimacaré were surrounded by an equally insistent group of older men. Jarivanau stood apart, still talking to the delighted old man I took to be his father.

'They want our packs,' said Chimo, looking uncharacteristically anxious. 'You must give out some presents, Reymono—*but not everything at once, or we're lost.*'

I unwrapped the Polaroid, found the bag of film, walked over to Jarivanau, claimed his protection by putting my arm across his shoulders and led him out to the hot, bright centre of the open arena. The huge lean-to roof enclosed us at a distance on all sides; in one of the sectioned dwellings behind us, the gaps between the regularly-spaced main support-posts, a middle-aged man was lying in his hammock with two small children perched on his stomach, his bow and arrows propped within reach against the low back wall, watching us, impassive. I was sure we were his first visitors from the outer world and yet, I realised, unnerved, such was his sureness in himself, so capacious the depths of his disdain, that he had not even bothered to swing his legs out and take a closer look.

I stepped back from Jarivanau, knelt down, took out a film from the waterproof bag, loaded the camera, and looked up again to take his picture. Jarivanau had changed: he was shaking all over as if he had malaria. He stared at me, but as if he could not see me, keeping his eyes blankly fixed on mine, not glancing away for a moment. Perhaps he could not bear to be photographed? Perhaps he thought I was about to capture his soul? Yet he had never objected before—in fact I knew he kept with him several of the Polaroids taken that night in his hut on the Siapa. And then I dimly remembered a passage in Chagnon and began to shake a little on my own account. I was now, unwittingly, obeying the dictates of Yanomami decorum which I had so signally failed to observe in the shock of our arrival (and perhaps that lapse of manners was why the old woman had given me her own aberrant greeting—there was nothing about *that* in Chagnon): the visitor must stand motionless in the centre of the clearing for two or three minutes with his weapons held vertically in front of his face; if someone has a score to settle (and a reputation to make) he must shoot the intruder there and then or not at all. So if this really was Jarivanau's first visit after the feud that split the village, he had every reason to shake, and so did I. I stared hard, in my turn, at the developing print in my hand, aware of the unbroken skin between my shoulder blades.

Jarivanau stood erect a moment longer, then bent forward and snatched his picture; we walked, fast, back to the crowd still gathered by the entrance. The photograph was passed from hand to hand, an object which Chagnon's people called noreshi, the same word they used for the most vulnerable part of the soul.

I beckoned everyone forward into the sunlight. The dignified man who, I decided, must be the chief, got out of his hammock and stood in front of the crowd, indicating that I should take his picture first and then place it at once in his hand. His portrait turned out perfectly and he gave me a lordly smile; excitement grew; I took everyone's picture in groups: only one film had become hopelessly blotched and speckled by its long journey in the heat and humidity; forty adults got a picture each and I still had twenty left for emergencies. The women giggled and pushed each other and compared their magical squares of card. They were beginning to be pleased to see us.

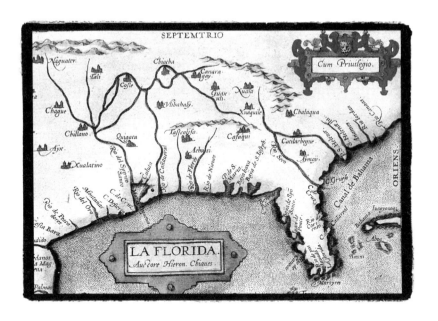

from Adventures in the Unknown
Interior of America
by Alvar Núñez
Cabeza de Vaca

Fortune-seeking nobleman Alvar Núñez Cabeza de Vaca (1490–1557) in 1527 joined a Spanish expedition to the New World. He wandered the wild and often brutal interior of America for eight long years, enduring unimaginable hardships at the hands of nature and man. Cyclone Covey's annotated translation of Cabeza de Vaca's account was published in 1961.

So we marched on for eight days, meeting no resistance until we came within a league of our immediate objective. Then, while we ambled along unsuspectingly, Indians surprised our rear. An *hidalgo* named Avellaneda, a member of the rearguard who had already passed the point of ambush when the attack broke, heard his servant-lad cry out and turned back to assist when, just at that moment, an arrow plunged almost all the way through his neck at the edge of his cuirass, so that he died presently.

We carried him to Aute, where we arrived at the end of nine days out of Apalachen. [Aute, as later French maps concur, appears to have lain a short distance above the mouth of the Apalachicola.]

We found the village deserted and all the houses burned. But corn, squash, and beans—all beginning to ripen—were plentiful. We rested there two days.

Then the Governor urged me to locate the sea, which was supposed to be so near and which we felt we had approached because of the big river we came upon and named Río de la Magdalena [doubtless the Apalachicola].

So I went forth the following day, with the Commissary, the captain Castillo, Andrés Dorantes, seven others on horseback, and fifty afoot. We traveled till the hour of vespers, when we reached an inlet of the sea. Oysters abounded, to the joy of the hungry men, and we gave thanks to God for having brought us here.

The next morning [August 1] I despatched twenty men to explore the coast. They came back the night of their second day out and reported that these inlets and bays were enormous and cut so far inland that it would be a major undertaking to investigate them properly, also that the coast of the open sea lay yet a long way off.

In view of this intelligence and of our limited means, I went back to the Governor. We found him and many others sick. The Indians had attacked the night before and, because of this illness, the soldiers had been desperately hard put. One horse had been killed. I reported on my trip and the discouraging nature of the country. We stayed where we were that day.

The next morning [August 3] we quit Aute and made it to the place I had just visited. The journey was extremely arduous. We did not have horses enough to carry the sick, who kept getting worse every day, and we knew no cure for the disease [undoubtedly malaria, probably complicated by dysentery].

By the time we reached my previous campsite, it was painfully clear to all that we were unprepared to go further. Had we been prepared, we still did not know where to go; and the men could not move, most of them lying prone and those able to stand to duty very few. I will not prolong this unpleasantness; but you can imagine what it would be like in a strange, remote land, destitute of means either to remain or to get out. Our most reliable help was God our Lord; we had not wavered in this conviction.

But now something happened worse than anything that had gone before. The majority of the cavalry plotted to desert, figuring they stood a better chance if unencumbered by the prostrated Governor and largely prostrated infantry.

Since, however, many of the cavalry were *hidalgos* and well-bred persons, they could not but inform the Governor and Your Majesty's officers. We remonstrated with the plotters on the enormity of their notion until they relented and agreed to share the common fate, whatever it might be. The Governor then called them all into his presence and asked their advice, one man at a time, on how to escape that dismal country.

A third of our force had fallen seriously ill and was growing worse by the hour. We felt certain we would all be stricken, with death the one foreseeable way out; and in such a place, death seemed all the more terrible. Considering our experiences, our prospects, and various plans, we finally concluded to undertake the formidable project of constructing vessels to float away in.

This appeared impossible, since none of us knew how to build ships, and we had no tools, iron, forge, oakum, pitch, or rigging, or any of the indispensable items, or anybody to instruct us. Worse still, we had no food to sustain workers. At this impasse, we agreed to consider the matter deeper and ended our parley for the day, each going his way, commending our future to God our Lord.

It was His will that next day one of our men should come saying he could make wooden pipes and deerskin bellows. Having reached that point where any hope of relief is seized upon, we bade him commence. We also instigated the making of nails, saws, axes, and other tools we needed out of the stirrups, spurs, crossbows, and other of our equipment containing iron.

For food while the work proceeded, we decided to make four forays into Aute with every man and horse able to go, and to kill one of our horses every third day to divide among the workers and the sick. Our forays went off as planned. In spite of armed resistance, they netted as much as 400 *fanegas* [about 100 bushels] of corn.

We had stacks of palmettos gathered, and their husks and fibers twisted and otherwise prepared as a substitute for oakum. A Greek, Don Teodoro, made pitch from certain pine resins. Even though we had only one carpenter, work proceeded so rapidly from August 4, when it began, that by September 20 five barges, each 22 elbow-lengths [30 to 32 feet long], caulked with palmetto oakum and tarred with pine-pitch, were finished.

From palmetto husks, also horse tails and manes, we braided ropes and rigging; from our shirts we made sails; and from junipers, oars. Such was the country our sins had cast us in that only the most persistent search turned up stones large enough for ballast and anchors. Before this, we had not seen a stone in the whole region. We flayed the horses' legs, tanned the skin, and made leather water-bottles.

Twice in this time, when some of our men went to the coves for shellfish, Indians ambushed them, killing ten men in plain sight of the camp before we could do anything about it. We found their bodies pierced all the way through, although some of them wore good armor. I have already mentioned the power and precision of the Indian archery.

Our pilots estimated, under oath, that from the bay we had named The Cross [their first Florida campsite] we had come approximately 280 leagues to this place. In that entire space, by the way, we had seen not a single mountain nor heard of any.

Before we embarked, we lost forty men from disease and hunger, in addition to those killed by Indians. By September 22 all but one of the horses had been consumed. That is the day we embarked [after consuming this last horse], in the following order: the Governor's barge, with 49 men; the barge entrusted to the Comptroller and Commissary, also with 49 men; a third barge in charge of Captain Alonso del Castillo and Andrés Dorantes, with 48 men; another with 47 under Captains Téllez and Peñalosa; and the final barge, which the Governor assigned to the Inspector [Solís] and me, with 49 men.

When clothing and supplies were loaded, the sides of the barges remained hardly half a foot above water; and we were jammed in too tight to move. Such is the power of necessity that we should thus hazard a turbulent sea, none of us knowing anything about navigation.

The haven we set out from we gave the name *Vaya de Cavallos* [Bay of Horses]. [Twelve years later, Indians led a detachment of De Soto's expedition to this cove of Apalachicola Bay, where scattered charcoal, hollowed-out logs that had been used for water troughs, etc., could still be seen.]

We sailed seven days among those waist-deep sounds without seeing any sign of the coast of the open sea. At the end of the seventh day we came to an island [probably St. Vincent's], close to the main. From my lead barge we saw five canoes approaching. When we went after them, the Indians abandoned them to us at the island. The other barges passed mine and stopped ahead at some houses on the island, where we found a lot of mullet and dried eggs of these fish, which were a grateful relief. After this repast, we proceeded a couple of leagues to a strait we discovered between the island and the coast which we named Sant Miguel [Saint Michael], its being that saint's day [September 29].

We passed through the strait and beached on the coast of the open sea. There we made sideboards out of the canoes I had confiscated, to raise our gunwales another half foot above water level.

Then we resumed our voyage, coasting [westward] toward the River of Palms [presumably thinking it closer or more certainly findable than their own ships to the south], our hunger and thirst growing daily more intense because our scant provisions were nearly exhausted and the water-bottles we had made had rotted. We wove in and out of occasional bays, which stretched far inland, but found them all shallow and dangerous.

For thirty days we went on like this, every once in a while catching sight of Indian fishermen—a poor, miserable lot.

The night of the thirtieth day, when our want of water had become insupportable, we heard a canoe coming. We stopped when we could make it out but, although we called, it went on. The night was too dark for pursuit, so we kept our course. Dawn brought us to a little island, where we touched to look for water but there was none.

While we lay [in the lee] there at anchor, a great storm broke over us. For six days while it raged we dared not put out to sea. Its already having been five days since we had drunk, at the time the storm erupted, our extreme thirst forced us to drink salt water. Some drank so unrestrainedly that five suddenly died.

I state this briefly because I think it superfluous to tell in detail what we went through in those circumstances. Considering where we were and how little hope we had of relief, you may sufficiently imagine our sufferings.

Our thirst was killing us; the salt water was killing us. Rather than succumb right there, we commended ourselves to God, and put forth into the perilous sea as the storm still raged. We headed in the direction of the canoe we had seen the night we came here [back, off the Alabama coast]. The waves overwhelmed our barge many times this day, and none of us doubted that his death would come any minute.

It was the will of God, who often shows His favor in the hour of total despair, that as we doubled a point of land at sunset we found ourselves sheltered in calm waters [apparently near Pensacola]; and many canoes of big, well-built Indians—unarmed—came out to speak, then paddled back ahead of us.

We followed them to their houses at the water's edge close by, and stepped ashore. In front of the dwellings stood many clay jars of water and a great quantity of cooked fish, all of which the *cacique* of this land offered our Governor before leading us to his "palace." Their dwellings were made of mats and, so far as we could tell, were not movable. When we [officers] entered the *cacique's* palace, he regaled us with fish. We gave him some of the corn we had brought, which his people ate in our presence and asked for more. We gave them more. The Governor also presented the *cacique* some trinkets.

In the middle of the night, the Indians fell on us without warning— not only the Governor's party in the *cacique's* lodge, but also our sick men strewn on the beach. [The *Joint Report* says three men were killed.] The Governor got hit in the face with a rock. Some of us grabbed the *cacique,* but a group of Indians retrieved him, leaving us holding his robe of civet-marten skins.

(These are the finest skins in the world, I believe. Their fragrance seems like amber and musk and can be smelled a long way off. We saw other robes there, but none to match this one.)

Those of us in the vicinity where the Governor got hurt managed to put him in his barge and to hasten all but fifty of our force aboard theirs. The fifty stood guard high up on the beach. Three times that night the Indians attacked, with such ferocity as to force us back more than a stone's throw each time.

Not one of us escaped injury. I was wounded in the face. If the Indians had had more than their few arrows, they undoubtedly would have done us serious harm. At their third onset, Captains Dorantes, Peñalosa, and Téllez with fifteen men ambushed their rear, at which the aggressors broke and fled.

Next morning [October 28] I broke up thirty of their canoes, which we used for fire; the north wind, which raised yet another storm, confined us to land in the cold. When the storm subsided, we returned to sea, navigating three days [three or four, says the *Joint Report*]. We had only a few containers to carry water, so could take but a little supply. Soon we were reduced again to the last extremity.

Continuing along the coast, we entered an estuary [Mobile Bay] where we saw a canoe of Indians coming toward us. We hailed them and, when they drew close to the Governor's boat, he asked for water. They showed themselves willing to get some if we furnished containers. That Greek, Doroteo Teodoro, whom I spoke of before, said he would go, too. The Governor and others failed to dissuade him. He took along a Negro, and the Indians left two of their number as hostages.

It was night when the Indians returned, without water in the containers and without the Christians.

When these returning Indians spoke to our two hostages, the latter started to dive into the water; but some of our soldiers held them back in the barge. The canoe sped away, leaving us very confused and dejected over the loss of our comrades.

[De Soto's soldiers some twelve years later learned from Indians in this vicinity of the arrival of the barges in need of water, and of the two men who had remained behind. The Indians produced a dagger that had belonged to Teodoro. One suspects that Teodoro insisted on accompanying the canoemen for water because he thought it his best hope to survive; i.e. he had no intention of returning to the barges. He and his servant may, in fact, have lived for some time longer and migrated as slaves to tribes farther inland].

With morning came Indians in many canoes [twenty—*Joint Report*], calling on us to give up our two hostages. The Governor replied that he would when the Indians brought the two Christians.

Five or six chiefs were distinguishable in the array of natives, who looked comelier, more commanding, and better disciplined than any Indians we had yet seen, although not as big as some spoken of before. Their hair hung loose and very long, and they wore marten robes like those we had lately taken, except that some of the robes exhibited a strange combination of marten and lion skin in a handsome pattern.

They entreated us to go with them, saying they would give us the Christians, water, and many other things. All the while, additional canoes kept reinforcing the first-comers, obviously bent on blocking the mouth of that inlet. This avenue closed and the country apparently hazardous to remain in, we betook ourselves back to open sea.

There the canoes and our barges floated side by side till noon. As the Indians would not return our men, we would not release theirs. They began to hurl stones and darts as us (using slings for the stones) and threatened to shoot arrows, though we saw no more than three or four bows among them. In the midst of this commotion the wind freshened and they departed.

We went on that day [two days, says the *Joint Report*] till nightfall, when my barge, which kept the lead, discovered a promontory, on the other side of which flowed a vast river [the Mississippi]. Off a little island at the point, I anchored and awaited the other barges.

The governor did not want to stop there but went into a nearby bay dotted with islets. The other barges joined him, and we found we could take fresh water from the sea, the river emptying into it in a torrent.

To parch corn—which we had eaten raw for two days now—we scrambled onto an island, but found no firewood, so decided to go to the river, one league distant behind the point. All our efforts to breast the violent current resulted only in our getting carried farther out. The north wind rose from shore to drive us the rest of the way to the high sea in spite of anything we could do. About half a league from shore we had sounded and found no bottom even at thirty fathoms, convinced that the current somehow interfered with our measurement. [True; the normal delta depth in this vicinity in the 20th century is ten fathoms, or sixty feet.]

For two days we toiled to gain the shore. Awhile before dawn of the third, we saw smoke rising at several points and worked toward it. We found ourselves in three fathoms of water, but it was still too dark to risk landing where we had seen the columns of smoke. So we held up till daylight.

When it came, the barges had lost sight of each other and I found mine floating in thirty fathoms. Keeping my course all day, to the hour of vespers, I at last sighted two other barges. As we neared them, I recognized the closer one as that of the Governor.

He asked me what I thought we should do. I said, join the barge ahead; by no means abandon her; so the three might go where God willed, together. He said that could not be done; the lead barge was too far out to sea and he wanted to get to shore. If I wished to follow him, he continued, I should order my men to the oars, since only by arm work could the land be gained. His old cohort, Captain Pantoja, had advised him thus. Pantoja claimed that if we did not make land that day, we would not in six more, by which time we would have starved.

The Governor's will clearly divulged, I took up my oar, and all my men theirs, and we rowed till nearly sunset. But, the Governor having the healthiest and strongest men in his barge, we could not keep up. I yelled to him to throw me a rope so we could stay with him. He called back that if he were to do what he hoped that night, he must not further sap his men's strength. I said that since we were too feeble to carry out his orders to follow him, he must tell me how he would that I should act. He replied that it was no longer a time when one should command another; that each must do as he thought best to save himself; that that was what he was doing now. So saying, he pulled away in his barge.

Unable to follow, I steered toward the barge at sea, which waited for me. When fairly close, I found her to be the one commanded by Captain Peñalosa and Captain Téllez.

Our two barges continued in company for four days, each man eating a ration of half a handful of raw corn a day. Then the other barge was lost in a storm. [The *Joint Report* says this loss occurred the day after the two barges joined.] Nothing but God's great mercy kept us from going down, too.

It was winter and bitterly cold, and we had suffered hunger and the heavy beating of the waves for many days. Next day, the men began to collapse. By sunset, all in my barge had fallen over on one another, close to death. Few were any longer conscious. Not five could stand. When night fell, only the navigator and I remained able to tend the barge. Two hours after dark he told me I must take over; he believed he was going to die that night.

So I took the tiller. After midnight I moved over to see if he were dead. He said no, in fact was better, and would steer till daylight. In that hour I would have welcomed death rather than see so many around me in such a condition. When I had returned the helm to the navigator, I lay down to rest—but without much rest, for nothing was farther from my mind than sleep.

Near dawn I seemed to hear breakers resounding; the coast lying low, they roared louder. Surprised at this, I called to the navigator, who said he thought we were coming close to land. We sounded and found ourselves in seven fathoms. The navigator felt we should stay clear of the shore till daylight; so I took an oar and pulled it on the shore side, wheeling the stern to seaward about a league out.

As we drifted into shore, a wave caught us and heaved the barge a horseshoe-throw [about 42 feet] out of the water. The jolt when it hit brought the dead-looking men to. Seeing land at hand, they crawled through the surf to some rocks. Here we made a fire and parched some of our corn. We also found rain water. The men began to regain their senses, their locomotion, and their hope.

This day of our landing was November 6.

[Cabeza de Vaca's approximations of the days after leaving the Bay of Horses add up to eight or nine more than the 45 or 46 allowed in his inclusive dates September 22-November 6. He could have experienced the hurling ashore a week or so later than he remembered; but his track of time while battling starvation, Indians, and the periphery of a Gulf hurricane would have been understandably faulty.]

After we ate, I ordered Lope de Oviedo, our strongest man, to climb one of the trees not far off and ascertain the lay of the land. He complied and found out from the treetop that we were on an island. [This was Galveston Island.] He also said that the ground looked as if cattle had trampled it and therefore that this must be a country of Christians.

I sent him back for a closer look, to see if he could find any worn trails, but warned him not to risk going too far. He went and came upon a path which he followed for half a league to some empty huts. The Indians were gone to shoal-flats [to dig roots]. He took an earthen pot, a little dog, and a few mullets and started back.

We had begun to worry what might have happened to him, so I detailed another two men to check. They met him shortly and saw three Indians with bows and arrows following him. The Indians were calling to him and he was gesturing them to keep coming. When he reached us, the Indians held back and sat down on the shore.

Half an hour later a hundred bowmen [*Joint Report:* 200, with joints

of cane stuck through holes in their ears] reinforced the first three individuals. Whatever their stature, they looked like giants to us in our
fright. We could not hope to defend ourselves; not half a dozen of us
could even stand up.

The Inspector and I walked out and greeted them. They advanced,
and we did our best to placate and ingratiate. We gave them beads and
bells, and each one of them gave us an arrow in pledge of friendship.
They told us by signs that they would return at sunrise and bring food,
having none then.

As the sun rose next morning, the Indians appeared as they promised,
bringing an abundance of fish and of certain roots which taste like
nuts, some bigger than walnuts, some smaller, mostly grubbed from
the water with great labor.

That evening they came again with more fish and roots and brought
their women and children to look at us. They thought themselves rich
with the little bells and beads we gave them, and they repeated their
visits on other days.

Being provided with what we needed, we thought to embark again.
It was a struggle to dig our barge out of the sand it had sunk in, and
another struggle to launch her. For the work in the water while launch-
ing, we stripped and stowed our clothes in the craft.

Quickly clambering in and grabbing our oars, we had rowed two
crossbow shots from shore when a wave inundated us. Being naked
and the cold intense, we let our oars go. The next big wave capsized the
barge. The Inspector [Solís] and two others held fast, but that only carried them more certainly underneath, where they drowned.

A single roll of the sea tossed the rest of the men into the rushing
surf and back onto shore half-drowned.

We lost only those the barge took down; but the survivors escaped
as naked as they were born, with the loss of everything we had. That
was not much, but valuable to us in that bitter November cold, our
bodies so emaciated we could easily count every bone and looked the
very picture of death. I can say for myself that from the month of May

I had eaten nothing but corn, and that sometimes raw. I never could bring myself to eat any of the horse-meat at the time our beasts were slaughtered; and fish I did not taste ten times. On top of everything else, a cruel north wind commenced to complete our killing.

The Lord willed that we should find embers while searching the remnants of our former fire. We found more wood and soon had big fires raging. Before them, with flowing tears, we prayed for mercy and pardon, each filled with pity not only for himself but for all his wretched fellows.

At sunset the Indians, not knowing we had gone, came again with food. When they saw us looking so strangely different, they turned back in alarm. I went after them calling, and they returned, though frightened. I explained to them by signs that our barge had sunk and three of our number drowned. They could see at their feet two of the dead men who had washed ashore. They could also see that the rest of us were not far from joining these two.

The Indians, understanding our full plight, sat down and lamented for half an hour so loudly they could have been heard a long way off. It was amazing to see these wild, untaught savages howling like brutes in compassion for us. It intensified my own grief at our calamity and had the same effect on the other victims.

When the cries died down, I conferred with the Christians about asking the Indians to take us to their homes. Some of our number who had been to New Spain warned that the Indians would sacrifice us to their idols. But death being surer and nearer if we stayed where we were, I went ahead and beseeched the Indians. They were delighted. They told us to tarry a little while, then they would do as we wished.

Presently thirty of them gathered loads of wood and disappeared to their huts, which were a long walk away; while we waited with the remainder until near nightfall. Then, supporting us under our arms, they hurried us from one to another of the four big fires they had built along the path. At each fire, when we regained a little warmth and strength, they took us on so swiftly our feet hardly touched ground.

Thus we made their village, where we saw they had erected a hut for us with many fires inside. An hour later they began a dance celebration that lasted all night. For us there was no joy, feasting, or sleep, as we waited the hour they should make us victims.

In the morning, when they brought us fish and roots and acted in every way hospitably, we felt reassured and somewhat lost our anxiety of the sacrificial knife.

That very day, I saw an Indian wearing a trinket which I knew we had not given. Inquiring whence it came, we learned from our hosts' signs that it had come from men like ourselves, who bivouacked farther back. At this, I sent two Christians, with two Indians for guides, to contact them.

It so happened that the latter were at that moment on their way to see us; for the Indians had told them of us as us of them. My detail met them therefore nearby.

They turned out to be Captains Andrés Dorantes and Alonso del Castillo with their entire crew [of 48]. When they came up, they were appalled at our appearance and sad that they had no other clothes than what they then wore.

They told us that their barge had capsized a league and a half from here the 5th of this month [i.e., the day before Cabeza de Vaca's barge was cast ashore] and that they escaped without losing a thing.

We decided to repair their barge, so that those who were strong enough and willing could resume the voyage, while the others stayed until their health allowed them to walk along the coast, and one day God our Lord should bring us all alike to a land of Christians.

We set directly to work but, before we could wrest the barge out of the water, Tavera, a gentleman of our company, died; and then the unseaworthy barge sank.

With most of us naked and the weather discouraging walking or swimming across rivers and coves—also with no food supply or even anything to carry one in—we resigned ourselves to remaining where we were for the winter.

We did, however, decide that four of our most robust men should set out now for Pánuco, which we believed close. Should God our Lord prosper them, they could report our destitute existence on this island. The four were: Alvaro Fernández, a Portuguese carpenter and sailor; a certain Méndez; Figueroa, an *hidalgo* from Toledo; and Astudillo of Zafra—all excellent swimmers. They took with them an Indian of the island of Auia [which presumably was the Indian name of Galveston, though another island could possibly have been meant].

Within a few days of the departure of the four Christians, the weather turned so cold and stormy that the Indians could not pull up roots; their cane contraptions for catching fish yielded nothing; and the huts being very open, our men began to die.

Five Christians quartered on the coast came to the extremity of eating each other. Only the body of the last one, whom nobody was left to eat, was found unconsumed. Their names were Sierra, Diego Lopez, Corral, Palacios, and Gonzalo Ruiz.

The Indians were so shocked at this cannibalism that, if they had seen it sometime earlier, they surely would have killed every one of us. In a very short while as it was, only fifteen of the eighty who had come survived. [Strictly speaking, there must have been more than ninety who made it to the island, and sixteen of them proved later to be living].

Then half the natives died from a disease of the bowels [doubtless infected with the soldiers' dysentery] and [the rest] blamed us.

When they came to kill us the Indian who kept me interceded. He said: If we had so much power of sorcery we would not have let all but a few of our own perish; the few left did no hurt or wrong; it would be best to leave us alone. God our Lord be praised, they listened and relented.

We named this place *Malhado*—the "Island of Doom."

The people we came to know there [Capoques and Han, as identified later in the narrative] are tall and well-built. Their only weapons are bows and arrows, which they use with great dexterity. The men bore through one of their nipples, some both, and insert a joint of cane two and a half palms long by two fingers thick. They also bore their lower lip and wear a piece of cane in it half a finger in diameter.

Their women toil incessantly.

From October to the end of February every year, which is the season these Indians live on the island, they subsist on the roots I have mentioned, which the women get from under water in November and December. Only in these two months, too, do they take fish in their cane weirs. When the fish is consumed, the roots furnish the one staple. At the end of February the islanders go into other parts to seek sustenance, for then the root is beginning to grow and is not edible.

These people love their offspring more than any in the world and treat them very mildly.

If a son dies, the whole village joins the parents and kindred in weeping. The parents set off the wails each day before dawn, again at noon, and at sunset, for one year. The funeral rites occur when the year of mourning is up. Following these rites, the survivors wash off the smoke stain of the ceremony in a symbolic purgation. All the dead are lamented this way except the aged, who merit no regrets. The dead are buried, except medicine-men, who are cremated. Everybody in the village dances and makes merry while the pyre of a medicine-man kindles, and until his bones become powder. A year later, when his rites are celebrated, the entire village again participating, this powder is presented in water for the relatives to drink.

Each man has an acknowledged wife, except the medicine-men, who may have two or three wives apiece. The several wives live together in perfect amity.

When a daughter marries, she must take everything her husband kills in hunting or catches in fishing to the house of her father, without daring to eat or to withhold any part of it, and the husband gets provided by female carrier from his father-in-law's house. Neither the bride's father nor mother may enter the son-in-law's house after the marriage, nor he theirs; and this holds for the children of the respective couples. If a man and his in-laws should chance to be walking so they would meet, they turn silently aside from each other and go a crossbow-shot out of their way, averting their glance to the ground. The woman, however, is free to fraternize with the parents and relatives of her husband.

These marriage customs prevail for more than fifty leagues inland from the island.

At a house where a son or brother may die, no one goes out for food for three months, the neighbors and other relatives providing what is eaten. Because of this custom, which the Indians literally would not break to save their lives, great hunger reigned in most houses while we resided there, it being a time of repeated deaths. Those who sought food worked hard, but they could get little in that severe season. That is why the Indians who kept me left the island by canoe for oyster bays on the main.

Three months out of every year they eat nothing but oysters and drink very bad water. Wood is scarce; mosquitoes, plentiful. The houses are made of mats; their floors consist of masses of oyster shells. The natives sleep on these shells—in animal skins, those who happen to own such.

Many a time I would have to go three days without eating, as would the natives. I thought it impossible that life could be so prolonged in such protracted hunger; though afterwards I found myself in yet greater want, as shall be seen.

The [Han] Indians who had Alonso del Castillo, Andrés Dorantes, and the others of their barge who remained alive, spoke a different dialect and claimed a different descent from these I lived among. They frequented the opposite shore of the main to eat oysters, staying till the first of April, then returning.

The distance to the main is two leagues at the widest part of the channel. The island itself, which supports the two tribes commodiously, is half a league wide by five long. [Whether computing by the 2.6 or the 3.1-mile league, this is a fairly accurate estimate of the actual 1.8-mile average width of Galveston Island and the 5.4-mile maximum distance from the mainland; but the treetop estimate of the length is only about half the island's actual 29.6-mile extent.]

The inhabitants of all these parts go naked, except that the women cover some part of their persons with a wool that grows on trees [Spanish moss], and damsels dress in deerskin.

The people are generous to each other with what little they have.

There is no chief. All belonging to the same lineage keep together. They speak two languages: Capoque and Han.

They have a strange custom when acquaintances [distantly separated?] meet or occasionally visit, of weeping for half an hour before they speak. This over, the one who is visited rises and gives his visitor all he has. The latter accepts it and, after a while, carries it away, often without a word. They have other strange customs, but I have told the principal and most remarkable of them.

In April [1529] we went to the seashore and ate blackberries all month, a time of *areitos* [dance ceremonies] and *fiestas* among the Indians.

The islanders wanted to make physicians of us without examination or a review of diplomas. Their method of cure is to blow on the sick, the breath and the laying-on of hands supposedly casting out the infirmity. They insisted we should do this too and be of some use to them. We scoffed at their cures and at the idea we knew how to heal. But they withheld food from us until we complied. An Indian told me I knew not whereof I spoke in saying their methods had no effect. Stones and other things growing about in the fields, he said, had a virtue whereby passing a pebble along the stomach could take away pain and heal; surely extraordinary men like us embodied such powers over nature. Hunger forced us to obey, but disclaiming any responsibility for our failure or success.

An Indian, falling sick, would send for a medicine-man, who would apply his cure. The patient would then give the medicine-man all he had and seek more from his relatives to give. The medicine-man makes incisions over the point of the pain, sucks the wound, and cauterizes it. This remedy enjoys high repute among the Indians. I have, as a matter of fact, tried it on myself with good results. The medicine-men blow on the spot they have treated, as a finishing touch, and the patient regards himself relieved.

Our method, however, was to bless the sick, breathe upon them, recite a *Pater noster* and *Ave Maria,* and pray earnestly to God our Lord for their recovery. When we concluded with the sign of the cross, He willed that our patients should directly spread the news that they had been restored to health.

In consequence, the Indians treated us kindly. They deprived themselves of food to give to us, and presented us skins and other tokens of gratitude.

After Dorantes and Castillo returned to the island [from the Han oyster-eating season on the main], they rounded up all the surviving Christians, who were living somewhat separated from each other. They totaled fourteen. As I have said, I happened to be opposite on the main at that time participating in the Capoque blackberry-eating season. There I fell desperately ill. If anything before had given me hopes of life, this dashed them.

When the other Christians heard of my condition, they gave an Indian the wonderful robe of marten-skins we had taken from the *cacique* [in that midnight brawl near Pensacola], to bring them over to visit me. [The robe could have been, in reality, a bribe to make their getaway down the coast but, in any case, they would still need a guide to show them where the channel was shallow enough to wade, or a canoe if they were ferried.] Those who came were: Alonso del Castillo, Andrés Dorantes, [his cousin] Diego Dorantes, [Pedro de] Valdevieso [another cousin of Andrés], Estrada, Tostado, Chaves, Gutierrez, Asturiano (a priest), Diego de Huelva, Estevánico the black [a Moor from the west coast of Morocco], and Benitez. When they reached the main, they found another of our company, Francisco de León [evidently a survivor of Cabeza de Vaca's barge, also kept by the Capoques].

The moment they had crossed, my Indians came to tell me and also brought word that Jerónimo de Alaniz [the notary] and Lope de Oviedo remained on the island. But sickness kept me from going [south] with my comrades; I did not even get to see them.

I had to stay with the Capoques more than a year. Because of the hard work they put me to, and their harsh treatment, I resolved to flee to the people of Charruco in the forests of the main. [Perhaps Cabeza de Vaca's illness bore on his change in status from a kindly treated medicine-man to a harshly treated slave; but he does not trace the transition for us. His comrades, living most of the time apart with the Han, apparently underwent the same drastic reduction in status.] My life had become unbearable. In addition to much other work, I had to grub roots in the water or from underground in the canebrakes. My fingers got so raw that if a straw touched them they would bleed. The broken canes often slashed my flesh; I had to work amidst them without benefit of clothes.

So I set to contriving how I might transfer to the forest-dwellers, who looked more propitious. My solution was to turn to trade.

[Escaping to Charruco about February 1530,] I did my best to devise ways of making my traffic profitable so I could get food and good treatment. The various Indians would beg me to go from one quarter to another for things they needed; their incessant hostilities made it impossible for them to travel cross-country or make many exchanges.

But as a neutral merchant I went into the interior as far as I pleased [the consensus is that he got as far as Oklahoma] and along the coast forty or fifty leagues for at least, as Hallenbeck points out, between the impassable Sabine marshes to the north and perhaps not quite to Matagorda Bay to the south, where he would have learned far sooner than he did of three Spaniards who survived in that vicinity].

My principal wares were cones and other pieces of seasnail, conchs used for cutting, sea-beads, and a fruit like a bean [from mesquite trees] which the Indians value very highly, using it for a medicine and for a ritual beverage in their dances and festivities. This is the sort of thing I carried inland. By barter I got and brought back to the coast skins, red ochre which they rub on their faces, hard canes for arrows, flint for arrowheads, with sinews and cement to attach them, and tassels of deer hair which they dye red.

This occupation suited me; I could travel where I wished, was not obliged to work, and was not a slave. Wherever I went, the Indians treated me honorably and gave me food, because they liked my commodities. They were glad to see me when I came and delighted to be brought what they wanted. I became well known; those who did not know me personally knew me by reputation and sought my acquaintance. This served my main purpose, which all the while was to determine an eventual road out.

The hardships I endured in this journeying business were long to tell—peril and privation, storms and frost, which often overtook me alone in the wilderness. By the unfailing grace of God our Lord I came forth from them all. Because of them, however, I avoided the pursuit of my business in winter, a season when, anyway, the natives retire inside their huts in a kind of stupor, incapable of exertion. [Hallenbeck reasons that Cabeza de Vaca wintered on the Trinity River or one of its western branches; the red ochre he acquired somewhere in that area is found in the woods around Nacogdoches.]

I was in this [general coastal] region nearly six years [but in this particular vicinity from early winter 1528 to early winter 1532, a merchant for perhaps 22 months], alone among the Indians and naked like them. The reason I remained so long was my intention of taking the Christian, Lope de Oviedo, away with me. His companion on the island, Alaniz, whom Castillo, Dorantes, and the rest had left behind, died soon after their departure. To get Oviedo, the last survivor there, I passed over to the island every year and pleaded with him to come with me to attempt the best way we could contrive to find Christians. Each year he put me off, saying the next we would start.

At last, [on the fourth visit, in November 1532] I got him off, across the strait, and across four large streams on the coast [Bastrop Bayou, Brazos River, San Bernardo River, and Caney Creek]; which took some doing, because Oviedo could not swim.

So we worked along, with some Indians, until we came to a bay a league wide and uniformly deep. From its appearance we presumed it to be Espíritu Santo [the name Pineda gave Matagorda Bay in 1519; Pineda's map, with which Cabeza de Vaca was familiar, mentions the conspicuous white sandhills beyond. They were guided not across the bay but across the Colorado River which flows into it.]

We met some Indians on the other side who were on their way to visit our late hosts. They told us that three men like us lived but a couple of days from here, and said their names. We asked about the others and were told that they were all dead. Most had died of cold and hunger. But our informants' own tribe had murdered Diego Dorantes, Valdevieso, and Diego de Huelva for sport because they left one house for another; and the neighboring tribe, where Captain Dorantes now resided, had, in obedience to a dream, murdered Esquivel [who had been in the Comptroller's barge] and Méndez [one of the four excellent swimmers who had set out, back in 1528, for Pánuco]. We asked how the living Christians fared. Badly, they replied; the boys and some of the Indian men enlivened their dreary idleness by constantly kicking, cuffing, and cudgeling the three slaves; such was the life they led.

We inquired of the region ahead and its subsistence. They said there was nothing to eat and that the few people [who evidently had not yet joined the nut-gathering exodus] were dying from the cold, having no skins or anything else to cover themselves with. They also told us that if we wished to see those three Christians, the Indians who had them would be coming in about two days to eat nuts [pecans] on the river bank a league from here.

So we would know they had spoken the truth about the bad treatment of our fellows, they commenced slapping and batting Oviedo and did not spare me either. They would keep throwing clods at us, too, and each of the days we waited there they would stick their arrows to our hearts and say they had a mind to kill us the way they had finished our friends. My frightened companion Oviedo said he wanted to go back with the women who had just forded the bay with us (their men having stayed some distance behind). I argued my utmost against such a craven course but in no way could keep him.

He went back, and I remained alone with those savages. They are called Quevenes and those with whom he returned, Deaguanes. [This is the last that was ever heard of the strongest man who had sailed in Cabeza de Vaca's barge.]

Two days after Lope de Oviedo departed, the Indians who had Alonso del Castillo and Andrés Dorantes reached the place we had been told of, to eat pecans. These are ground with a kind of small grain and furnish the sole subsistence of the people for two months of the year— and not every year, because the trees only bear every other year. The nut is the same size as that of Galicia; the trees are massive and numberless. [According to the *Joint Report*, these groves where the Indians began nutcracking were ten or twelve leagues above the Bay, i.e., on the lower Colorado, and tribes converged there from a distance of twenty and thirty leagues. In the course of the gathering season they worked a great distance up-river.]

An Indian [not one of those who had been manhandling Cabeza de Vaca but a recent arrival] told me secretly that the Christians had arrived at the appointed place and, if I wished to see them, to steal away to a segment of the woods which he pointed out and that there he and his relatives would pick me up as they passed by. I decided to trust him, since he spoke a dialect distinct from the others. Next day, they found me hiding in the designated place and took me along.

As we approached their abode, Andrés Dorantes came out to see who it could be; the Indians had told him a Christian was coming. When he saw me, he was terrified; for I had been considered long dead and the natives had confirmed my demise, he said [without mentioning that he was guilty of deserting a superior officer whom he had passed by without seeing in his presumed final illness]. But we gave many thanks to be alive together. This was a day of as great joy as we ever knew.

from The Dogs of Paradise
by Abel Posse

Argentinian Abel Posse (born 1934) in his novel
The Dogs of Paradise retells the story of
Admiral Cristóbal Colón's (Christopher
Columbus') first voyage to America. The book
takes as points of departure the explorer's
deeply religious and mystical convictions, and
the notion that those beliefs drove his passion
for discovery. The result is a hallucinatory vision
of the great voyage, which included the terrible
passage through the Mare Tenebrarum—the
Sea of Darkness.

Horrifying griffins. The Giant Octopus. The Killer Whale. Now, now it must be confronted. The abysses of the unknown Sea. The fury of the wind; the realm of demons.

It seemed to a distraught Colón that God had unleashed His wildest fantasy. Divine perversity, that punishes as it bestows. Let pain be your triumph. Curiosity your damnation.

Espinoso brought him a bowl of beans with sausage and dried beef. A glass of harsh wine, the kind that has no effect. As a sweet, a handful of almonds and raisins.

"You will be hard pressed, Admiral, to maintain this course."

"Did I ask your opinion?"

"No, but the men say that this route can only lead to warm lands, whether those of the Great Khan or someone else. They say it's madness, that it's as if you were going out of your way to find dry, barren lands like those we left behind in Trujillo and Badajoz and Extremadura. Pure madness! Such land will only yield olives and garlic. And with prices already so low! If your excellency does not correct the course there's going to be hell to pay. Admiral: get it in your head: in warm lands, in the tropics, all you'll find is people too poor to cover their nakedness. Where it's hot, it's *poor*."

It was easy to see he was a messenger. That he was speaking the opinion of Pinzón and his men. Ants! Dwarfs! What could they know of the Voice? Of the secret mission of the descendant of Isaiah?

SUNDAY, SEPTEMBER 9. The crewmen have not steered a steady course, but veered a quarter northwest. Sometimes as much as ninety degrees.

They seek a northerly course toward temperate and fertile lands.

They believe either that the admiral will not notice, or that he is too weak to discipline them. They are mistaken. This is the one point he cannot concede. He signals the ships to approach, and summons their captains and pilots. For a real tongue-lashing.

Rodríguez de Escobedo, the secretary, is called to the bridge. He checks his appearance in the mirror tacked to the mainmast. Combs his beard. Solemn, always with his Homer in his pocket.

The Pinzóns arrived, Niño, de la Cosa, Quintero. All the Genoese and the royal paymaster, Sánchez de Segovia. Colón wants his wishes to be clear, stated in black and white in the presence of the Scribe of the Realm. No ruses from now on. There will be no change in the course herewith solemnly noted and in accord with the mandate of their royal highnesses; *due west*. Due west along the line of the Tropics.

Discontented faces. But now deception and unauthorized variations in course will be difficult.

The official document is signed. The meeting is called to an end.

The admiral returns to his roundhouse. He climbs into his tub. He meditates on the forces of the sea.

ELEMENTARY AMPHIBIOLOGY, SEPTEMBER 10. Word of the admiral to his officers: nothing worse than to forget. Yet men, even sailors, forget their amphibian origins. Have they never studied their feet, the palmiped hands that have lost their membranes? Their buttocks, stubs of vanished dorsal fins. Are they blind to the evidence?

They will never learn to navigate if they do not return to their essence. Men must forget what they praise as the mark of a good sailor.

The admiral orders the main course to be rigged so the ship rides low in the water. He wants the ships to blend into the substance of the sea. For them not to be dry, mere visitors on the ocean.

He orders that several leaking seams not be caulked. He wants water in the bilge, wants the men to hear it sloshing with the roll of the ship, the way he listens to it splash over the edge of the tub and run along the cabin deck.

Navigate like gulls. Like sailors from the Bay of Biscayne. Never far from the mass of the sea. Never in opposition to it. Never dry. He recommends that the men not try to keep dry, to stay wet, if possible. They will avoid colds, although they do not believe him.

The gull—the admiral preaches—does not look to the winds to change. It *is*, whatever the wind. He has similar praise for the nautical adaptability of Galician fishermen.

"Any other way of thinking," he proclaims sententiously, "is for the French."

Juan de la Cosa starts to reply, but refrains.

Colón submerges his head in the tub and floats face downward, like a dead man. All that is visible is an arse as soft and white as the buttocks of a Belgian nun raped by soldiers and drowned in a Flemish canal.

He floats a long time; he amazes them.

Then he states that in the bosom of the water he communicates with the Ocean Sea, and that only challenge can conquer fear.

Sing in cemeteries, he recommends. Whistle in the moonless forest.

The wind is howling and the ship is breasting heavy seas. The bow shattering teeth of foam. Fringe is flying, lace, the slobber of a madly galloping colt.

When the admiral steps out of his cabin, the insolent wind whips his hair mercilessly.

Drenching drops of salt. Strings of melted silver.

Shrouds and halyards are humming. The billowing spritsail, the "nose bag," tugs valiantly at the bowsprit. It is a stubborn mule straining in harness, its ears laid back by the rain and wind.

As soaking halyards are whipped by the sail, they are wrung out and dried. They smoke from friction with bitts and belaying pins.

The reins of a runaway horse.

Deep sobs were wrung from the mast holes of the foresail, mainsail, and mizzen—strained to capacity. The masts are again slender tree trunks standing amid the fierce thrill of the storm.

Thudding hoofbeats as the hull pounds the seas.

"Look lively! Man the sails!" shouts the admiral. He runs down the ladder from the quarterdeck to the main deck. He shouts orders to the uninspired men, who act as if they do not hear him. They loaf about as if waiting their watch. Staying out of the spray. Somber, bored, playing cards. "Get up! At once! All of you! Sheet the sail! Tighter! Heave away!" he cries. He himself takes the forestay.

The ship shudders. A filly in season. A stringed instrument in a passionate *allegro.*

Now the wind is singing hoarsely through hatches and lockers. The stays and shrouds are chords of an enraptured harp.

The wind moans and sobs.

The admiral shouts, exhorts. He longs for a whip, anything to shake up the loafers. Wretches!

He climbs to the forecastle and receives a benediction: foaming waves, cool on his face and chest. He stretches his arms before him, face streaming water. He feels he *is* the ship.

"Yahweh! Yahweh! Yahweh! Hallelujah!" he shouts. "Sheet the sail! Tighter! Look to the mainsail! Haul the main topsail higher, that's it!"

Tumultuous gallop across the fields of the sea. Abandon. Celebration. Ecstasy. Capitulation to space.

As he returns, soaking, to his cabin, he sees them exchanging grins and winks. They think he is mad. Most of them are lolling against stores on the poop deck, picking their teeth, dreaming of an orchard of their own, or of stealing pearls from the idol in the Imperial Palace.

Blessed common sense.

SPACE AND TIME, SEPTEMBER 13. The return to Heaven from Earth must be affected along the same path Adam followed in his ignominious and deserved expulsion.

The world in which we think we live is writing that must be read in reverse, before a mirror.

Space and Time are the names of the exterminating angels that expelled us from Eden. They must be watched with great cunning. Only they can indicate to us the return path to the desired Gates.

("Is that what you want, Adam? To measure? Count? Till you can't count on anything? To study the science of Good and Evil? Stubborn geodesist! *This* is Space, and Time is *here*. Get it straight, stupid! Take care, or they will crush you. They will roll you flat, squeeze you dry, like the dear departed—God rest her soul—Felipa Moñiz Perestrello. She ended up a portrait her ungodly husband hung above the carving board in the dining hall. Adam: entangle yourself for all time, if you wish, in the net! Or exclude yourself, if you want. Measure carefully!")

But there will be one, one of the line of Isaiah, who will lead them all. Never will so many have owed so much to one man. The Hero.

He will liberate them from their unique suffering.

Christ was a minor demiurge. He could have done much more. Save bodies, for example. Save here on Earth. Here in the pain on Earth. All he did was show the path by which souls might return.

But this is understandable, given his celestial nature: his body was pro forma, a virgin born of a Virgin. His flesh insipid. Christ did not sweat. (The admiral notes this with the greatest respect. He recognizes that Christ was the God of the Jews' best possibility to make himself known throughout the world.)

The sea is still strong. The wind, safe. Time, variable. Occasional clouds and drizzle. The men lick their hands and the wet brass. Some hold out the blade of their knives to receive the angel of the rain.

Mess is announced. General jubilation concentrated about the firebox. Stewards are filling the wine jugs.

Officers—the secretary and the paymaster—sit at their table near the helm; the seamen lounge against the coamings of the hatchways or coils of rope. They all have a favorite place, their territory. Like cats.

A ship's boy runs up and down the decks with a little bell (as if everyone were not already waiting!).

"To table! To table! Sir Captain and Master and good company. Table is set. Food is ready. Long live the King and Queen of Castile, on land and on sea!"

Merriment. Laughter. The usual disorder around the firebox and cooking pots. Jokes.

A good day: mutton stew with lentils. Soup of rice and dried fish. Roast peppers. Large pieces of biscuit.

Harsh wine, not yet turned bitter.

They gnaw the bones happily. Use their bread to wipe the last grease from the plate.

Dried figs.

Cards, a siesta, or watch duty.

SEPTEMBER 14. THE BRANCH OF FIRE ON THE SEA. Toward dusk the skies cleared. That night they saw stars they had not seen for several days.

A moonless night. The awesome movement of the stars. (The men whisper that many constellations seem to be falling below the horizon. The pilots try to clarify matters. Calm the men.)

Incredible splendor. An abyss that humans can see from the spine of their dark planet.

In the west, they watched a marvelous branch of fire fall from the sky into the sea.

The men point to it with fear. They believe it is an exploding star.

Several arms of fire around the center. It is the unmistakable sweep of the flaming sword. The swastika of fire.

The admiral falls to his knees in the dark solitude of the bridge, in response to that clear and direct manifestation from the Divinity.

"Oh, God. You Who cast us out from Your house now are indicating the way home. All praise be to Your name."

Devoutly, he closes his eyes and sees in the night of astral space the unequivocal movement of the sword, just before the bow, almost a projection of the center line of the ship.

> *Arise, shine; for thy light is come,*
> *is risen upon thee . . .*
> *but the Lord shall arise upon thee,*
> *and his glory shall be seen upon thee.*
> *(Isaiah 60: 1, 2)*

The sea is ever deeper and more foreboding. Its calm does not soothe anyone's terror.

The Admiral, conscious that they are disheartened and alarmed, enters false information. Each morning, for the day's run, he reckons fewer leagues than they have made. You have to put blinders on a horse when you expect to confront fire, or a savage bull.

This is not the sea they have known, the Mare Nostrum that man plies with relative confidence. This is the Mare Tenebrarum in all its grandeur.

It is a living animal that only human ingenuity can domesticate. It needs no special malevolence to destroy men: its mere being—a mammoth, savage deity—is sufficient.

At dawn, off the bow, they sight two or three whales followed by a clientele of sharks.

Their presence is menacing. The sailors stand in small groups, whispering terrible tales, superstitions heard in the ports. (Are the monsters in the sea or in their souls?)

The realm of demons is best left undisturbed. The admiral recommends discreet silence. Leave off the boasting and foolishness of days on land: the laughter, the quarreling. He has little success. They do not understand.

The spider, the scorpion, the serpent, are aware of their evil. The creatures of the sea, who conserve the dimensions of a different era on earth, work their evil automatically, like mindless children; in short, like Dutchmen.

Griffins, which fly from undiscovered islands to devour sailors' flesh, are a hybrid of eagle and lion. The Giant Octopus, which so often has dragged ships down into its abyss, is a squid with eight tentacles. It is known that it prefers the light of the full moon, but if it devours men it is from extreme hunger, for lack of anything better.

They enter a spatiotemporal region never seen by human—except accidentally or in the unconscious. The admiral understands that it is natural that in this intermediate zone between nothing and being, between the known and mystery, the dead—at times with true insolence—make their appearance.

The admiral has experience, and knows what to look for. They walk constantly among the living, but it is at dusk when their milky color is most defined.

He knows the dead must be denied, and that if allowed they will claim all the space and time of the living, driving them mad. Treat them like dogs: ignore their threats; never show fear.

They are clinging, opaline presences. Astral protoplasm with an unholy nostalgia for life on earth. Nothing more.

At close quarters, the dead have the stale smell of cloistered nuns, like slightly damp snails.

The admiral refuses to acknowledge the dead, to know them any better. Even though he knows they are there. He senses them from his cabin: perched in the rigging, legs swinging; sardonic, demanding, calculating. Unable, basically, to tell what they have seen, if, in fact, they have seen anything. Indecent exploiters of the somber reputation of death. Always with an insistent desire to scatter signs and portents.

But the admiral will not look at them. His fear is stronger than his curiosity. He knows that the dead abduct, but never liberate. That they spread fear and disdain for life, when actually they are devoured by a rabid envy of healthy bodies and senses.

The admiral stares at the deck. If it is night he squeezes his eyelids tight. He tries to sleep, thinking of bright scenes filled with people.

When he feels he is about to lose the battle, that they are about to emerge in all their milky splendor, he rushes from his cabin, hurries down the ladder, and begins talking with the helmsmen on duty.

These are the only times when he expresses himself freely, speaks of pleasant, even entertaining and sincere, subjects.

Because of his fear of the dead.

To the degree they are increasingly insecure, the men find propitious signs tailored to their desires.

They bring the admiral seagrasses borne on the currents, and show him a live crab nesting in them. They place it on the planking of the deck and nudge it to make it move. They feed it crumbs. They splash it with seawater. They adopt it. It becomes a talisman to ward off their fear.

They estimate that the coast—the fertile lands they seek—is very close. They believe they see flocks of migratory birds (on that auspicious September 18). With exuberant cries they welcome the sighting of an aged pelican, surely lost or abandoned by the flock.

On the 20th there came to the ship, about dawn, two or three land birds, singing, but before sunrise, they disappeared.

Their eagerness is so great that the eyes of many shine as if bewitched.

The compass declines northwest: unmistakable proof that they are approaching a region of the world where the usual spatiotemporal schemes are disrupted. The needle always seeks the true, therefore they are uneasy.

The sea rises very high. A dark sea, heavy as mercury. Strong seas, but in the absence of wind; this disturbs the pilots, who communicate by shouting from the crow's nests of the three ships.

They do not understand. They have never seen such a phenomenon. But the admiral welcomes it as another unspoken but unequivocal sign from God. As in the times when Moses led the Jews out of Egypt, the sea is parting, rising into walls of water, even though there is not a breath of air.

The admiral gives thanks, eyes half closed. The Dialogue continues; that is the important thing.

SEPTEMBER 25. THE FALSE ISLANDS. The wish is so strong that it becomes illusion: finally someone shouted from the *Pinta,* commanded by Martín Alonso Pinzón, that land has been sighted.

Visions of their fear. The admiral capitalized on the opportunity. He accepted the mirage, and joined in the exultation. He dropped to his knees on the bridge, in a pathetic pose, and led the chorus singing *Gloria in Excelsis Deo.*

Men swarm up the rigging. Wave their hats. They all see the islands of golden sand. "Just like Guinea." They see palm trees. They name several species of phantom trees.

Taking advantage of the sudden calm, some dive from the rigging. The Mare Tenebrarum is behind them!

They mistreat the sea as if it were a sleeping lion, kicking and splashing. They are convinced the worst is over.

Their thoughts turn to self-interests and dreams of what they will find ashore.

Even the most excited sleep with calm. They are no longer thinking of mutiny, but of plantations (at sea, they want to be ordinary husbandmen; in the fields and tailor shops, they dream of the sea).

But the dawn reveals no coastline. They sail on.

Bikpela Hol

by John Long and
Dwight Brooks

Fearless climber, adventurer and writer John Long (born 1953) loves to visit the places others avoid. Here, he and buddy Dwight Brooks (born 1954) offer a tag-team account of their hair-raising visit to Papua New Guinea in search of just such a spot—and what happens when they find it.

Dwight: The thorny business of entering Papua New Guinea from Irian Jaya involves leaving a police state—where the Colonial administration's main activity is contending with the daring guerrillas of the OPM freedom fighters—and entering an independent nation, booming and upbeat. PNG welcomes visitors, has ethnological and topographical diversity surpassing Irian's, and places few, if any restrictions on those keen to explore the wilds. Many have done just that. The twentieth century has crept in nearly everywhere, largely due to aggressive missionary activity, but a few pockets remain, so isolated that no outsider has yet climbed up or down into them. The problem is to find out where these pockets are.

While kicking around a bottle shop in Goaribari, we met and befriended a formidable individual, vacationing with a steel axe in his belt. Describing himself as an "Assistant to the Sub-Assistant District Commissioner," he pre-accommodated us with a wide-ranging sub-elucidation of why the Enga Province was the most barbaric, least-developed in Papua New Guinea. Following this conversation, we ran out into the street, hopped a Public Motor Vehicle and hung on for two days, hell-bent for a census post called Birip, in South West Enga.

We spilled into the little bush village only to learn that the provincial government had been suspended due to its failure to control the constant tribal fighting. A disgusted Tasmanian anthropologist told us there were no "first contacts" left in Enga, everyone there having been chased from a battle scene by the police chopper at least once. True, there was a certain allure to the plan of photographing Enganese against a ubiquitous backdrop of arrow showers, but we hung on to our initial goal of seeking out unexplored areas.

We did take the time to insinuate ourselves into the Official Satellite Record Bureau of the Suspended Provincial Government. Alone in the office, we read through volumes of patrol reports, apprising ourselves of the current situation, and devouring the exploits of forgotten explorers. The name, T. Sorari, came up again and again, this officer chronicling an unforgettable spate of hair-raising escapades. Assigned to routine village tours, Sorari repeatedly contrived farfetched pretenses for heading off his designated patrol routes into what was then (late 60s) unpenetrated bush. We daubed our brows, packed our mouths, and excitedly agreed that this guy was the real thing.

We were unpleasantly rousted then by one angry Mr. Clementine Warulugabibi, informed by his secretary, Ululiana—whose breasts resembled ripe Wau pumpkins—that "two pela in de" had been rifling government files for more than three hours. He ordered us out, stiffly, threatening to "rifle and shoot" us. John suddenly whirled, and with unusual fervor in his voice, asked, "But, who is this man, Sorari?" Twenty Enganese gathered at the shouting of that name.

"Sorari?" Mr. Warulugabibi barked, astonished, ejecting his quid of betel. "How would two breadloaves like you know about . . ." He paused, a stern, somnolent expression stealing over his face. "I take it," he resumed with studied gravity, "that you rubbercoconuts have been looking at Sorari's reports. I could calaboose you both. How would you like to sweat it out in the hot-box and eat sago for a month?"

"We ate sago and less for nine weeks in the Strickland Gorge, wantok," John growled intemperately.

I had a Biami sago pounder inlaid with fine slivers of human bone which I produced and invited Mr. Warulugabibi to examine. I hoped this might quell the tension. It didn't.

"Oh, so you think you're a couple of real bush kanakas, do you?" Mr. Warulugabibi jabbed with an ominous, punishing rise in tone, while flipping the pounder in his hand. All along, the number of steel axes in the immediate vicinity had been swelling.

"You might say that, " John replied. "Besides, those bare feet of yours look plenty soft to me. Where you been lately?"

"Steady, John," I barked.

"No place you'd stay alive very long," Mr. Warulugabibi roared, then suddenly cut himself off, pausing a moment to consider something.

"Mi no laikim go long calaboose," I courteously declaimed to Mr. Warulugabibi, taking advantage of the pause. I'd spent a night in the swamp jail at Daru the previous year, and had no interest in sampling a highland facility.

Mr. Warulugabibi grinned and laughed malevolently. "A service to Papua New Guinea, yes, yes. I've changed my mind. You'll find Sorari in the Gulf Province: our Siberia. That is where the board who drafted his thirtieth reprimand sent him. A patrol post called Kaintiba. Of course, to get in there you may have to face Kukukuku along the way. You'll need more luck than I can wish you, but," he looked thoughtfully at the blackening sky, "I am not going to wish you any luck!"

The door slammed. We knew about the Kukukuku. Once the most feared tribe in the highlands, they are still treated very cautiously by the government, and isolated, uncontacted groups of them are rumored to inhabit nearly inaccessible nether regions of the Gulf Province.

It took some doing, but we made our way up to Kaintiba from the malarial coastal village of Moveave, swallowing gooey sago and sidestepping puk-puks (crocs) along the route. We saw no one.

Kaintiba gained, we made for the village men's house, inside which were stacked some thirty-seven cases of South Pacific Lager, the pride and joy of the District Commissioner, Tsigayap-twektago Sorari. Initially surprised at our arrival, he soon welcomed us emphatically, inviting us in to inspect the hang, and in particular, its trove. The vestibule was guarded by a Sergeant Wanyagikilili, who brandished an M-1 rifle of Second World War vintage. While in no way inclined to refuse the ninth bottle offered him, purchased by us from his stock, the Australian-educated Sorari proved himself an astute, witty, and fascinating conversationalist. He sized us up quickly and began talking about various patrols he had made in the surrounding bush. Although cutting a deceptive pose, grinning wildly, constantly-traveling bottle in hand, he had turned an attentive ear to the enthusiasm escalating in our voices the further out his narratives led us. After several minutes we were grilling the man for a unique destination. He suspended all frivolity, composed himself, and made us an offer we could not refuse.

"First of all, boys, no guarantee. You may go a very long way hunting down what may be only rumor. But, I'll tell you, I think there's something to this. For many years, stories have trickled back here about a cave called the Kukuwa Wantaim Kapa Ston, a very gigantic cave; very, very gigantic: truly a bikpela hol."

"Ya-Wa! Nogat! Nogat!" shouted Sergeant Wanyagikilili with fervent dismay. "Duk-Duk, i stap de! Em i got wanpela bikpela *sinek* em i gat sixpela het, fipela tail, em i tausen foot long. Nogat! Me no laikim lukim! Mi nogat tok! Mi go long haus bilong me!" With this, he thrust the rifle in to Sorari's hands and bailed.

I dropped a kina coin into the skull-bank and withdrew another bottle for our friend as John exclaimed, "Man! What was that all about?"

Sorari laughed, pried the cap off with his teeth, handed John the rifle, and took a long pull. "Well, that's the problem. The local people are afraid of the cave, the bikpela hol, and not one of my officers will patrol out to determine whether or not it even exists. Supposedly, it lies ten days walking from the nearest habitation, and that place, about seven days from here, is not a village, only what we call a liklik ples. Most everyone there has died from malaria and sorcery." Sorari shrugged, smiling inscrutably. "Now, Sergeant Wanyagikilili said there is a ghost in the cave, and a snake. The snake is a thousand feet long, with six heads and five tails. He said he is going home because he and this talk about the cave cannot sleep in the same village. His home is twelve miles from here. I am a fairly civilized man, but I do not know what to think. I would love to go, but I can't get away. They'd catch me absent, and I'd be sacked. I'm chained to the radio nowadays, relaying messages from out-stations to Moresby."

The next morning Sorari drew up papers making us temporary Government Patrol Officers (which he had no authority to do) and provided us with a guide willing to lead us as far as Hapayatamanga, the last Kukukuku village before the linik ples, but not one barefoot step further. In Hapayatamanga, we were to seek out Irtsj, who was under government employ and who would lead us on to the liklik ples, Imanakini. "Irtsj is a sort of a good-for-nothing," Sorari casually added. "He won't want to lift a finger, and you have my orders to be as firm with him as you feel is necessary." From Imanakini we would have to rely on an elusive individual called Ofafakoos, who lived with four wives and many children, some of whom, it was said, had recently been killed and eaten on a payback raid.

We stomped out of Kaintiba on a muddy track that snaked wildly along the contours of a luxuriant ravine. Soon, we were trudging up and down wearisome inclines choked with skin-slashing vines and seething with primordial leeches. Walking on newly fallen diptero-carps was fine. Those recently fallen, still hard though shorn of bark, were slick nightmares indeed. Trees long fallen usually looked recently fallen, which meant we had as good a chance of enacting cartoon cart-wheels as we had of plunging into rotted, pungent trunks to our knees, and mingling with the translucent larvae of rhinocerous beetles, dis-creetly squirming in the friable wood. Mazes of steep rivulets ran every-where, and were soothing to climb or descend in. Orchids, lianas, moss, were everywhere, large flying things constantly startled us, and our evasive dives were monitored by intelligent lizards. We slogged up to Hapayamaka after only five days.

The enthusiastic reception the machine-gun-speaking Kukukukus gave us was encouraging. That good-for-nothing Irtsj, a gangly beast with a walking stick on his shoulder, earnestly translated as much talk as we cared to hear, but he flatly refused to march on to Imanakini: a dangerous place, he said, where the people were controlled by vicious bush spirits who made them harm each other. But, Sorari had sent orders for him to lead us! "Samting Nating!" He did not care. But we had hiked two hundred hours to get there! He laughed. We had trade goods with which to pay him. He said he was sure we would leave Hapayatamanga without them, and laughed again. We didn't, and only after John had threatened his very life did he agree to roust a couple of bolder village boys to lead us off.

Nippongo and Timbunke, perhaps fifteen and seventeen, had just returned from a forty-day cruise in the Western Province, apparently all the way to the Irian border, and, well, maybe a little further, since the ragged clothing they returned with bore labels reading "Dibuat di Jawa" (made in Java). They did backflips when their fathers cut them loose again so soon. They didn't want money, just buai (betel), tobacco, and any excuse to get right out into the bush again. These guys were unbelievably industrious. They'd lead, chattering and laughing, firing back at us exotic fruits and sweet nuts we wouldn't have found if our lives had depended on it. They built rafts in minutes for the gear, then swam the rivers, never just once, but four or five times each. Of course, they'd also have to run half a mile up the bank to ride the river down, and all this only after they'd speared a string of barramundi and whipped up an impromptu barbecue. Rice? They'd rip the bark off a certain tree, fold it into a sturdy trough, build a fire and boil it up. The trough never caught fire. Their bushcraft was ingenious, and we began to see there really wasn't any limit to how resourceful one could be. They were having so much fun maxing themselves they got euphoric. The going was treacherous, no doubt about it, but Nippongo and Timbunke completely transformed our way of looking at the jungle.

During the last twenty minutes before the liklik ples irregular snaps and rustlings convinced us we were being shadowed, paralleled, actually, by men with stealthy gaits. John was tense as a pit viper. Anyone watching the execution strokes of his bush knife could plainly see it. We paused a moment together and strained our ears: nothing. John made it clear he had little interest in establishing a listening post, and blasted off anxiety by screaming up the last incline like a cruise missile. Toward the end I couldn't match the clip, so I brought up the rear in wide-eyed spirals, figuring I'd run straight at anyone making a hostile move and nail him.

Then we hit Imanakini:, all two huts, two men, thirteen wives, and nineteen kids of it. They were jittery, freaked by us we thought, but soon guessed not when no one had relaxed a whit an hour after our arrival, and every kid old enough to run was kept prowling on the perimeter. Whoever they were, we never saw them. That they might have been a group of Kukukuku devolving on the hovel for a raid, only to be spooked-off by the odd double white sight was eminently plausible. Fatigue supplanted anxiety later on, however, and we took turns sacking out beneath a teetering lean-to on a bed of fronds, food for every fly, mosquito, ant, mantis, beetle, scorpion, spider and kissing stabber in the whole territory. One old, bedizened fellow, betel eyes out in the Crab Nebula, sat up all night chanting protective spells and exercising his horrendous hacking cough. Another, his toothless mouth a bloodbin, was so paralyzed by fear he never suffered himself to move, save for the spasmodic demands of his frame. The women, naturally, did all the work. We swapped watches, slapping bugs, eventually giving up, hosting all arthropods, desperate by turns to doze. As the night wore on we convinced each other no one was out there, each of us fully aware that in the Asmat, headhunting raids usually took place right before dawn. Then we both went flat. Worse, however, than falling victim to any skullhunt was putting up with the infuriating jibberish of a cock pecking tediously six feet behind our heads. Once home, I would buy a rooster for the sheer pleasure of shooting it.

We slipped out of Imanakini before dawn, following Nippongo along an inobvious brawl of rotting trunks that gave passage through hectares of flora deep enough to swallow a man whole. Eventually we arrived at the bush hut (haus bilong bus) of Ofafakoos, the bitter-end habitation. Queried about Kukukuku raiders, he acknowledged they did sweep through there from time to time, but usually harmed people only when fruit trees they considered their own had pieces missing. Upon being offered one kina per day to lead on to the cave, purportedly eight days away, Ofafakoos grinned extravagantly, thick lips framing a mighty red orifice and two rows of black teeth. He said betelnut offerings tied to certain trees would assure the Kukukuku of our good intentions. He snatched up his bow, six types of arrows, his bush knife and bilum bag of buai, chatted with each of his four wives in turn, glanced askance at John's hand ferreting out a few of the stimulant bulbs for the white man's consumption, then took off through the dripping sawblades like a track athlete. The unrelenting flurry of machete slashes plied against the untracked jungle by this superb bushman filled us both with enthusiasm and admiration, and distracted us from the starchy, spiceless, boiled gunk of forest tubers we'd gagged down at Imanakini.

Six days followed, during which we traveled in great arcs and weaves, typically climbing a gooey wall adrip with flesh-blistering poisons, needle-like vines, and invidious foot-snaring creepers. We'd top out on choked razorbacks, rest the duration of a smoke, then improvise descents down walls where pitching off meant a 100-foot fall. The only white men who had ever been within fifty miles of these locales were the bold Aussie patrolers who slogged around from Kerema, Kikori, and Malalaua during the sixties.

Ofafakoos would lead a knee- or waist-deep wade for an hour or so, only to step out with spooky acuity and start up another hideous wall. We were truly amazed by his sense of direction. Fathom it? Nogat! Wall, ridge, wall, river: over and over and over.

Understandably, we both began to wonder if he did indeed know where we were going, other than into unfrequented reaches, laced with odoriferous bogs and impenetrable clumps of pink lotuses, fourteen inches across. Day six gave us a view of a forbidding limestone escarpment, a sign which rejoiced us, hinting as it did at cave territory. Next day, after scaling a mud wall on which ice tools and crampons would have been sumptuous aids, I looked at where Ofafakoos had elected to descend. Two Urama Taboo Goblins, ten feet high, their bamboo, human hair, spiderweb, rattan, human bone, sennit, hornbill-headed, pig-tusked, red and gray spiral-beaded eyes frankly terrifying, were staked out as an explicit warning not to continue.

"Dispela olgat det longtim," Ofafakoos remarked uneasily, then spun around convulsively at what proved to be only the loud, chugging huff-huff of a hornbill. Apparently, the people who made these effigies were all dead now, having succumbed to the raids of the uncontacted Kukukuku. With an upward flick of his blade he severed the fibrous weave linking the eerie totems and bolted through.

John: We hurtled down, legs moving like pistons so momentum couldn't start us cartwheeling toward the creek, a thousand feet below. Slipping, bashing and heel-digging through ripe mulch, we took the final 100 feet on our asses, sailed off a mud bank as if on toboggons and splashed into the creek. After plodding downstream for an hour, under triple canopy, Ofafakoos zagged left into dense thicket. Twenty paces and we ran into a limestone wall stretching overhead for 500 feet and melding into a tilted mesa carpeted with ferns.

Around us loomed the strangest topography imaginable, as though God had grabbed this craggy jungle and twisted it into a green jigsaw. The land flowed in and out of itself with such confusion that getting a bearing was futile since one's other points of reference appeared upside down or backwards. Huge trees grew askance from cliffs and buttresses teetering at impossible angles. Waterfalls looked to fall sideways, creeks ran the wrong way and grass hung down from the ceilings of mottled grottos. This natural labyrinth felt almost four dimensional, possessing the queer geometry of an M.C. Escher drawing. We'd be lucky to cover a mile a day in such terrain, and likely would end up where we started.

Skirting right along the stone wall, we finally gained a clearing and collapsed. Ofafakoos pointed to a tiny black hole. The cave entrance? Hardly the Gothic job we'd expected. More like the entrance to a dog house.

Native eyes peered in for sineks as we wiggled out from underneath our packs and exalted that, for a while anyway, the trudging was over.

D.B. dug out some dried swine from his pack as Nippongo, who never tired, laid his bush knife into a sixty footer, showering us with wedges of meaty wood. Timber! He ran to the high bough and plucked just the right leaf with which to scroll his black tobacco.

"Nogat" said Timbunke: too green. Nippongo shrugged and laid into a hundred footer, felling it only after a pumping ordeal.

"Nogat," said Ofafakoos: too dry. Running sweat, Nippongo smirked, then went for a mammoth hardwood, stopping only when I tossed him a pack of Djarums, ferried with much devotion from the Indonesian pirate port of Ujung Pandang. We all howled. Nippongo bounced a pebble off my head, once it was turned.

After twenty minutes, when our legs stopped cramping and we had some food on board, we couldn't wait any longer. D.B. and Ofafakoos dove into the little cave entrance as Nippongo stared, carping about the thousand-foot sinek. "Nogat!" echoed from the chasm. Let's go. Nippongo and Timbunke queued up behind me. We wiggled in.

The tight entrance immediately gave way to a stupendous tunnel, where manifold veins shot off into velvet nothingness. Thousands upon thousands of bats were startled into wayward flight. And the hues: ochre walls, stripes of red and orange, swirling dikes of Pan-Ethiopian ivory. Down, down we went, through crawlways into vast, dripping arenas where fang-like columns, seemingly half-melted, loomed enormously. The Papuans were forever on guard for the bikpela sinek or its traces. Onward, we squirmed past clusters of golden stalagmites, crawled through odorous guano under a two-foot ceiling, treaded around oceans of vicious quickmud. We long-jumped over bottomless clefts, hooking into warehouse-sized antechambers and dead-end vestibules. I paused at a clean pool, pointing wistfully. Confused, Nippongo trained his gaze, just long enough for me to boot him in.

We'd been inside six hours, wandered two, maybe three miles. Though the way meandered, sporting many aberrations, all now explored, we invariably returned to the principal shaft. The tunnel ahead looked uniform, extending beyond eye-shot, but in two hundred feet it started shrinking, the corrugated floor angling down at a ten-degree rake. The bats were gone, likewise the guano, so our little passage was hospital clean. Bubbling potholes appeared—little carbonated springs—with the overflow racing down the incline into pitch darkness. Water dripped from the seamless roof. It was probably pouring outside. A squall could trigger an interior flood, but we figured this cave too vast to cause a problem. As Nippongo rolled a smoke, we washed off layers of mud from sweat-soaked bodies. The beastly humidity made our breath thick as cigar smoke.

We'd marked strategic bends with chalk—about forty times so far—but now everything was soaked so we simply pushed on, the rays of our flashlights swallowed fifty feet beyond. The shaft angled down sharply, maybe fifteen degrees. Worse, the ceiling was now only eight feet above and the walls barely ten feet apart. After one hundred yards the water ran knee-deep, with wall fissures belching blades of clear juice into our dwindling passage. Suddenly, Nippongo stepped into a pothole and disappeared. Ofafakoos shrieked, "Bikpela sinek em i kai-kai (eat) liklik Nippongo!" Nippongo popped back up, laughed, pointed down the tunnel and said, "Yumi go now."

This kid Nippongo—we wanted to slap him silly half the time. But in fact Nippongo was the most game person I had ever seen and a source of confounding amusement guaranteed to lighten us up when legs grew weary and the leeches too thick to bear. The struggles we had in that cave might some day fade to black, but never Nippongo. He was already black.

Nippongo led the way down the dark corridor. We followed.

In fifty feet we were chest-deep, and in twice that we were treading water, the walls six feet apart and the ceiling only three feet overhead.

Just beyond, the ceiling curved down to the waterline.

"Fudge," I said. "Dead-end."

"Lot of ground we covered . . . just to bail," D.B. said. "I say we try and swim for it."

"Swim for what?" I asked. Nippongo and Ofafakoos must have

caught the drift because they started spewing out incomprehensible tok ples (place talk = dialect), afros flush to the ceiling, mouths taking in water. A novel sight, all our bobbing heads, like apples in a barrel.

"I really don't know about swimming," I said. "We got no line and no idea where the thing heads, if it leads anywhere. Plus once you're under, you can't see shit."

"I'll just have a look," said D.B., who drew a deep breath and slipped into the underwater tube. D.B. re-emerged five seconds later, wild-eyed and rambling.

"Man, is that spooky! We'll have to work it out, five feet at a time. Just draw your hand along the wall so you don't lose direction." I guess that meant it was my turn. Nippongo shouted that the tube was the gullet of the thousand-foot sinek, then laughed. Glug, glug, and into obsidian, free floating in liquid space. When my stomach turned to stone, I reversed.

"Wow, now! I don't know about this one!"

But soon, the familiarity of repetition allowed more serious efforts, and in half an hour we'd ventured out a dozen times each. The shaft ran straight—simple to reverse so long as we turned around with enough air. But we weren't really getting anywhere. We needed another approach. Yes, forget feeling the wall, I thought. Put in a few big strokes and see where it puts you.

"Okay," I said. "I'm going out ten seconds, taking two big strokes, and coming back." One stroke out, gliding directionless through this ink, and I freaked, clawed for the wall, then groped back to the fellows.

"That's it. That's my threshold. I'm finished, and that's final." Ten minutes later, we'd both gone in twice more, taking three stokes each. Still, we were only staying under about twenty seconds, max. I decided to push it a little more.

"All right. I'm going for four strokes." I dove back under. Ten seconds, one stroke, two strokes, three, gliding blindly, untethered in space. My arms dovetailed forward and I pulled hard for this last thrust, bringing my arms to my sides, knifing further into . . . Bonk! A stalagmite! My hands wrapped my ringing head, and for several seconds I drifted on the shadowline between consciousness and unconsciousness. I grasped for the stalagmite, which was nowhere, then for the wall, which I found. But what now? The situation overwhelmed me: I didn't know which way was up, or which way was back. With seconds of air left, I stroked out right. Wait! My left hand felt odd, different, and my head raised instinctively into an air pocket, black and soundless.

I broke down, gasping, hyperventilating, rubbing my dazed head. Sweet Jesus, I've done it now, I thought. I'd known some lonely places in 32 years, but that air pocket—dark as the Devil's heart—made the North Pole feel like Trafalgar Square. Then a thought. Find the stalagmite! That was my best hope, believing as I did that the air pocket was past the stalagmite. Finding it anew would at least point me in the right direction. A sound plan, but even brief exits from the pocket were terrifying. Finally I found the stalagmite, fifteen feet away. Then back to the pocket. After a minute of big breaths, I glided out, slithered past the stalagmite, hand dragging the wall—but soon as I realized I might still be going in the wrong direction, I panicked and started stroking for all I was worth. My arms shot out and heaved back, then out again; but with this last pull, I hit something, something moving. It's alive! The sinek! Some massive freshwater eel! I reflexively grabbed the snake, or the eel—which turned out to be D.B.'s leg. Seconds away from sucking water, he hauled me to the thick air.

The light was heaven attained, but my nerves were shot and not until grappling to a dry porch and gasping for minutes could I start talking. Nippongo thumbed a thin trickle of blood from my forehead, then rolled me a smoke—which I zipped in about four draws. D.B. reasoned that since the air pocket was so close to the stalagmite, he'd go have a look. I was too whipped to argue. The few minutes waiting seemed an hour, and my mind cooked up all kinds of crazy things. Then D.B. burst back, his face awestruck.

"It's there! It's true! No myth!" Ofafakoos's eyes popped, thinking D.B. found the sinek. "The shaft ends just a few seconds past the air pocket—inside the bikpela hol! There's a river the size of the Mamberambo flowing through the bottom of it. You gotta check it out!"

"Okay," I said. "Just give me a minute." I had no idea what I was saying, and wouldn't till I was fixing to swim back into the black tunnel.

Without hesitation, D.B. swam back under. Ofafakoos, Nippongo and Timbunke set off immediately to find their way out, for the water level was rising by the second. I wasn't entirely sure I'd talked myself into going back under. But now I was alone, which is so spooky in such a place that you're urged to action, however crazy. Finally, my mind went blank and I dove back into the inky tunnel, too frightened to stop at the pocket, finally popping up with a swift revivifying lunge to the flash of D.B.'s Nikon, feeling like I'd just been born.

"What's with the light?" I asked out loud as we scrambled from the pool. We were clearly inside something very large, yet the cave was full of subdued natural light. A little easy climbing over mossy blocks and we were onto solid ground. The bikpela hol! That first open vista defied words. I honestly felt I knew what the Spanish conquistadors must have felt when first gazing into the Grand Canyon, or when antique Miwok indians first entered Yosemite Valley and peered up at El Capitan. It took many looks, this way and that, to fathom the size, later calculated at eleven million cubic feet. We'd been treated to the rarest find—a natural wonder of the first magnitude. Several years later, once the word got out, a New Zealand team battled to the cave and conducted a proper survey. The following year D.B. and I were credited with "discovering and exploring the world's largest river cave." Nippongo, Ofafakoos and Timbunke were not mentioned. Not that they would care. For D.B. and I, the real payoff was that first view.

The river, some 150 feet across, entered through a 400-foot rainbow arch, flowed through a half mile of open cave, then exited through a 200-foot arch. Between the giant arches the versicolored ceiling soared to an ultimate apex of eight hundred feet above the water. A one-hundred-foot maw slashed the roof at centerpoint, rife with flying foxes maintaining a clockwise circuit between the dark ends of this massive gash. The swim had gained us a balcony of sorts, three hundred yards long and extending at a gentle angle one hundred yards ahead, ending sharply at a suicidal plunge straight into the river, slow and wide, hundreds of feet below. Light flooded through the colossal entrance and exit, taking us back to the stone age. Never before or since have I felt such awesome natural forces, or felt the earth's great age, as when we first stood on that parapet and beheld the Bikpel Hol!

At the balcony's far right margin, D.B. discovered a tree-lined tunnel exiting to the original limestone buttress, one mile downhill from our entry point: we could walk in and out of the main chamber easy as climbing a flight of stairs.

"Too bad," I said. "Everyone should have the pleasure of swimming in."

After a hour's gawking (and trundling boulders into the river), we exited into a downpour for the forty-five-minute trek back to the entrance. After two nervous hours, Nippongo and Ofafakoos emerged, battered, with horror stories of their own. Constant rain had made for treacherous flooding, and twice they'd nearly been whisked into oblivion by rising currents. I quickly dressed wounds more painful than serious, then we charged for a bivouac in the main chamber, vast and dry. En route, we marveled over how the terrain could mask our perception of both the cave and its river. The river, so distinct a quarter mile upstream, flowed through a twisted maze of upheaved crags and ledges overgrown with trees and shrub so thick that even the huge cave entrance was noticeable only if one was looking straight at it.

Later, stretched out on pads in the titanic chamber, I told Nippongo if he didn't rustle up some food, he'd soon find himself diving into the river several hundred feet below. He said if I could find so much as a seed pod, he'd give me his widowed sister and her four daughters.

The starved march back to Hapayatamanga thrashed us into hallucinations and slurred speech. The final hours were hateful uphill battles, our only aid the knowledge that we'd stashed four tins of Torrid Strait mackerel in the hut of a Hapayatamanga sorcerer. One tin lay conspicuously open: Nippongo's sister told us that some of the men had been dipping their arrow tips into the uneaten fish. The other three went down faster than we could wince.

The Gulf Province averages twenty-plus feet of rain a year, and I swear we got half that in the following days. Bivouacs were sleepless disasters and the food was long gone. After seven days, we finally plowed into Kaintiba, and I literally dropped, not rising for twenty hours. We later snagged a lift on a Pilatus Porter from a Kiwi mate bound for Lae, a coastal haven, and spent the next four days at a ritzy expat yacht club, eating and drinking and drinking and eating.

Crazy in the Congo
by Michael Finkel

*Writer Michael Finkel (born 1969) accompa-
nied environmental activist Bruce Hayse on an
extremely ambitious, uncomfortable and dangerous expedition down the Congo's Chinko
river in 1999. The team planned to navigate
the entire length of the river—a feat probably
never before attempted, let alone achieved—
and document the impact of poaching on the
region's wildlife. Hayse is known for leading
trips that inflict great pain on his companions;
this one proved no exception.*

Bruce ended up on the floor, shivering and semi-delirious,
wrapped in an afghan on a 100-degree day. This was nothing to
be alarmed about. He had caught malaria twice before—once
in Gabon, once in Congo—and had apparently reached a sort
of détente with the disease. "The nice thing about having malaria," he
said, during what may or may not have been a moment of lucidity, "is
that when you get over it you feel so damn good."

Mike's condition did not have such a cheery prognosis. His back
looked as though a sizable army of tsetse flies had used it for target
practice, which in fact is precisely what had happened. He returned
to the United States as soon as we left the river, spent a week in the
hospital, and lost 30 pounds. Also, it turned out that he, too, had
malaria.

As did Christian.

And Hank as well.

With Louise, it was her legs. If Braille dots were red, her legs would have appeared to be a treatise for the blind. Ants, I believe, were responsible—ants or termites; I forget which.

Chris, I'm pleased to report, seemed well on his way to straightening himself out from what can only be described as an extraordinarily bad acid trip, except without the acid.

Randy's right elbow had something growing from it that had a surprising resemblance, both visually and texturally, to a racquetball.

Rick was fine.

Brian had a possible case of worms.

My face, thank you very much, was healing nicely from the killer-bee attack.

And that's everyone—all ten of us. Raymond and Thomas, the two Central Africans who joined the group, had their own scars, but they were relatively minor. So it seemed that nobody would die. Which is one good thing. Another is that nobody got shot. I'm still pretty surprised about that. Even without a fatality or a bullet wound, however, it's safe to say that we'd finished a reasonably difficult trip.

It is not exactly fair to blame Bruce Hayse for everything, but that is what I intend to do. The idea, after all, was his. He was the expedition's leader; I was merely its chronicler. When I accepted the assignment, I did not know who Bruce Hayse was or what a Bruce Hayse expedition typically involved. Before departing, I had spoken with him several times, but I'd caught no more than oblique hints of his idiosyncrasies. We were already en route to Africa when a fellow member of the group, a friend of Bruce's from his hometown of Jackson, Wyoming, attempted to clarify our leader's reputation. "Just about everyone in Jackson has gone on a trip with Bruce," he said, "but not many have gone on a second trip."

Gratuitous pursuit of danger isn't what scares people off. This much was clear to me within a few hours of meeting Bruce. He is quiet and introspective and endlessly inquisitive. He is neither propelled by testosterone nor obsessed with points on a map. Ask him about extreme sports and he will pucker his face as if he has just bitten into a lemon. What inspires him, rather, is something far more potent and infinitely more hazardous than adrenaline addiction or summit fever. Bruce is powered by belief.

What he believes in is wilderness. He believes in uncontrolled, ungerrymandered, unsullied wilderness—the type of wilderness where native species are able to follow natural migration patterns without bumping into boundary lines or suburbs or ecotourism lodges. A wilderness of this magnitude, sometimes called a frontier forest, is so rare, Bruce says, that only five such tracts remain: central Siberia, the plains of Tibet and Mongolia, the Alaska/Yukon region, the Amazon rain forest, and the Congo Basin.

Only the last of this tenuous quintet provides sanctuary to a full raft of the planet's megafauna—hippos and elephants, lions and leopards, giraffes and buffalo. After the Amazon, the Congo Basin is also the most endangered of the frontier forests, and almost certainly the most difficult and hazardous to explore. This area is the seat of Bruce's passion, a region he has visited, off and on, for two decades.

Bruce Hayse is 51 years old. He is a doctor by profession, the proprietor of a family-practice clinic in Jackson, but his roots are in environmental activism. He was raised in rural Oregon, in the town of Burns, where his father was both mayor and, according to Bruce, the dealer in a backroom gambling den. Bruce completed a master's degree in plant ecology at the University of Wisconsin, and then, in 1980, became one of the charter members of Earth First!, where his tireless, and apparently not always legal, campaigns earned him the nom de guerre Dr. Doom. He was close friends with the writer Edward Abbey—he is one of the few people who knows precisely where Abbey is buried—and Bruce is widely rumored to have been the inspiration for a character in *The Monkey Wrench Gang* (Doc Sarvis seems a possibility). His manner of travel appears patterned after Thoreau; certainly, he has taken "Civil Disobedience" to heart. He is notorious for what the authorities at several national parks call illegal trespass and what Bruce terms "walking in the woods, away from the trails."

He also shares Thoreau's enthusiasm for water voyages. In 1998,

Bruce led the first descent of Gabon's Ivindo River, in an effort to initiate a movement to protect the region—a proposal currently under consideration by the Gabonese government. He is the president of the African Rainforest and Rivers Coalition, a group dedicated to preserving the Congo Basin and surrounding areas. When pressed about the ethical conundrum of saving wildlands in a place where people are often suffering, Bruce responds instantly and unequivocally: The preservation of the last swatch of African wilderness takes precedence over the protection of human lives. It takes precedence, he implies, over the protection of his own life.

Little surprise that few of his travel partners seek an encore.

Last fall, Bruce organized his most ambitious expedition yet. The journey centered around a region in the Congo Basin called the Haut Chinko, which is located in the eastern half of the Central African Republic, almost in the exact crosshairs of the continent. The Haut Chinko, 36,000 square miles with scarcely a human living in it, was at one time the Congo Basin's crown jewel. It is bisected by the Chinko River, also known as the River of Elephants, which flows more than 400 miles from the highlands near Sudan south to the Congo border. An estimated 50,000 elephants, including some of the largest ever observed, once roamed the savanna woodlands, along with vast herds of buffalo, and giant elands, and waterbuck and hartebeest and reedbucks and duikers.

Then came the slaughter. It started in 1979, when gangs of Sudanese poachers, armed with military weapons and leading teams of donkeys, rolled unimpeded over the northern border and slashed their way into the heart of the Chinko. Prior to this, the French, who had colonized the Central African Republic, had maintained a sizable border patrol. But in the late 1970s, the French pulled out and the Sudanese strolled in.

They began with elephants. Ton after ton of ivory was tied to the donkeys' backs, carted to the Sudan, and sold overseas. Then, when virtually every elephant had been shot, it was the hippos' turn. The prize this time was the animal's skin. Likewise with leopards and lions.

Finally, the poachers went for meat: buffalo, bushpig, warthog—basically, anything that moved. All of it was strapped to the donkeys and hauled away.

During the rainy season, when the savanna grasses are too high to hunt, the poachers continue to raid villages at the outer edges of the Haut Chinko. Women are raped, men enslaved, supplies stolen. Some villages have been abandoned. There is little the government can do. The Central African Republic is a relatively undeveloped country, completely lacking in infrastructure. Money is too scarce to fund even the most basic of hospitals or schools, let alone border patrols in a remote, unpopulated area of the country. The poachers have reign over the Chinko. The situation has become so sketchy that by the time we arrived, no non-African was known to have ventured into the Chinko region for at least five years.

Bruce's plan was straightforward. A suicide mission, said some, but even so, a straightforward one. He wanted to navigate the entire length of the Chinko River (something that had in all likelihood never been done); document which animals, if any, remained in the region; and then, upon our return, initiate a drive to eliminate the poachers and protect the Chinko. Bruce was not blind to the dangers. He merely chose not to dwell on them. He realized that in order to trumpet a cause he felt so strongly about, people would probably have to suffer. It was possible there would be martyrs. It did not escape my attention that, in Bruce's world, the publicity attending a martyrdom or two might actually help the cause.

Those who do travel with Bruce more than once tend to be of like-minded obsession. The Chinko expedition included four Hayse regulars, three men and a woman, all friends from Wyoming: Christian Guier, an orthopedic surgeon; Rick Sievers, a professional river guide; Brian Whitlock, a sound engineer; and Louise Lasley, a seasoned wildlife spotter. To bolster the group's conservationist credentials, Bruce added three high-ranking activists: Mike Roselle, the cofounder of Earth First!; Randy Hayes, the San Francisco-based founder of the Rainforest Action Network; and Hank Morgenstern, a Florida lawyer specializing in Endangered Species Act enforcement. The media contingent consisted of myself and a photographer named Chris Anderson, a fearless globe-trotter who seems to have made a parlor game of getting himself into trouble—in Kosovo, in Siberia—and then charming his way out of it.

We met for the first time in Charles de Gaulle airport, in Paris, where we awaited one of the twice-weekly flights into Bangui, the Central African Republic's capital. We landed in Bangui just after dawn. It was October 3. Stationed at both ends of the runway were United Nations tanks, each with a soldier poking out of the top hatch and gripping a machine gun. There have been four coup attempts in the CAR in the past four years, all of them violent. We'd arrived three days after a contentious presidential election, and intimations of an uprising were again in the air.

I walked around the city with Chris Anderson. The coups had inflicted heavy damage, and much of Bangui appeared as if a tornado had recently swept through. The number of tourists who visit each year is approximately zero. Some of the city's intersections were marked with military barricades constructed of sandbags topped with razor wire, and as I walked by each one I could see an assault rifle being trained at my head, which is something I took very little comfort in. (It wasn't just me; this happened to everyone who passed by.) Bangui's prostitutes were both numerous and predaceous—they were hookers who literally hooked themselves to you—and it took no small effort to pry yourself free. In an intriguing, Ransom of Red Chief-style twist, I later learned that two members of the expedition actually paid prostitutes to leave them alone.

We stayed only one night in Bangui, in a fortress-like compound owned by a South African diamond-mining company called CAMCO. Before leaving the States, Bruce had contacted CAMCO, which does much of its mining in the CAR. For $14,800, cash only, the company agreed to fly us and our small mountain of gear to the headwaters of the Chinko River.

• • •

The first leg of the trip was in a Russian plane, which transported us several hundred miles east, to the village of Bria. The view from the plane's windows was inspiring: thousands of square miles of pea green forest, punctuated only by scattered collections of mud-brick homes. Although on a map of Africa the CAR appears diminutive and sort of chipped away by its neighbors, the nation is fairly large, nearly the size of Texas. The population is 3.4 million. There are no railways and few drivable roads. Women give birth to an average of five children; life expectancy is 47 years.

In Bria, we were met by CAMCO's cargo helicopter. We transferred our gear to the chopper and were joined by the final two members of the expedition, both of whom live in Bria: Thomas Kolaga and Raymond Yakoro. Thomas had worked as a tracker for French hunting guides for three decades before the poachers put an end to his livelihood. Bruce had employed him to help us detect wildlife.

Raymond, a special forces soldier, was the expedition's one-man security detail. We had hired him through CAMCO, for whom he occasionally freelances when problems with diamond bandits arise. For bandit hunting, Raymond said he is paid by the head—literally—and there is a rather graphic photo at the CAMCO compound of Raymond holding up four such receipts, blood still dribbling from the severed necks. When he got into the helicopter, he was wearing full jungle fatigues and carrying an AK-47 assault rifle with a banana clip in place. From his belt hung two grenades. "One for the men," he told me, "one for the truck."

The helicopter performed an unsettling tussle with gravity before managing (unenthusiastically, it seemed to me) to achieve loft. We flew for two hours. The jungle thinned to savanna, and all signs of human inhabitation vanished. We landed in a field of elephant grass beside the river and unloaded our gear, and the helicopter took off. I was as far from civilization as I have ever been, or am likely ever to be. As that thought was working its way through me, invigorating and disquieting at the same time, there arrived among us the first bee.

• • •

It's funny. Of all the things I'd been warned about before leaving, African killer bees were not on the list. I was warned, of course, about poachers—poachers with machine guns, poachers with machetes. I was warned about worms. There would be worms in my intestines, I was told, and worms in my eyes—river blindness, it's called—and worms poking themselves out of my skin. Apparently, there were a lot of worms to worry about. Also, viruses. It was pointed out that I'd be traveling in the same general region that had produced Ebola. There were tsetse fly warnings and leopard warnings and hippo warnings and crocodile warnings. I was alerted about malaria and filaria and giardia. If a black mamba snake were to bite me, I learned, I'd have 30 seconds to live.

The presence of Raymond, somehow, reassured me. Raymond would protect us, I figured, and failing that, we'd use our satellite phone, with which we could conceivably call the CAMCO people, who, for a significant payment, cash only, might be willing to send their helicopter into the area to try to find us.

With bees, though, we weren't sure what to do. It is very difficult to shoot bees, and yet they are not a call-in-the-helicopter offense. We simply had to cope. As we sorted our gear, the number of bees seemed to increase, exponentially, by the minute. It was not unusual to have 40 or 50 around you at once. The sound they made was Harley-like in its ability to aggrieve the eardrum. Head nets provided little protection: Bees are attracted to sweat, and will squeeze through even the most minuscule of openings to get at it. A bee trapped inside a head net tends to panic, and then sting. Even 100-percent DEET, sprayed directly on a bee's head, was impotent at best; often it served as an agent of provocation. The most common reaction—the layperson's term for it, I believe, is "freaking out"—was worst of all. When a bee's body is crushed by swatting, it releases an odor that incites other bees to partake in a sort of sudden insectile jihad.

The sting of an African killer bee feels more like a burn than a sting—it radiates a burn's throbby, almost dizzy-nauseous sensation—and often leaves behind a welt that would require a bandanna to fully cover. I know this because during the 19 days we spent on the Chinko River I was stung 67 times (I kept precise count, in my journal). Within three hours of the helicopter's departure, two of my fellow travelers, Hank and Christian, had pretty much lost their minds: They leaped into the Chinko fully clothed, and submerged themselves to their nostrils, in Hank's case with his camera and binoculars still around his neck, both of which were ruined beyond repair.

Night brought relief. Bees observe, innately, a strict curfew, and at dusk they departed en masse. We set camp. To do this, we first had to flatten the grass. This does not sound particularly difficult until you consider that the savanna grasses are ten to twelve feet tall, with the stalks of some species as sharp as razors. I learned very quickly to wear a long-sleeved shirt and to seek out only the soft grasses, which I'd stomp in a crop-circle pattern, the stalks all bent inward, providing a duff for my tent as thick as a down comforter. In places where sharp grasses were unavoidable, I borrowed Thomas's machete and hacked madly away. I found this intensely satisfying—macheteing, much like chopping wood, is a wonderful, legal method of assuaging pent-up frustrations.

Entering my tent, however, was always disconcerting. The absence of bees in the evening was more than compensated for by the company of mosquitoes and sand fleas and chiggers and no-see-ums and gnats. I'd unzip my tent door and they'd pour in like a gas seeking equilibrium. The next 20 minutes would be spent ridding my sleeping area of as many of these visitors as possible. My tent walls, over time, became festooned with an impressionistic mélange of splattered bug innards.

On our first morning in the Haut Chinko, before we'd even placed a boat on the river, I emerged from my tent and heard a sudden, thunderous blast. Instinctively, I threw myself to the ground. Poachers had found us, I was certain. A shot had been fired. My surroundings acquired the crystalline sharpness and slow-motion feel that often accompanies moments of terror. I can recall, with precision, the blade of grass rubbing against my nose, and the feel of my heartbeat strong in my fingertips. There was no shouting, no commotion. I crawled, unarmed, toward the source of the blast. I saw five of my expedition mates huddled football style around what I was convinced was a body. I stood up. No. It was one of our inflatable kayaks, which had been baked by the sun and had blown a seam.

We had six boats—actually, now five and a half. There were catarafts, each of which consisted of an aluminum-and-rubber platform lashed to a pair of banana-shaped pontoons. These held all our gear. The others were two-person kayaks, lighter and more maneuverable than the catarafts, and therefore better able to explore the Chinko's side channels. Once we'd fixed the blown seam, using a needle and dental floss, Bruce produced a bottle of champagne, popped it, and passed it around. We climbed aboard our boats and headed downriver.

The Chinko has a strong current, three or four miles an hour, and most of the time it was unnecessary to paddle. We simply drifted, and observed. The bees would harass us for maybe five minutes and then turn around and go home. The river water was sandalwood brown and congested with bits and pieces of unidentifiable flotsam, like hot-and-sour soup. Bruce had timed the trip to coincide with the end of the rainy season, when the water is at its swiftest, the savanna grasses are at maximum height, and the trees bordering the river are dense with foliage. This is the time of year when the likelihood of being sighted through a poacher's rifle scope is at a minimum. In an unavoidable compromise, it is, for the same reasons, also the season when spotting large game, at least from the river, is nearly impossible.

This is not to imply that there was little to see. You simply had to narrow your focus. The Chinko, it turned out, is an avian sanctuary. The first day's sightings included herons and parrots and kingfishers and egrets. I watched a flock of weaverbirds, bright yellow and endlessly chattery, use bits of grass to sew their hollow, snail-shell-shaped nests. I saw hawks and eagles and bee-eaters and owls. I spotted a dozen prehistoric-looking hornbills commuting to and fro across the river in their whimsical, follow-the-bouncing-ball flight patterns.

Butterflies were even more numerous. I was tailed by a pair of monarchs with wings like Chagall windows, and soon acquired a personal cloud of gray-blue butterflies, their ticklish wings continually brushing against cheeks and ears. They stayed with me all afternoon, and at one point I held myself perfectly still and watched as ten butterflies alighted, one at a time, upon my ten bare toes.

Entertainment was provided, gratis, by monkeys and baboons. The first time we passed an acacia whose branches were swaying with monkeys, I grabbed a water-level limb, lay back in my boat, and studied a family of colobus. There were seven of them, each covered in silky black fur that I'd have loved to run my hands through, their faces framed in white and ornamented with Santa Claus beards. They performed a circus act's worth of improbable, inconceivable leaps, at times accompanied by burpy roars. When one colobus determined that I'd overstayed my welcome, it plucked a few seeds off the acacia and hurled them at my boat.

An hour later I was parked beneath a wide-limbed kava tree, where a troop of savanna baboons had been resting. When they saw me coming, rather than race to the topmost branches, like the colobus, the baboons dropped to the forest floor. The largest male in the 20-member troop displayed both his extensive vocabulary—a bark, a grunt, two screeches, and a growl—and his lipstick-red genitals. He determined that I was not a threat, and led his troop back into the tree. When everyone had reached an appropriate perch we embarked upon a lengthy staring session, which endured until the big male stood up, stretched, and then crawled onto a limb over my boat and urinated on me.

As I floated off, I waved good-bye; two of the smaller baboons, I swear, waved back. I convinced myself that I'd imagined this, and didn't record the incident in my journal until three evenings later, when Bruce revealed that he, too, had been waved at by a baboon.

On the first few days of the trip, when many of us were still learning to maneuver our crafts, we covered only a dozen or so miles. Mornings and late afternoons the weather was pleasantly temperate; midday, however, the equatorial sun often microwaved me into catatonia.

Initially, the heat was mitigated by taking long swims in the river. Many of us did this. Then, on day four, our swims abruptly came to an end. As I emerged from a dip, it occurred to me, for the first time, to ask Raymond and Thomas why they never swam.

"Because of the crocodiles," Thomas replied, speaking French. Raymond nodded. We'd seen, along the muddy shoreline, several of the unmistakable skid marks where crocs had slipped into the water. Raymond and Thomas had assumed, incorrectly, that those of us who swam had assessed the danger and deemed it an acceptable risk. In truth, we had all somehow failed to put one and one together.

"So there's a chance I could be eaten while I'm swimming?" I asked.

"No," said Thomas.

"Why not?"

"Because crocs don't eat in the water," he said.

"They don't?" I was starting to feel optimistic.

"No. When a croc is hunting, he hits you with his tail. Then he drags you to the bottom and lays on top of you until you are drowned. Then he hauls you to the shore and eats you there."

Our expedition was not a scientific mission. Mike Roselle, the Earth First! cofounder, told me that he considered the trip an "action," which is conservationist-speak for a task undertaken strictly to promote awareness of a larger cause—in this case, to halt the pillaging of the Haut Chinko. Nonetheless, if we wished to convince people that the area should be saved, we had to present compelling evidence that it *could* be saved.

We gathered such documentation by embarking on hikes. The first took place on day two. Around noon, with the heat on the water overwhelming, we tethered our boats to shore and began tromping through the tall grass. Thomas took the lead, wearing his white plastic sandals and floppy hat, his machete tucked under his left arm like a baguette. The pointer finger of his right hand fluttered at his side, acting as a sort of subconscious compass needle, indicating the direction in which he thought we might find animals. Raymond followed,

Kalashnikov at the ready. We pushed at the grass until we discovered a game trail, which we followed until we came upon a clearing.

Here, Thomas knelt down and gestured for us to do the same. He pinched his nose, drew in a breath, and made this . . . noise. It was a strange, trilly sound—the closest I can come to a transliteration is *Muick! Muick! Muick!*—that seemed to reverberate through the forest. It's a curiosity call, Thomas explained, one that has been passed down through generations. Practically every animal that hears the cry is drawn to it, even snakes. Silently, we waited for a minute. Nothing. Thomas called again, and there was a rustle in the grass and we all swiveled our heads and caught a momentary glimpse of the rear end of a yellow-backed duiker, a small African antelope. But that was all.

In Thomas's mind, the Chinko was still as it was in his youth—a place teeming with game—and he could not disguise his bitterness at what the poachers had done. "It's strange," he whispered. "I feel like I'm in an abandoned garden." Still, there were reasons for hope. During the first hike we saw tracks of elephant, hippo, bushbuck, and forest hog. Thomas's expertise was such that he could reliably estimate how many animals had passed through a particular area and how many days old a certain track was—fundamental information that could determine whether the Haut Chinko should be given up for lost or safeguarded for rebirth.

Bruce typically strayed toward the rear during these excursions, and I often followed him. When Bruce is walking, his elbows and shoulders and hips pantomime a sort of belly-dancer motion—the constant readjustments of a person wrestling against a bad back. He is six feet three inches tall. His hair, black and unbarbered, has achieved a degree of curliness of ramen-noodle proportions. A walrusy mustache partitions his face; he hasn't shaved it, he said, since it began to grow 34 years ago. Every day on the river he wore a set of surgical scrubs decorated with cartoonish, multicolored crocodiles.

Tailing Bruce in the wilderness was like witnessing a piece of performance art. On day six, after we'd floated south into a more temperate zone of mixed savanna woodlands, I followed Bruce for 15 minutes and vigilantly recorded everything he did. During this span, he picked four species of fungi and carefully sniffed each one. He reached into a tree to pluck an intriguing fruit, patterned like a soccer ball, and then cut it open with his knife and took a nibble. He pointed out an attractive arrangement of lichen on a kapok leaf, and an aesthetically pleasing orchestration of vines garroting a fig, and the faint hoofprint of a duiker. He came upon a pile of lion scat that resembled a mat of hair one might fish from a clogged drain, then poked his forefinger into it, attempting to discern which type of animal had been ingested. Upon spotting a column of army ants, he wondered, aloud, whether he could actually hear them crawl, and then kneeled to find out. He could. He discovered a wild lemon tree and proceeded to fill his pockets. He pointed out three colobus monkeys squatting silently on a branch, and when I remarked that I couldn't tell the difference between colobus males and females he looked at me with an expression of utter earnestness and said, "Then you probably shouldn't go to dances with them."

My Waterloo with the killer bees took place the next afternoon. The topography in the Chinko basin is fairly flat, and when we came upon a decent-size hill during our hike, Bruce, Rick, Randy, Chris, and I decided to scale it, in order to take in a panoramic view. Thomas and Raymond and the others remained at the base to rest.

I was the first to reach the top. I removed my pack and stood on the summit rock. Immediately, bees began landing on my face. By this point, I'd become habituated to such things—it was a hot day, and the bees wanted to gather my sweat. I knew that if I didn't swat at them, they wouldn't sting me.

This time, though, was different. These bees had not come to gather. The first sting, into my right cheek, surprised me, as did the second and third. By the time I thought to react, I'd been stung five times. My instinctive response, unfortunately, was the wrong one. I covered my face, trapping more bees. I was promptly stung five more times before I hatched a plan: I needed to get my head net. This, too, was a poor idea. As I groped blindly in my pack for the net, I was stung another five times, all on my face. I could hear nothing but the sound of bees. My head gonged with pain. I started to panic.

Randy had been climbing behind me. He witnessed what was happening, and shouted what seemed like the obvious thing to do, except that in my frenzy I hadn't thought of it. He shouted, "Run!"

And that is what I did. I ran. I ran over boulders and bushes and termite mounds. I ran as fast as I could, down the side of the hill, and after a minute or so there were no more bees. The swarm had let me go. Judging from the number of stingers in me, I'd been nailed 22 times in less than a minute. If I'd been even mildly allergic to bee stings, I probably would have been killed. And I still had to retrieve my pack. I borrowed a head net from Randy and put an extra pair of socks over my hands, but I was still stung three more times during the rescue. The attack was, without question, the most frightening minute of my life.

It retained its ranking for two days. The event that surpassed it happened on the river. I was alone in an inflatable kayak, drifting along the right bank, a little comatose from the sun, when I noticed an unusual assemblage of rocks on the shore. The transition from rocks to hippopotamuses was swift and startling. There were four of them—two big ones, two smaller ones. I was maybe 50 feet away. I snapped out of my reverie and glanced downstream to read the current. It would sweep me quite close to the shore, near the hippos, and then carry me back out to the center of the river.

At this point, I had two choices: I could paddle out of the way and almost certainly disturb the hippos, or I could remain absolutely still and attempt to slip past them. I selected option two. I braced myself against the sides of the kayak. I didn't so much as breathe. Silently, I broadcast all the most positive and peace-loving hippo vibes I could muster. I was 40 feet away. Then 30. It was at this point that the largest of the four hippos opened his eyes. He raised his dinosaur head and rotated it slowly in my direction. I was still moving toward him. We locked eyes.

I was raised wrong regarding hippos. When I think of hippopotamuses, I think of George and Martha, the hippo characters in a series of children's books that, as I recall, I absolutely worshiped. Martha wore a purple tutu, if I remember correctly, and both hippos walked around on their hind legs. In truth, hippos are the meanest sons of bitches in the forest. Seriously. Don't be fooled by the vegetarian diet. A male hippo can weigh four tons, and his bite can sever a 15-foot crocodile. Actually, if you want to use the correct terminology, you don't get bitten by a hippo—you get "stapled." Among African game, hippos are the number one killer of humans, responsible for as many as 200 fatalities per year.

The big hippo and I stared at one another for maybe three seconds. During this time, it seems, I was judged unfavorably. The male let out a sound like a high-pitched foghorn and suddenly four hippos were up and in the water, and four very large wakes were headed straight at my boat.

I'm not exactly sure how I managed to escape. There was something of a fireworks grand finale going off in my head, endorphins and peptides and adrenaline pumping through my system. I was still on silent mode. I didn't muster so much as a yelp. Rick was in the cataraft behind me, and he told me later he'd never seen someone backpaddle a kayak faster. Evidently, I reversed into the middle of the river, and when I looked up I saw four hippo heads still bobbing near the bank, looking at me with what appeared to be unmitigated disgust. Then they disappeared. I never saw them again.

These incidents were aberrations. Overall, my 19 days on the Chinko were perhaps the quietest of my life. Bruce encouraged silence on the river, so that wildlife wouldn't be spooked, and so that we could hear the buzz saw of the cicadas, and the boom-echo of distant thunder, and the baby-toy squeak of the crocodile, a sound wholly at odds with the animal's ferocity. I never wore a watch—we rose with the sun and slept with the dark. Except for the hikes, our days were mostly slow-moving and lazy. It was nice. My mind was open to sensory stimulants, but not deep interpretations. I saw dragonflies whose coloring was so emphatically red that they must've burned my retinas, for when I close

my eyes I can see them still. I experienced rainstorms of such intensity
that each drop's splash lofted high enough, if you were in a kayak, to
get you wet again. I spotted pastel-colored orchids as delicate as
origami; I saw crickets that could have tried my shoes on for size; I witnessed a school of silvery fish perform a seemingly choreographed jeté.
I composed epic-length poems, more or less nonsensical, every line
rhyming with Chinko.

It was only the tsetse flies that disrupted our idyll. They'd come in
gangs, often while many of us were napping, and stab without warning. It was quite amazing. A pre-bite female tsetse (only females bite)
is sleek as a cigar tube, with veiny, wax-paper wings. When the bug
lands, its wings sit flat on its back like an open pair of scissors. You
don't feel a thing. If you're not paying strict attention, it's too late. With
its abdomen stuffed like a blood sausage, a post-bite tsetse looks like a
crimson zeppelin struggling to gain altitude. That's your blood in there,
you realize, and the sight of it in someone else's abdomen perturbs
you. Then you see another tsetse blimp. And another. Killing one now,
you realize, is a waste of energy. Still, you do it. Your palm comes away
sticky with plasma. It makes you feel better, but only a little.

At night, we'd typically set camp in a tight circle of pup tents—"our
village," Thomas called it. Dinner was dehydrated food we'd brought
with us, a dozen different varieties, most of which tasted like wood
chips. Afterward, we'd hold court around the campfire. Bruce's preferred tales involved macabre emergency-room stories (the woman
who accidentally lobotomized herself with the tip of her fly rod was a
favorite), or trips that went unexpectedly wrong (it seems he is constantly walking all night to get back to the trailhead). Personal questions, though, were deflected by Bruce with a flurry of amusing asides,
and even a query as direct as his marital status was left unclear.

Bruce, I came to learn, has developed an internal logic that is simultaneously airtight and counter to almost everyone else's sense of nor-
malcy. He does not like music—any kind of music, with the possible
exception of classical. He's been known to walk into friends' homes
and turn off the stereo before saying hello. He has not been to the

movies in almost ten years. He has never owned a television set. He traveled the Chinko with no fewer than 21 hardcover books.

He loves to ski, but never at ski resorts. "I'm not inclined toward recreation that involves large numbers of people wearing bright clothes," he told me. He is, I believe, a failed misanthrope—one who has the great misfortune of being adored by almost everyone he meets. (Not long ago, he was named Jackson's Citizen of the Year.) He is pacifistic nearly to the point of irrationality. When an ant nest materialized in the pocket of his life jacket, rather than rinsing it out he protected it with almost parental concern. He kept track of the number of different species of moths that landed on his paddles and the types of spiders that were attracted to his tent fly. Once, when I accused him of killing tsetses, he scowled and said, "No, I'm just stunning them."

A nagging concern, over the first two weeks of the trip, was what the Chinko's rapids would be like. Such is the nature of an unknown river. Bruce had somehow acquired a set of Russian spy maps of the Central African Republic—Chinko, on the maps, was spelled "Illukho"—and on these sheets, where rapids supposedly churned, were a series of slashes. The slashes were a source of much speculation. What did they mean? Were these riffles? Waterfalls? Would we have to portage for miles? By the 14th day, the Chinko was more than a quarter-mile across and bounded by patches of closed-canopy rain forest—and that's when we came upon the area that matched the first set of slashes.

The rapids were large. The water progressed in a series of increasingly virulent waves, culminating with a ten-foot drop. Class III at least, probably Class IV. Thomas took one look at the white water and assumed we'd portage. The ten Americans held a vote. It was unanimous: We'd attempt to run them. "This is a very serious sport," said Thomas, his eyes as big as pinballs. He left the group and began walking through the forest, heading downstream of the rapids. "I don't want to get my gun wet," said Raymond, clearly rattled. He trotted off to join Thomas.

My kayak partner was Mike Roselle. Mike, who is 45 years old, is possibly the most dedicated environmental activist in the U.S. He has been arrested during actions more than 40 times, and once spent the better part of four months in prison for draping a banner that read "We the People Say No to Acid Rain" across Mount Rushmore. He lives in Berkeley, in a yurt whose only furnishing is a futon mattress he found on the street. "I've been married four or five times," he told me, "though only twice legally. " He looks, as much as a human is able to, like a sea lion. His diet on the trip consisted of Slim Jims (he brought a hundred from home) and Marlboros. His slapstick joviality in times of duress singlehandedly kept the group from each other's throats. Raymond and Thomas revered him. Thomas's sole request for a souvenir, in fact, was a large, framed photo of Mike: "I want to hang it in my house," he said, "so that I can be sure I'll laugh at least once a day."

Mike and I were perhaps not the wisest of pairings, although we didn't know this until we were very much committed. We attacked the first set of waves with brio, our strokes in sync, the boat neatly perpendicular to the whitecaps. Then something happened. As we came closer to the drop, we began drifting sideways, imperceptibly at first, and then, all of a sudden, quite noticeably. In an effort to correct our position Mike and I both paddled furiously, which might have solved the problem, only we were paddling in opposite directions. At the edge of the lip we were completely sideways—the worst possible position. There was nothing we could do. We went over.

Boaters sometimes use the term "May-tagged" to describe what happens to a kayak that is poorly situated at the bottom of a waterfall. It is an accurate verb. Remarkably, though, when our kayak was ejected from the hole and the churning ceased, I was still in the boat. It took me a moment to realize that Mike was not. I looked around and saw him bobbing in a nearby eddy. The evening before, around the campfire, Bruce had mentioned that crocodiles are particularly attracted to eddies in rapids, where it is relatively easy to troll for fish. Two frantic strokes and I was at Mike's side. I lifted him by the lifevest straps, dumped him ingloriously into the kayak, and we were safe. The other teams made it through without incident.

• • •

That was it for rapids. It had been an unusually rainy summer and the Chinko was running near flood stage, which smothered the remaining rapids into little more than ripples. We completed the final hundred miles in less than four days. This turned out to be a good thing. While it's true that we gelled as a group—we instantly formed bucket-brigade lines when unloading gear; we gave one another unfortunate haircuts—individually, I believe, we started to disintegrate. Even Raymond, our personal Rambo, came unglued. On the morning of the 16th day, I awoke to a crazed shriek. I peered out the tent and saw Raymond running through camp, arms flailing, head swaying. He ran to the fire and put his head so close to the flames I thought he was attempting suicide. It turns out that a bee had flown deep into his ear. Thomas had tried to fish it out with a match-stick, which worked exactly as well as you can imagine. Bruce eventually located a pair of tweezers and removed the insect, but from then on Raymond began wearing a head net, which is not the best accessory for someone attempting to exhibit a tough-guy demeanor.

In the final days, the malaria started kicking in. With malaria, though, it is sometimes hard to tell which is worse, the disease or the prevention. Lariam, the most common anti-malarial medication, triggers a peculiar psychosis in some of its users. The medicine is ingested once a week, and for most people the side effects consist of one night of strange and sometimes unpleasant dreams. Brian, on one of his Lariam days, leaped out of his tent and ran about camp warning everyone that we were being invaded by baboons. We were not. Lariam delirium got the better of Chris, and one evening he began speaking in tongues, pacing back and forth and spouting gibberish and then, occasionally, writhing on the ground. It got so disturbing that Bruce eventually had to tranquilize him. Chris seemed dazed for the better part of a week.

The finish, however, was as fine as we could have imagined. During the entire journey we did not see any poachers, or any people at all, in fact.

Our first encounter—an elderly man in a hooded robe, staring mutely in disbelief—came as we floated into the village of Rafaï, which consists of a few dozen mud huts tucked amid tropical trees. We were told that we were the first visiting white people, except for a missionary, since 1964. Rafaï is one of the towns that has been terrorized by poachers, and when we mentioned we were on a mission to help put an end to the poaching, a village-wide celebration ensued. Grapefruits and papayas were plucked from trees. A cow was slaughtered and barbecued. We were handed generous servings of *ngbako*, a sinus-clearing moonshine made of honey, cassava, and corn.

A xylophone of papaya logs was assembled, drums were produced, and the local musicians began pounding out a hypnotic beat. A full moon rose in a cloudless sky, and I began to dance, we all did, the whole village did, and the music was rapture in my head and the ngbako made my body feel as light as a bird's, and I knew with absolute certainty that if I could have been anywhere on Earth at that moment I'd have chosen to be right where I was.

In the morning Bruce called CAMCO on the satellite phone, and a plane came and landed on a dirt strip and took us back to Bangui. We spent a week in the city, meeting with government ministers, presenting our findings and outlining a possible solution. The Chinko, Bruce explained, is fully savable. There is no industrial giant trying to tear it apart, there are no humans to transplant, and most major species are still in existence. In the course of our hikes, we had observed enough tracks to conclude that poachers had exterminated only giraffes and rhinoceroses. Sufficient wildlife remained, Bruce predicted, so that if poaching were halted immediately the area could reach sustainable population levels in as little as five years. With a moderate expenditure—build a few roads along the Sudan border, arm a few units of soldiers, have an airplane occasionally fly over—poaching could at least be dramatically reduced. The animals would return, and the Chinko would again become one of the richest wildlife areas on the planet. It's really not more complicated than that.

Uncomplicated, though, does not mean easy. Even if all funding and materials were provided by private groups, the cooperation of the Central African Republic's government would still be essential. And in the CAR, political instability is virtually a given. Take our experience in Bangui, for example. All the ministers we met were excited about our trip, delighted with the protection plan, willing to do whatever they could to help. They were going to talk to the president, they said, and tell him of our findings.

A week after we flew home, every minister was abruptly fired, without explanation. The situation in Bangui had intensified; another coup seemed likely. Bruce, however, was unfazed. The Haut Chinko, he told me, was too precious to allow political uncertainty to destroy it. He planned to take matters into his own hands. Next year, during hunting season, Bruce is determined to return to the Haut Chinko and meet some poachers himself, face-to-face, to see if he can broker a deal. Only Bruce could come up with a notion even more foolhardy than our river trip, and possibly more fascinating. A few weeks ago, he called and asked if I'd consider joining him on this second trip. I didn't hesitate. I told him I'd go.

from The Indian Alps and
How We Crossed Them
by Nina Mazuchelli

Struck tents this morning as soon as we could arouse our poor weary people, who lay huddled together under the rocks, each with his blanket round him, and often a stone for his pillow.

The messengers we sent to Yangting so long ago have neither overtaken us with supplies of food, nor followed us with tidings as to why the Kajee has so miserably failed us. Great and hourly increasing depression, therefore, reigns in camp, and the poor coolies have lost all their natural exuberance of spirits. We are besides very unfortunate in the weather, which adds not a little to our discouragement. A great deal of mist is hanging about the higher ridges—a very inauspicious thing for our march through deeper snow, which we shall have to encounter to-day on the heights. I take care this time not to go on in advance of F——, but keep near him, our attendants and ourselves forming one continuous line.

For a considerable distance we passed beneath a mountain, which effectually shut out the west as with a tremendous battlemented wall;

down the side of which we saw a frozen cataract, whose waters, gradually congealing as they fell, had formed themselves into icy shafts and columns, clearly distinguishable even at this distance, fully a mile away.

We now begin to ascend the steep face of a mountain, following carefully the footsteps of our Guide, and zig-zaging to render it less steep. Heavy masses of vapour continually roll past, now enveloping us completely, and then dispersing for awhile, affording glimpses of clear blue sky, which helped to raise the spirits of us all, giving hope of a bright day for the remainder of the march. At length it dissolved entirely, and the sun showed himself, a well-defined disc of mellow fire, out of the darkest blue sky I ever beheld, for at this elevation the azure becomes almost purple in its intensity; and then Junnoo, clad in his glittering mantle, the one object above us, towered majestically heavenwards. How wonderfully near it looked! We could even see the crystals sparkling in the sunshine, and I felt more than ever, with Alpine pictures in my memory, how utterly impossible it is for human hand to represent, as it is for mortal speech to express, the purity and loveliness of snow.

Not only were we ourselves elated by the glorious sight, but our men also; and the fact that we had at last reached the snowy range we had travelled so many weary miles to visit, sent a thrill of satisfaction through our hearts. The novelty of the scene, too, seemed for awhile to make us all forgetful of one great anxiety. Moreover, were we not to reach Yangpoong at the end of the day's march, and be within reach of food?

Being now in very deep snow, we have to be careful to follow the footsteps of our Guide, and of the goodly number of coolies who have preceded us, lest by forming a new track, or even one contiguous to it, we inadvertently mislead the remainder of our camp, and cause them to lose their way—by no means an improbable result should the mist again surround us.

A little further climb, and we find ourselves on the summit of an extensive and slightly concaved plateau, hemmed in on all sides by small snow-clad peaks, through which jagged portions of madder-tinted gneiss are visible, and over which the unsullied Junnoo, its head now shrouded in mist, reigns supreme. As far as eye can reach stretches one livid field of snow, so vast that we feel quite lost amidst it, the colourless waste apparently seeming interminable; yet not colourless either, for each undulation along our pathway casts its pale blue shadow, sharp and well-defined, and there are exquisite gradations of light and shade everywhere, to rob it of an absolute monotony.

Across this plain we march quickly, for, the snow being deep, all irregularities of surface are smoothed over, and it is too hard to clog the feet. What an exhilarating sight it is, to watch the coolies with their loads hurrying along in single file!—their various and many-coloured costumes contrasting strongly and vividly with the white world around, against which they stand out in bold relief, whilst at almost every instant some amusing adventure occurs, to call forth peals of laughter from Nautch-wallah and the merry Lepchas, and in fact from the whole party. Now one man falling, hammers the ice with his head, the contents of his basket scattering themselves hither and thither in every direction. Now another is seen idiotically sliding forwards, endeavouring to clutch the air to save himself, and of course failing in his endeavours, with the usual result. Then Tendook himself, walking solemnly and sedately by my side, is suddenly seen to submerge, as he falls into a hole, where nothing is seen of him but his head, pigtail, and little round Chinese cap with its scarlet top-knot, and whence he has to be dragged out, unhurt I am thankful to say, but with no small difficulty.

We now begin to lament bitterly the loss of our dark glasses, the light reflected from the snow already affecting our eyes most painfully. Some of the baggage coolies, I observe, are provided with these necessary preservatives of the sight, wearing spectacle made of yâk's hair finely plaited.

The elevation also is again beginning to tell upon some of us. A little further on and we overtake C——, who, sitting down in a state of utter collapse, is apparently suffering from vertigo. I, too, have a return of palpitation of the heart and laboured breathing; others feel intense pain in the head, attended with nausea; but F——, with the exception of feeling very tired, seems happily quite himself.

Hitherto the glare had not been at all greater than we had anticipated; but soon we were enveloped by a semi-transparent mist, through which the sun, like a ball of fire, could be distinctly recognised. The light became so intolerably dazzling as we proceeded, that we could neither see before nor around us. The very atmosphere itself seemed to vibrate and be composed of floating spiculæ of snow— glittering atoms, through which the sun appeared a great scorching eye, most painful to gaze upon.

The effect of the glare upon our sight was greater now than I have power to describe, and the effort to keeping the eyes open such torture, that they were streaming with enforced tears. Had there been but a particle of blue sky, we might have found relief, but this dazzling mist which enclosed us, seemed but to serve as a corradiation for the sun. We had all, of course, heard of snow-blindness; but anything so distressingly painful to the sight as this we never had imagined. The poor coolies who had not provided themselves with spectacles, taking off part of their clothing, now cover their eyes, and lunge along almost blindfold. Following their example, we do likewise, only uncovering the eyes now and again, to assure ourselves we are in the right track; then for one instant only can we discern the baggage coolies in advance, and all is darkness as before. At length a time came when we could not see our way at all, and Tendook, who was near us, having called a halt, Catoo stooped his head almost to the ground as he endeavoured to discover whether there were any footprints in advance of us; but to our dismay he declared there were none, and it consequently became but too manifest, that we had deviated from the right track.

It was an anxious moment; but, after some search, the path was traced by marks of blood in the snow, which some poor fellow whose feet the ice must have sorely cut had left behind. We, therefore, retrace our steps for a short distance, and, opening my eyes for a moment, I recognise our host being led by one of the coolies, overcome with blindness as well as vertigo.

Not a little discouraging was it to find him—the strongest of our trio, on whom we one and all so greatly depended—give in thus; but had this fearful state of things lasted much longer, we must all have thrown ourselves down upon the snow, and awaited our fate, the sight of each becoming worse and worse every instant. We were rapidly losing even the momentary glimpses of surrounding objects which we had had previously, almost total blindness seizing us for the time being. At length my bearers, declaring themselves too blind and giddy to carry me, set me and my dandy on the ground, without further ceremony. But, happily, just as we were beginning to despair of being able to proceed on our journey, the mist began floating away, and, to our inexpressible relief, the sky showed itself above as an opaque and vast purple dome overshadowing us.

Then gradually, and by slow degrees, we regained our sight. One by one distant objects became visible, the sombre purple affording incalcuable rest to the eye; and we now find that we have almost traversed the snow-field, and that a steep ridge of black rock is shutting us in northwards, and, oh joy! beneath this, we recognise our Guide and advanced party awaiting us.

Anything like the intense relief this rock afforded us, wearied as we were with the field of glistening white, cannot be conceived by those who have not similarly suffered. It was truly like the 'shadow of a great rock in a weary land,' and I doubt whether this beautiful simile, so often made use of, was ever so applicable even to travellers in the scorching desert as to us at that moment, whilst the feeling of security, in once more finding ourselves in the presence of our Guide, was scarcely less inspiriting. On reaching this spot, we climbed the ridge, and found we were standing on what appeared to be a gigantic snow drift, the snow which had blown hither for ages having lodged against the rock, until it had become almost as hard as adamant itself.

It was a sight worth immortalising in deeper tablets than those, alas! of memory, and one which an artist would have gone far to paint. The trackless wastes of snow throwing into relief the picturesque figures, some of whom were standing in groups, whilst others reclined upon their loads. There is an unconstraint and natural grace in all Orientals, whether dwellers in the plains or hardy mountaineers, and they often pose themselves in attitudes which are perfectly statuesque, of the beauty and dignity of which they are themselves, of course, wholly unconscious, but which makes one long to tarry and portray them.

Here we rest awhile, and C——, now quite himself again, tries to dilute some cognac with snow for the general benefit; but, instead of its becoming amenable to our necessities, and melting as we naturally expected it would do, it refused to liquefy, and instantly transforms the spirit into a solid lump of ice! Whilst halting we try to gauge the depth of the snow with our alpenstocks, which are seven feet long, but do not succeed in reaching the bottom of it; we also make some deep holes, and the colour of the snow, on looking into them, is that of the most perfectly exquisite and liquid azure it is possible to conceive.

The order to resume the march being now given, the coolies take up their loads, and the Guide, looking more sinister and Mephisthophelean than ever, precedes us. A steep ridge has to be descended on the other side. This descent Tendook and C—— resolve to accomplish by sliding down like two schoolboys, an example followed by many of the baggage coolies, with various results; whilst others, rashly attempting a glissade, get overbalanced by their loads, and may be seen in all directions tumbling head over heels to the bottom of the descent, where they are eventually picked up more frightened than hurt, but with a complete dislodgment of the contents of their baskets. My dandy, however, is ingeniously converted by Catoo into a kind of sledge for my behoof but F——, as an old and experienced Alpine traveller, wisely decides to do the thing scientifically or not at all and, planting his alpenstock firmly in the ground, determines upon descending by a series of dignified leaps. Hatti had just given my sledge an impetus, and I was proceeding in my downward career as satisfactorily as could be desired, when half way I caught sight of F——, who, benevolently turning round, bade me 'hold on' whatever I did. But the effort proved too much for him. He first made one desperate and agonising grab at the snow, then felt for some mysterious hand in mid-air to save him, and heeled over, reaching the end of the declivity in a more rapid manner than he had anticipated; whereupon, once safely landed, I made a pencil sketch of him, which, out of regard to his wishes, I forbear to introduce here—a waste of genius, for which he is wholly responsible!

Then journeying on over the same kind of snowfield out of which rise jagged peaks a few hundred feet above us, and which hem us in completely, I cannot help mentioning to F——, who is walking by my side, that this seems quite unlike what we imagined the approach would be to Yangpoong, which is a yâk station, about the height of Singaleelah; here, on the contrary, we seem surrounded by perpetual snow. He, too, says he has been marvelling, and that we seem rather to be travelling right in the midst of the splintered snow-covered rocks, above the line of congelation, which lie at the west base of Junnoo, and which from Darjeeling appear like the uneven teeth of some animal. There was another circumstance also that struck us as very extraordinary, viz. when we began the ascent this morning, Junnoo was not only close above us, but we were slightly to its left—that is to say, *west* if it rather than east—in which latter direction we imagined we should have to journey to reach Yangpoong. Major Shirwell's map is in C——'s possession, but no doubt hidden in the depths of some portmanteau, for since we had been under the leadership of a guide, we had hardly consulted it, trusting him implicitly.

Following the camp in single file—for we too are far behind C—— to talk with him on the subject—we are once more shrouded in mist, and this time the sun entirely disappears. Still we plod on, wondering if we shall ever begin to descend the long-wished-for Yangpoong, when suddenly there is a halt called from the front, and overtaking C—— we learn, to our horror, that the line of men who went on in advance of us is nowhere to be seen.

Accustomed to call each other from mountain to mountain, these nomad tribes have a peculiar and prolonged cry, that may be heard from a great distance—this they now sustain for a considerable time; but still no response reached us from our missing people. Again another shout, louder than the first, followed by a breathless silence, and then the unwelcome conclusion forced itself upon our minds that we must have wandered considerably from the track.

A proposition was then made to fire a gun, trusting that its report might reach them as a signal of distress, and induce them to return to our help. Accordingly, C——, advancing some paces, fired his rifle in the direction which we believed they must have taken, although it was more than possible that we had lost our bearings entirely by this time.

At the same moment the brave Tendook, penetrating the mist, went off himself to endeavour to find the track. Most of the coolies laden with tents and stores happened to be amongst the number of those in advance, and the harrowing thought at once suggested itself to our minds that if *they* had also lost their way, and we ourselves managed to reach our destination in safety, we should be in a sad plight, without either food or shelter in these dreary wilds.

I do not know how long we remained in this terrible suspense, for one cannot estimate such periods by time, which loses all proportion when one is tormented by such agonising fears, and when each moment seems to stretch into a whole lifetime. Thoughts of what might be our fate came crowding thick and fast, every possibility rising before us. At length we heard the muffled sound of voices, and the shadowy form of Tendook appeared, bearing the cheering news that our Guide and party were returning; and the little spectral band were soon visible through the darkling mist.

Once at our side, we ascertained that, having lost all sight of us, they were already endeavouring to retrace their steps when the report of the rifle reached them; but our joy and relief, alas! were doomed to be but of short duration, for they gave us the discouraging intelligence that our Guide knew no more in what direction the village of Yangpoong lay than we did ourselves!

At this announcement, cutting off as it did the possibility of our reaching that place upon which we had set our longing hearts for so many weary days, a panic seized the whole camp. The Lepchas, relieving themselves of their loads, sank down upon the snow, and burying their faces in their hands in mute despair, appeared to have given themselves up as utterly lost in a way that was very heart-rending to witness.

Not so the Bhootias, however, most of whom stood erect in excited groups, with looks bold and defiant, talking together, but not low enough to prevent our hearing that they were blaming *us* for having brought them hither, 'where,' as they said, 'they must starve and die,' not seeming to realise that we ourselves were in the like danger. Nor did they hesitate to imply that we had purposely so brought them; whilst the impulsive and child-like Nautch-wallah, standing apart from the rest, lifted up his voice and wept.

At that moment we were completely in their power, and, had they chosen, the whole camp might have broken out into open mutiny. As for ourselves, we felt like shipwrecked mariners in an ocean of snow; but neither gave utterance to the fears which possessed him, as, having summoned Tendook, whom we feel to be quite one with us in this terrible emergency, we took solemn council together as to the best thing to be done.

'Are you sure you don't know at all where we are?' enquired C—— of the guide, whom he summoned to our side.

'We are now in the district of Yangpoong, Sahib,' he replied; 'but in this mist I cannot take you farther, for I know not in what direction the village lies.'

It was then suggested that several detachments of coolies should be sent down the hollows, in different directions, to ascertain whether any camping ground could be found, where wood might be obtained; but this was soon discarded as extremely dangerous. The coolies might fall over precipices, and the risk to their lives was far too great to justify our subjecting them to it, even were it probable—which it was not—that a place of the kind could be found sufficiently near to enable them to return with the intelligence before nightfall.

It was then proposed that we should encamp where we were; but this proposition was as quickly dismissed as the previous one. Not a particle of wood was obtained, and without fires we must all have become frozen before morning. Moreover, it was very doubtful whether tent-pegs could be made to hold in the snow; and besides all these discouraging considerations, it seemed to be threatening for a snowstorm. There was that peculiar feeling in the atmosphere which usually precedes snow in lower elevations; and if it should come, and our track hither were obliterated, we might wander for days over these mountains without food or shelter, and must inevitably perish.

The suggestion therefore of halting here was, for various reasons, at once abandoned. Very palpable signs of insubordination were beginning to manifest themselves, not only amongst the Bhootias, but the Nepaulese also, to which we dare not shut our eyes, whilst the Lepchas were taken possession of by those notions of fatalism which render them quite powerless in times of danger.

These symptoms more than aught else determined us upon taking decided action of some sort; and whilst F——, C——, and Tendook were parleying on the feasibility of our pushing on, with the hope of getting out of the mist, and once more ascertaining our bearings or remaining in our present position awhile, trusting to its clearing away, I realised the situation and all its terrors. I felt that not an instant should be lost. To travel further into the lonely heart of these mountains with the mere possibility of discovering our whereabouts, or lingering where we were on the miserable chance of the mist clearing, would alike be running a tremendous risk. What if it should not clear? What if, in the event of its doing so, our Guide—in whom we have now lost all confidence—were unable after all to indicate the direction of Yangpoong? It would be too late then to retrace our steps while daylight lasts. With a woman's natural instinct I believe I arrived at the only safe course to pursue.

'Let us return at once; don't hesitate for a moment,' I cried, stamping the snow with my foot in my vehemence. 'It is the only thing to save us.'

After a few moments' solemn and earnest consultation—there was no time for more, for evening was approaching—they yielded willingly to my proposal; the men were informed that we proposed retracing our steps, and encamping at the very first place where we could discover wood. It was truly a neck-or-nothing kind of thing to do; we had come thus far in quest of food, and were now to relinquish all hope of finding it. At that moment, however, we could hardly heed the future, the present was all we dared contemplate.

For one instant a terrible pang shot through me. Was I destined to be the means of bringing sorrow on others? *I would come:* these three words pierced my very soul like a red-hot iron. Had I been less anxious, the expedition would not have been undertaken at all. I thought of C——'s wife and his little children; I thought too of my mother and her letter of warning, on being informed of our proposed tour:—'I dread your travelling in a mountain region so little known to Europeans, and so far removed from civilisation. Do not attempt too much, and, above all, avoid the many dangers to which you will be exposed by travelling in the region of perpetual snow. Rest satisfied with the lower levels. I think you are rash in attempting to explore so vast and unknown a country.'

The announcement of our decision was received in various ways: by some few, with signs of satisfaction, by others with surly and ill-suppressed mutterings, but one and all seemed unwilling to resume their loads. We had been leading them on, day after day, with the assurance that at Yangpoong they would find sustenance; it was no wonder, therefore, tired and disappointed as they were, they should lose pluck and even confidence in our words, and we felt that nothing we could now say would inspire them with hope for the future.

The gentle Lepchas remained in the same position, scarcely lifting their heads when this last propostion was made. In common with Mahomedans and Hindoos, they entertain a blind belief in *kismut* (fate), and having once made up their minds that a thing is inevitable, they will endure it with an indifference that is perfectly stoical; but there was fearful despair written in some countenances notwithstanding, and it needed all the energy and decision we could muster, and every argument we could think of, to imbue them with the courage necessary for beginning another weary and hopeless march.

Wandering in and out amongst the groups of baggage coolies, with my own hands I helped some to lift their loads, endeavouring at the same time to arouse others who had relapsed into a state of lethargy, trying to speak words of comfort and encouragement to all; feeling that if *I*, a woman, set the example of exertion, there was enough chivalry existing in the hearts of these poor ignorant creatures to make them not only obey but help me. F——, C——, and Tendook, meanwhile, by exercise of authority, were doing *their* share amongst the Bhootias and Nepaulese, which answers far better with these tribes than simple persuasion, and in ten minutes' time every load was resumed, and their faces turned in the direction whence we had come.

Then followed a scene of such dire confusion as I shall never forget. Some of the more reckless and headstrong of the coolies began rushing madly forwards, quite regardless of the track. But C——, alive to the danger this threatened, was in pursuit in an instant; whilst Tendook, whose voice was so seldom heard, now loudly and sternly commanded them to remain stationary until everyone should be ready for the start. All were then made to advance in single file, C—— heading the camp, I coming in the middle, the faithful Tendook by my side and F—— bringing up the rear. Feeling something like the force of military discipline, they now became more orderly; but it was not without violent efforts, and alternate scolding and encouragement, that we succeeded in urging our poor footsore fellows onwards with their burdens, from the weight of which, in their weakened state, many seemed to be sinking. In several places, too, our path was made sadly conspicuous by marks of blood, as they plodded slowly along.

Although suffering greatly from difficulty of breathing, I tried to make light of everything, bidding them remember that if *I* were not despairing for the future, they who were men should not be so either. With the same purpose I made the mountains echo with many an assumed laugh, at every little adventure by the way, in which even the Lepchas who were near me, forgetful of all for the moment but their love of fun, tried to join. By such small subterfuges did we strive to relieve the tedium of the march; but they were, after all, such a sorry and sepulchral counterfeit, that we soon relinqueshed them, for they seemed to relapse into greater sadness than before. How completely sanguine we had been on starting in the morning! but how had all changed! Our day-star of hope had given place to an evening of utter despair.

At length, as we went on, the mist grew less dense, and yonder, straight ahead of us, about two miles distant, we recognised the rock beneath which we had halted on our way hither, thrice an oasis in our desert now, for we thereby not only knew that we had not mistaken the track, but that being once reached, we should be within a very few miles of our last camping-place. I shouted to F—— behind me, but he had already caught sight of it himself, and there ran a murmur of general satisfaction through the whole length of our long line. It was like an electric shock, and had the poor fellows been less weary and sorrow-stricken, I feel sure they would have got up some kind of cheer.

To the phlegmatic Tendook I exclaimed, 'We are saved!' But he, less impulsive than I, after a short pause, deliberately, and as I thought sorrowfully, replied, in the concise and epigrammatic style of all these Eastern people, *'Jism fani aur ruh baki hai, mem sahib'* ('The body is mortal, the soul is immortal') . . .

Arctic Discovery

by Lawrence Millman

Lawrence Millman (born 1948) took a canoe trip on the remote Meta Incognita Peninsula of Canada's Baffin Island with an Inuit guide who promised to show him something extraordinary. The guide kept his promise—and Millman was enlightened as well as surprised.

In travel, as in life, context is everything. It's not likely that anyone would pay much attention to a traffic jam in Manhattan, whereas a traffic jam in Tiniteqilaq, East Greenland, would be a remarkable event, maybe even a disturbing one. For there are no roads in Tiniteqilaq. No cars, either.

I've never actually witnessed a traffic jam in the Arctic. But I have set foot on an arctic beach, Labrador's Porcupine Strand, which was as perfect as any beach featured on a travel poster . . . except, of course, for its dead whales. And the best tan I've ever gotten did not come from the usual tanning zones in the Caribbean, the Greek isles, or the Pacific; it came from the Greenland Ice Cap.

Context, I've learned, has a way of making the ordinary seem extraordinary.

Last summer I found myself in the Arctic again—this time on Canada's Baffin Island. Accompanied by an Inuit guide, Peter Tunnillie, I was canoeing a segment of the Soper River on that island's remote Meta Incognita Peninsula.

River trips usually put me in mind of Huck Finn paddling the murky Mississippi or Thoreau enjoying a gentle meander on the Concord or Merrimack. But this one did not call up such comfortable literary associations. For the Soper is neither murky or gentle. Nor does a single human being live along or even near its frigid 60-mile course.

River trips also call up images of vines, creepers, and lavish flora for me. But the country on either side of our canoe seemed nearly as bare as an old golf ball. It bore this bareness with rock-ribbed dignity, however. Greenery you can always get in the facile tropics, it seemed to say: I can offer you naked geology such as the earth itself possessed when its crust was first squeezed into shape. As I silently regarded this geography, Peter said: "There's something really interesting I want to show you."

"What's that?" I asked him.

"Oh, I can't tell you now. It's a surprise. But you'll find out soon enough."

My mind raced through the possibilities: Perhaps Peter had discovered the skeletal remains of Martin Frobisher's so-called "Five Missing Men"—five crewmen who disappeared on this peninsula while serving on an expedition with Frobisher, a sixteenth-century arctic explorer. Or maybe there was a group of uncontacted Inuit somewhere in the vicinity. Or maybe a significant archaeological site . . . But he merely shook his head, smiling mysteriously, in response to my questions. After all, this was supposed to be a surprise.

When we put ashore for lunch, I gave Peter some dried whale meat I'd gotten a week earlier in Iglulik; he gave me some of his noodle soup. *Qallunaaq* (white man) and Inuk, we seemed to be moving inexorably toward the other's diet.

Later we walked inland a short distance. I gathered some small, reddish mushrooms which, according to Peter, the local lemmings use as an aphrodisiac. Then we visited a lapis lazuli mine that'd been abandoned many years ago. Scattered over the ground was a veritable mosaic of dusky blue lapis gemstones.

I asked Peter if this unexpected beauty was in fact his surprise. He shook his head again. It wasn't.

Now we returned to the canoe. Shortly after we moved on, I began to notice caribou by the hundreds browsing the mossy banks along the river. They would lift their heads and stare at us with utter bewilderment, as if they'd never encountered non-antlered beings before.

This wasn't the surprise, either. For Peter knew that I, as an old arctic hand, had seen plenty of caribou in my day.

Immediately after we negotiated a series of loops in the river, Peter pointed to a lofty escarpment in the distance. "See the rock that looks like a woman with a baby in her *amauti?*" he said. "Just below it is where we're going."

Putting ashore again, we began to hike toward this woman-shaped rock. The suspense, I admit, was killing me. I tried to remember if any of Sir John Franklin's ill-fated crew had ended up on Baffin Island . . . or if I'd read about an endangered species which nested, denned, or burrowed in these parts.

We hiked into a valley where the vegetation seemed altogether luxuriant compared to before. I saw the gossamer tufts of arctic cotton, Lapland rosebay, harebells, saxifrages, moss campion, and several different types of berries. Meanwhile, hordes of mosquitoes were mobbing my every pore, even probing the eyelets of my boots.

At last we arrived at a clump of arctic willows not quite ten feet high.

"There!" Peter exclaimed triumphantly. "The only trees on Baffin Island!"

Over the years I had seen plenty of trees, of course. But to find trees in such hard country—even stunted, minimal trees like these—seemed to me almost unimaginable. In fact, I was as surprised by this wisp of a forest as I would have been by a herd of caribou on Boston Common.

"Photo?" Peter asked. I nodded and handed him my camera.

And now, over a year later, the picture he took occupies pride of place on the bulletin board above my desk. It shows me standing in front of a tangle of branches that look not unlike chickenwire. On my face is an expression of distinct astonishment.

How, friends ask me, can you be astonished by such a seemingly ordinary scene?

Context is everything, I tell them.

Upland Stream

by W. D. Wetherell

Exploration doesn't always occur on the wind-blasted ice of the Arctic or in the deepest jungles of the Amazon. Writer and fly-fisherman W. D. Wetherell (born 1948) makes discoveries in the woods near his New Hampshire home.

There can't be too many places in the world where it's possible to stand in all four seasons simultaneously and be uncomfortable in each. The hills above my home are one of them—the oddly beautiful, oddly tortured New Hampshire hills of granite and spruce, brook trout and beaver, bogwater and Frost. By late April the snow is almost gone there, though enough remains to trap, squeeze, and soak heavy boots. The leaves, last autumn's crop of them, lie in slick matted heaps on the forest floor, their red and gold blended into an amber in-betweenness with the treacherous texture of mud. The sun, with no shade on the trees, burns even faster than in July. The wind, the thawing vernal wind, slaps back and forth like a wet towel, adding a chill in your middle to go along with the chill in your toes. Add a few precocious blackflies, potholes of slush, and some fresh tangled blowdowns and you have a pretty thorough set of variations on one masochistic theme. Come spring and the start of the trout season I would be nowhere else.

It's Copper Run I'm talking about here, the small upland stream I've come to love in the course of five years' fishing. Never wider than ten feet, never deeper than four, it drains a small unspoiled corner of New England woods, leaching as it does so all the beauty to be found there, so that it becomes the liquid, flowing locus of the surrounding hills. Seldom visited, it's possible to walk along the banks the better part of a day without coming upon any human trace other than a rusty bolt or tinny water can dropped by a logger fifty years before. Not in every pool but enough to make it interesting there are trout—miniature brook trout that seem in their color and quickness to be essence of stream, spontaneously generated, living crystals of orange and black. To take even a single six-incher—for one short moment to be attached to something so vivid and alive—is reason enough to suffer the multiple discomforts of the April woods.

There are more mundane reasons, of course. The need once the weather warms to bolt from the prison a house can become. The need to justify the new graphite rod I treated myself to at Christmas. The need after a long winter's writing to be out and questing after something besides words. Around the third week in April these things reach their peak, and it only takes a gentle, triggerlike pressure—a surge of sunlight? geese returning? a southerly cast to the wind?—to make me shed the last of my inertia and make the five-mile migration that separates a Copper Run longed for and imagined from a Copper Run stood beside and real.

Last April's trip could stand for any. There was the busy rummaging in the closet for leaders and flies, the casual "Think I'll try a few casts up on the mountain" to a knowing Celeste, the raid on the refrigerator for nuts and oranges, the hydroplaning, swerving ride up our dirt road that in mud season passes for driving—the abrupt dead-end when the ruts became frozen and the joyride stopped.

The stopping point varies each year, but I'm usually left with an uphill walk of at least a mile. On this trip it was a little more than that; I made it to the frozen pond where the deep woods begin, parked on an icy pull-off, pushed my rod into a rucksack, and started off on foot.

It had been a hard winter, and the earth in the middle of the road was still in the process of turning itself over, lined with the stiff petrified creases that are, I suppose, the earthy equivalents of groans. There by the marge the ground was softer, potted with moose prints. I've seen moose here in the past on their journeys from pond to pond—great lumbering browns wearing a look of perpetual bafflement, as if they can't quite figure out who or what they are or whether they should care.

At about the same time the hardwood starts giving way to spruce there comes a perceptible flattening as you emerge on the height of land. There's a bridge here, nothing more than a rude corduroy, and it's possible to walk right across it without realizing a trickle of water flows beneath. Leave the road—follow the trickle through the first tangled briars—and in less than twenty yards you come to the start of Copper Run proper at the towering Gateway Arch.

I call it this quite deliberately for the drama of the May evening I discovered it. Celeste was pregnant, and in the course of one of our evening walks for exercise we crossed the corduroy bridge on our way to a small pond whose star attraction, besides its wildness, was a resident loon. I had my rod with, me, of course; I caught perch in the pond's shallows as Celeste readied our picnic and poured out our tea. After dinner, curious, I left her admiring the sunset while I walked back to the bridge and followed the trickle upstream to see if I couldn't find where it began.

It began in a beaver pond, as it turned out, and a big one; on the far shore, framed by the fingers of dying tree trunks, rose the gray bulk of Slide Mountain, emphasizing the vastness even more. There were insects hatching everywhere; between their rings, the wake left by the resident beaver, and a slight evening wind, the surface of the pond buzzed with as much activity as Lake Sunapee on a weekend afternoon. I managed to balance along the beaver dam to a place I could cast, but if there were trout in the pond they were occupied elsewhere and I soon gave up.

So back to the bridge then. Back to it—and then off into the woods downstream. I'm not sure what prompted me to do it; it was close to dark and the stream was more shreds and tatters than a definite flow. But the future has a magnetism all its own, and there in the twilight, in the mountain stillness, with the sensitivity toward omens even a vicarious pregnancy brings, I was more attuned to it than usual, and it would have taken a deliberate act of violence not to have given in to its pull.

"Just a little way," I told myself—the old indisputable justification. There by the bridge the bank was all briars, and it was hard enough to make any way. Since the future not only tugs us but shapes us into the correct posture to meet it, I was bowing my way (a low, reverential bow) through a particularly bad tangle when the watery tatters suddenly gathered themselves and changed from a pedestrian pewter to a rich, luminous copper; the effect was that of stepping into a sunset turned molten. At the same time, or perhaps a split second earlier, I noticed a darkening overhead, and looked up to see the branches of two white pines meet high above the stream, forming with their intersection a perfect proscenium or arch.

A Gateway Arch—the expression came to me the moment I saw it. It wasn't just the perfection of the framing, the changing color, but how both came embellished with a roll of drums—with a deepening and staccato-like increase in what had been until that moment nothing more than a vacant gurgling. Just past the arch, where color and sound were richest, was a small pool formed by the junction of two smaller streams—the outlets of the two ponds already mentioned. Waving my rod ahead of me like a Geiger counter—like the antenna of a probing ant—I shook my Muddler down into the pool's center, letting it sink toward the sharp rocks that lined its sides. Immediately there came a pull, and then a moment later a six-inch brook trout was splashing across my boots, sending up a little shiver of happiness toward my neck. I let him go, then tried another cast, this time a little farther downstream. Again, a six-inch trout, this one even deeper-bodied and more brilliantly speckled, with a soft coppery cast on his back that seemed the water's undertone.

I caught six trout in all that first evening, each a yard or so downstream of its predecessor. In the twilight, in my twilight mood, it was

clear they were deliberately tugging me deeper into the woods, the better to ensnare me in their enchantment. After the sixth I broke away
and waded back through the darkness toward the bridge. By the time I
rejoined a worried Celeste (who knew my Hansel-like susceptibilities
well enough), the experience had settled just far enough for me to realize I had stumbled upon what in flinty New England terms was a vir-
tual Shangri-la.

Something of this surprise, something of this ceremonial quality is
still present whenever I go back to Copper Run, and never more than
on that first April trip after a long winter away. Again, I slip and slide
my way from the bridge through those deceptively small riffles; again,
I bow through the hoop of briars; again, the arch of pine forms overhead, and then, after a quick clumsy cast, my fly line is uncoiling down
across the coppery water in floating *N*'s and straightening in a tug—*two*
tugs, the first as the Muddler swings tight in the current, the second as
a trout takes hold with what can only be described as a hearty hand-
shake of welcome. And just as the arch seems to beckon me each time,
so too when I've passed under the branches it seems to seal me in. Back
beyond the arch is noise and worry and confusion and doubt, but this
side of it—stream side of it—there is nothing but that shiny, exuberant
mix of rapid, riffle, and pool, and no requirement upon me but to
align myself with its inspiration and let the current lead me down.

So into the water then—away from the snow and slush and bad
footing and directly into it, frigid as it is. The banks along this first section are too steep and heavily forested to balance along, and there's no
alternative except to wade. I'm dressed for it, of course. Woolen under-
wear, wool pants, silk liners, heavy socks. For shoes, I wear old sueded
boots from my rock-climbing days, with hard toes and heels that
absorb all the bruises and enough insulation to hold the coldness at
bay . . . at least in theory. In actuality, with the water in the forties, my
toes lose their feeling about every fourth cast, and I have to climb my
way out of the stream and stamp up and down on the nearest boulder
for a good five minutes before the feeling is restored.

By the time I've fished through the first pool, if I'm lucky, I've caught my first six trout, perhaps even the same friendly sentinels that were there the evening I discovered it. By about the fourth one I begin to relax. Behind all the anticipation and excitement that lure me here each spring is a darker emotion: the nagging worry that something terrible will have happened and all of it will be gone. Copper Run, the dancing water, the iridescent trout—all gone. It always takes an hour of being immersed in it—of feeling those twin chills merge, the coldness of the water and the happy shivers transmitted by the trout—before my doubts finally vanish and I let myself wholeheartedly believe.

Below the entrance pool the banks taper together and the water drops between rocks in three distinct runs. They come together again at the bottom, then fan out across a broad shelf of granite into a second, slower pool. The water is darker-looking here, deeper, with large mossy boulders that absorb the sunlight rather than reflect it. A good place for trout, only there aren't any. I fish it each time to make sure, but never once have had even the suggestion of a nibble. Is it too exposed to otter and heron for a trout to be comfortable? Is there some hidden interplay of current that disturbs their equanimity? Or is it just that Copper Run trout are too cranky and original to place themselves in a place so obviously suited to their well-being? If nothing else it gives me something to think about, and lets me know the easy successes of the first pool won't be duplicated on the same lavish scale.

As pretty as it is, the first hundred yards of Copper Run are pretty much a warm-up for what comes next. The water spills from the fishless pool in one of those terracelike steps that are so characteristic . . . churns itself over a few times for good luck . . . then deepens to form a bowl that is so perfectly round and so tropically shaded it's impossible to look at it without thinking of Gauguin.

If Copper Run is essence of mountains, essence of woods, then this pool is essence of Copper Run. I've spent entire afternoons here trying to separate out all the strands that go into making it so perfect. The smell is one of them; besides the wet leaves, the thawing earth, there's a sharper, more acrid smell that is metallic and not at all unpleasant. The trace elements, I decided—gold and silver tinges scoured by water from rock.

A short way beyond the tropical pool a small tributary seeps in. I say *seep* quite deliberately—it's a damp, spongy wetness more than a definite flow, and it doesn't appear on any map. Copper Run itself *is* on the map, but only as a thin scrawl between contour lines, with only the most approximate relation to its actual course. It's too small to register properly; its improvisational, quicksilver meanderings are if anything anti-map. Were I the cartographer in charge of the New England hills I would acknowledge its chanciness, slap a Gothic *Terra Incognita* over the entire height of land, and let the curious and energetic go about discovering it on their own.

Which, in my stumbly fashion, was exactly what I was trying to do. The truth is that despite the visits of five years, I still had only the haziest notion of Copper Run's course. I knew where the water started: the combination of ponds there behind me on the ridge. I knew where, via a larger river, the water ended: an old mill town beside the Connecticut twenty miles farther south. But the things that happened in between— the twists of its channel, the dark woods it traversed, the possible waterfalls, its junction with larger streams—were for a long time as unknown to me as the headwaters of the Orinoco.

This was not due to any lack of curiosity on my part—quite the opposite. The water I came to seemed so rich in possibility that each yard deserved an afternoon of admiration to itself. My trips were of pilgrimage, not reconnaissance; each pool had to be sat beside, admired, and fished. What with revisiting the familiar pools and lingering over the new ones, about three new pools per visit was the fastest pace I could manage and still get home before dark. Add the fact that between bugs and low water I only visited Copper Run in spring and autumn— add a dozen tributaries that in their miniaturization and mystery were just as alluring—and you can see I had set myself a question mark the erasure of which was beginning to seem a lifetime's work.

That was my resolution for last year: to increase the tempo of my exploration, to force my pace downriver, to learn before spring ended where Copper Run came out. There would be less time spent exploring each pool, less time to fish, but a labyrinth has its own charms, and I was trying to focus back on it to reach some comprehensive understanding of the whole. I knew the spill where the water surged across a fallen hemlock, grooving the wood until its grain seemed to ripple; I knew the falls where the water washed sideways off a mica-flecked cliff; I knew the spots where the spray kicked high enough off the boulders to wet my face, the best fording places, the pools most likely to hold fish . . . and now it was time to thread these beads together in a necklace to marvel at, fasten, and share.

And if I was proceeding downstream in a pleasant geographical blur, I was proceeding in a pleasant historical blur as well. I knew little about the history of Copper Run, though there was little enough history to know. The stone walls that marked the limit of the early settlers' audacity—the stone walls that climb even Slide Mountain to heights awe-inspiring and tragic—end well below Copper Run. Even the surveyor's tape that dangles everywhere in the woods now, fluorescent and mocking, has only reached the fringes of this notch. Between these two limits—the patient, backbreaking husbandry of the past; the easy, land-grabbing mentality of the present—Copper Run sits like a lost world, removed for a good century and a half from the curse of events. The trees grew, then someone cut them, then they started growing again, and all along Copper Run danced its way south, oblivious to any imperatives but those of gravity.

Our exhaustive town history contains only one story from the height of land—the story of a woman who spent her life in the woods as her father's unpaid assistant in a small logging operation. The older people in town can remember seeing her drive a wagon full of logs past the common to the Connecticut—a straight-backed woman who teetered between proud dignity and shy wildness and never lingered long enough for folks to get to know her. I've seen her grave, the last one in a cemetery where everyone else had been buried seventy years before. It stands alone in one corner beneath some birch; in its simplicity, in its apartness, it could stand for all the solitary lives that have escaped history's record.

She died in 1957—more than thirty years now. In the decades since probably the only big thing to hit Copper Run have been the Vibram soles of my size-twelve boots, stirring apart the moss on rocks that are as old and untroubled as any on earth. Seen in those terms, I was an invasion—a whole new chapter in what so far had been, as far as man was concerned, a relatively blank book. This placed upon me a certain responsibility; it was up to me, in my short visits there, to conduct myself in a manner befitting an explorer—not an explorer hot for commerce, but an explorer out to record what he had found as faithfully as he could, the better to understand the hidden, threatened beauty of this one fragile place.

So what did I find there? What justified those afternoons along its banks that could have been more usefully spent writing short stories or splashing paint across the barn? What was the payoff for those icy immersions? All pretty stuff, but what—a skeptical Queen Isabella might ask—does this newfound land contain?

Pygmies. Bush pygmies eking out a precarious existence high in a forest remote from man. Copper Run trout, to complete my metaphor, are small, not stunted; independent, not docile; shy, but not so shy a properly placed bauble won't lure them from their haunts. Like mountain tribes, they are splendidly suited to their habitat, and have the happy knack of taking on its qualities—not only its coloration but its very element, so that catching a Copper Run brookie is like catching and holding a condensed length of spray.

And since it is pygmies we're talking about here, it's best to dispose of the size question right at the start. An average Copper Run brook trout is six inches in length; a good one, eight inches; a monster, nine. By the time you've adjusted to the miniature pools and miniature riffles, say fifty yards in, the scale has begun to right itself and you understand what a genius Einstein was when he spoke of relativity. In an eddy twelve inches deep, a six-inch trout takes up a not inconsiderable space; in a shadowy forest, it's copper richness is not an inconsiderable source of light.

There's another thing to keep in mind: small is not necessarily easy.

The trout come willingly enough to a fly, but they're quick, quicker than the current, and it takes near-perfect timing to connect. Then too, for all their innocence, these fish are not gullible rubes; a trout that strikes and misses will not come again. Add to this the sheer difficulty of placing a fly on the water—the protective overlay of blowdown and branches, briars and boulders—and you have fishing that is as challenging in its small way as any other.

For the fly-fisherman, this goes right to the heart of the problem: the chore of keeping your backcast free of the trees. After an hour and perhaps fifty collisions, it hardly seems like casting at all, but a particularly vexatious form of air traffic control; you spend more time looking back over your shoulder than you do looking in front, and any cast that manages to uncoil without hitting branches seems a pretty successful flight. Take a day of this, and you will be left with the illusion you haven't fished the water at all but the air, and your dreams that night are apt to be laced with hemlock-dwelling trout that mock you with their inaccessibility.

I've learned the hard way not to fight this, but to incorporate the obstacles as part of the challenge. Rather than bring a hundred flies along and moan each time one is broken off, I now bring only two— a Muddler and a backup, thereby assigning a definite limit to just how clumsy I can afford to be. I usually manage to snap off the first one by the third or fourth pool, but you'd be surprised at how long that last one stays on. I've climbed my share of Copper Run trees, plunged my hand deep into pools to work feather out of bark, and even occasionally twisted a hook from my earlobes, but never once have I headed home early for the lack of a fly.

The two-fly limit has another happy effect: it simplifies the process, and simplicity is what this kind of fishing is all about. All fishing, both sport and commercial, has about it something of a complicated hide-and-seek, but small-stream brook trout fishing—the fishing that fascinates me—retains the hide-and-seek quality in its most basic, childlike form. Mountain trout spend their lives hiding in an environment that is perfect for their concealment, and what I find so compelling and

interesting in fishing for them is the trick of waving a fly across the
water and thereby finding out exactly where they are. The fight, the
actual landing—for fish this size, none of that counts. It's the first flash
I'm after—the brief but exquisite pleasure that comes when a swirl of
water swirls suddenly faster and a life from out of nowhere firmly tugs
you, shouting "Here!"

In some pools the trout are just where they're supposed to be—the
satisfaction is the smug one of knowing their hiding places so thor-
oughly. In other pools the hiding places are there, but not the trout—
my smugness stands chastened. It's beyond these, in the unexplored
water downstream, where the game becomes most interesting. That
plinth-shaped rock in the current's fringe—there should be a trout
right in, front or right behind. Is there? A careful cast, the fly landing
perfectly, the current sweeping it down . . . No. That log aslant the bank
with the deep pocket along its head. There? Yes! and a good one, all
splashing iridescence, to be brought quickly to my feet, defeathered,
and urged gently home.

Once this simple curiosity is satisfied, there's room left for a whole
complicated superstructure of conjecture and wonder. Why do Copper
Run trout seem to migrate with the seasons and in a direction reverse
to what you might anticipate, heading upstream when the water turns
colder, downstream when it warms? What autumnal hint triggers their
color change, when their copper deepens toward crimson and their
spots take on a vivacity that makes even maple leaves seem dull? Why
does their size seem to diminish the farther from the road you go? Why
will they smash a dry fly and not rise, at least perceptibly, to a living
insect? Why this, why that, and then suddenly I've raced through three
new pools and some pretty connecting water, and my wondering has
run away from me and I find a dry, sunny spot to climb out of the water
and rest.

There are several of these resting places along the stream—flat,
grassy terraces just big enough to admit my outstretched body, slanted
so I can stare at the water while flat on my back. Removed from the ici-
ness, plied with oranges, I am free to devote myself, for a few minutes

anyway, to one of those vast metaphysical questions that only occasionally seem worth the asking. Why, if I am so enchanted with the sheer beauty of this stream, must I bring along a rod and reel in order to fully appreciate it? Why can't I just stroll down its banks in simple adoration? Why, when you come right down to it, fish?

There's a teasing, quicksilver-like quality to Copper Run—like any stream, the moment you try to grasp it, it's gone. And so too with any question posed on its banks; the best you can hope for is a partial, impressionistic answer that leaves in the air as much as it settles. Still, fishing for brook trout on a small mountain stream is about as simple and pure as the endeavor becomes, so that motives stand out with a clarity they lose in bigger, murkier waters.

Why fish? Leaving out on one side the obvious reasons like being outdoors and the healthy exercise, and leaving out on the other side the complicated reasons of blood lust and the ancestral promptings of our watery origins, I think I can begin to find the beginnings of an answer. It has to do with the exploring I mentioned earlier—that ritualistic, challenging version of hide-and-seek. Fly-fishing is the only means I have to enter into the hidden life of a stream and in a remarkably literal way, so that if my cast has been a good one and my reflexes sharp, that life—through the energy of its fishy emissary—pulses up a taut leader through a taut line down a curved rod to my tensed arm . . . to my arm, and by the excitement of that conveyance to my heart. A fishless stream might be every bit as beautiful as Copper Run, but it's the fish that whet my curiosity, stocking it with a life I need to feel to understand.

Discovery, and the vicarious thrill that comes with having my surrogate self—my Muddler, Royal Wulff, or Cahill—go swimming off through a pocket of rapids, being at one and the same time an extension of my nervous system and an independent, unpredictable agent of free will. Like *Alvin*, the tethered submarine guided by cables through the *Titanic*'s wreck, the fly answers our commands and does our probing; in some mysterious, sympathetic way we *see* through our fly and understand the water better beneath it than we do the water we're actually standing in twenty yards upstream. That little back eddy near the alders, what's under it? Sweep the rod to the correct angle and our surrogate drifts over and checks it out. That granite reef sunk beneath the brightness? Shake some line loose and our surrogate plunges down.

Our nerves are transmitted to a tethered cell of tinsel and feather— that and the added, exhilarating bonus of knowing any second we may be jumped . . . that our surrogate selves are liable to be eaten. Anyone who compares fishing to hunting has got it backwards; it's the thrill of *being* hunted that gives fishing its charm. For the few seconds our lures swim beneath the surface we recapture the innocence—the dangerous, stimulating innocence—of the days when man walked the earth not as master but as prey. It was, it is, a dangerous thing to be a human, and we need to be reminded from time to time not only of our abstract mortality, but of a mortality that springs from ambush and clamps down.

Why fish? Notes toward the start of an answer, not the answer itself. In this resting place, beside a small ribbon of water on a fine April day, it's the best I can do.

I balance my way onto a rock in the center of the current and begin casting again. With the sun going down, the chill more penetrating, it's time to admit something I've tried to keep from my story as long as possible. The fact, the sad inescapable fact, that Copper Run is threatened, and by the time you read this its miniature perfection will almost certainly be gone.

This will come as no surprise. Here in the last decade of the Twentieth Century it has become a given that something beautiful is something threatened. A beautiful marriage, a beautiful custom, a beautiful place. We cannot admire any of these without hearing a meter in the background ticking off borrowed time. If that something is remote, fragile, and cherished, then it is doomed even more—there are garbage dumps on Mount Everest, for instance, and the Borneo rain forest is being ground into pulp. Our century has extracted its share of payment over the years, payments social, political, and environmental, but not yet the full amount. The day of reckoning is approaching, and before it, like a glacial moraine, comes the huge debris of extinction, this heavy, pervasive sense of doom.

We're a race of Cassandras now, not Pollyannas, and I have no wish to gloss over the facts. For the corner of New England woods I love the threat is quite simple on one hand, quite complex on the other. The remote notch Copper Run drains is owned by a paper company that is in the business of selling trees. The trees along Copper Run, the trees that entangle my backcasts and darken the riffles, are fast approaching a marketable size. All winter long, as I sit typing, trucks roll past my house loaded with logs. It is too much to expect that none of them will be from Copper Run. The vague uneasiness I experienced last April was not without reason; here spring is approaching again, and yet when I think of returning I feel not anticipation but only dread.

This is not the place for a lengthy discussion of the pros and cons of timber management. Timberland, at least for the time being, is land not being developed or macadamized, and in this part of the country the paper companies have traditionally allowed public access to the woods. Still, any organization whose sole raison d'être is greed cannot be trusted to do anything except be true to that principle on any and all occasions.

As it turns out, I know the man who owns the company that owns Copper Run, at least by sight. He's in his fifties, balding, of average height and weight, fond of wearing the rumpled chinos and flannel blazer of the perpetual Ivy Leaguer. He doesn't appear particularly greedy; occasionally, I'll hear him joking with our postmistress when I go to pick up our mail. It's hard, looking at him, hearing him laugh, to connect his appearance with my happiness—to know at a word from him, at a tuition bill due for his son, some ready cash needed to float a new deal, a political contribution to be made, Copper Run and all its treasures could in the course of a day disappear . . . disappear, and that were I to protest, the whole weight of law and custom is there behind him to prevent any appeal.

And yet he looks perfectly harmless; he even drives a car smaller than mine. At night when I drive past his house all the lights are on in every room—every room, every light, no matter how late it is, and I feel a hollow spot in my stomach when I see this and know with a certainty beyond reason that Copper Run is doomed.

Taking the long view, I can reconcile myself to this, at least partially; cut forests eventually grow back. But it's another characteristic of our age that the threats come shot-gun style, so that even if you dodge one projectile, there are enough left to cause serious damage. The threat of development, constant road building, the dangers posed by the warming of the atmosphere and acid rain . . . all these make cutting seem positively benign. Even my own walks along the banks must be included in the dangers; as careful as I am, as gently as I bring them to hand, there are trout that die when you hook them, and the loss of even three or four good fish a season, in an environment so fragile, is the equivalent of a major kill. Like Steinbeck's Lenny, that animal-loving fool, we can hug the things we cherish until they die.

But here's where the complexity enters in. Just as there is a real Copper Run faced with real, mortal dangers, so too there is an abstract Copper Run faced with dangers that are abstract but no less mortal. I refer to the relentless, vicious attack on the beautiful that is going on all around—an onslaught so widespread and successful the only conclusion to draw is that its goal is the destruction of the very notion—the very *humane* notion—of Beauty itself.

Like the environmental dangers mentioned above, you can make your own list. The brutality and trivialization of popular culture; the abominations posing as architecture; the not-so-coincidental fact that the richest society the world has ever known is also its ugliest . . . all you have to do is look out the window. And though on one hand a sterile glass box designed for the entrapment of a thousand office workers in Indianapolis, Indiana, would seem to have very little to do with the fate of an upland stream in the New Hampshire woods—the mindless, flickering images these office workers watch with their children on a glass screen when they go home even less—the connection is a direct one, it being, when it comes to Beauty, one world after all.

For if Beauty dies in the mass, how can it be expected to live in the particular? How can I possibly describe to that caged-in, image-drugged man sitting there in Indianapolis what a hemlock twig looks like spinning its way down a Copper Run riffle—how the reflected sunlight welling up from the bottom enlarges it so the needles drift within their own delicate halo? How can I explain how a Copper Run trout, held against the palm in the moment before its release, will send a shiver through you that for one fleeting second reconciles you to everything? How to explain all my love for this? How?

A person who writes for a living deals in the raw material of words. And, like rivers, mountains, and forests, words themselves are under attack, so that even the means to describe the desecration are fast disappearing. The gobbledy-gook of advertising, the doublespeak of bureaucracy (*beautification* for something made uglier; *restoration* for something lost), the self-absorbed trendiness that passes for literature; the sheer weight of illiteracy . . . again, the wretched list. Words like *lovely* and *fragrant* and *natural* have been inflated so far out of proportion they form a kind of linguistic freak show where words that were once suggestive of all kinds of richness now mean something grotesque. Emerson's "Every word was once a poem" becomes, in our century, "Every word was once for sale."

Again, the connection to Copper Run may seem a subtle one, but again it is simple and direct. For the devaluation of words makes for a devaluation of the things words describe and sets up a vicious circle from which there is no escape. With fewer words left to describe our Copper Runs, it becomes harder to justify saving them; as the Copper Runs vanish, the need for a language to describe them vanishes as well.

To a writer—to a dealer in raw materials—a polluted, unreliable source is the worst of calamities. But while the assault on words is every bit as depressing as the assault on the environment, at the bottom is to be found a strange kind of exhilaration, at least for those with the spirit to fight back. For perilous, degenerate times put a great responsibility on those who care for what's threatened, and endow their actions with a significance that is not just symbolic.

Here is where the link between these separate conservations

becomes clearest—the conservation of Copper Run, the conservation of Beauty, the conservation of words. For just as the world has seen the wisdom of creating refuges that are as far as possible removed from the hand of man, the better to protect the lessons of untrammeled life, so too should writers seek to create a refuge of words where notions of Beauty and joy and solitude will endure in the very heart of a despoiled language, so that even if the worst happens and our methods of expression become as vacant as our method of living, there will still be books and stories and descriptions to go back to so we can see exactly what has been lost—so we can see these things and so there will remain a gene pool from which Beauty might flourish once again.

I spend my life writing fiction; among other things, it presupposes a certain ability of imagination. If I could, I would have no scruple in making Copper Run imaginary, giving it a make-believe course through make-believe woods protected by make-believe laws in a kingdom of my own design. But an imagination that seeks only escape is no imagination at all, and the best I can do . . . the best I can hope for in these twenty-odd pages of celebration and lament . . . is to state the dangers facing Copper Run as simply and directly as language can manage, and thereby protect, if not this wild upland province, at least this wild, upland province of words.

An ending, and yet not the end. For now it is April again, and I have gone back to Copper Run to find it only slightly changed. The trees are a little higher, a little thicker, but still uncut; the trout are smaller, but they seem just as plentiful; the water, while it may be more acidy, still vaults across the boulders in happy leapfrogs, and the sunlight still takes on that grainy, shaftlike quality as you go deeper into the woods. I retrace it pool for familiar pool, moving so slowly there's only time this first trip for a small portion of new water: a bright rapid surging between matching boulders overhung by a giant spruce.

Only one new step, but who knows? Maybe this will be the year I keep my resolution and follow Copper Run to its junction with the larger river to the south. It can't be far, and it's only my enchantment with what I've discovered that keeps me from pushing ahead at a faster rate.

Will I be disappointed to find an ending? I don't think so—well, only partially. For if the Copper Run I love is finite after all and joins a woods road or path I've already traveled, at least I'll have the solace of the pattern's completion. In the end, it's all we can ask of the unknown—that it leads us around at last to the familiar and sets us off on the trek once again.

from This Wild Darkness
by Harold Brodkey

Novelist Harold Brodkey (1930–1996), known

for intensely personal fiction that is by turns dark

and luminous, learned in 1993 that he had AIDS.

Brodkey set off to explore the unknown country

of his own dying, maintaining a painfully open

and lucid journal of the experience. This excerpt

from the journal begins on his 65th birthday

and ends shortly before his death.

Octotber 25, 1995: It is my birthday. And for the first time in my adult life, it matters to me that the age I have reached is a specific number. I am sixty-five years old, but it is not so much that I am sixty-five as the idea of birth and near old age and now death. I do not know at what rate of speed I am moving toward my death. The doctors cannot tell me—the only hard medical fact with AIDS is death. The hard social fact is the suffering. One approaches the end of consciousness—or the end of consciousness approaches one—and strange alterations of the self occur: a hope of cure, a half-belief in treatments that could extend life. (By a year, two years? Three years is so vast a time, one thinks of life as being extended indefinitely if one can hope to live three more years.) The less luck one has, the stronger is one's new conviction in one's luck. This while the doctors back away. They have nothing more to offer. They conserve their energies and the hospital's medical resources, but what it feels like is being locked out of the house when I was six years old. The experience is closer to the early angrier descriptions of AIDS than I had expected it would be for me or others after all these years.

I am sleeping without a detritus of dreams or symbols now, without images, not lions or tigers, not flowers or light, not Jesus or Moses—but a few memories, chiefly of childhood, perhaps because of the night sweats, which I have all day long sometimes. I am rolling down the grassy hill behind the house in Alton. It is twilight. Dark shapes flit in the air—bats, I say now, like a schoolchild answering a question in class. And the birdsong! The pre-DDT birdsong: I had no idea I missed it so harshly. Sing! Chitter! A train travels on the tracks below the cliff, below the limestone bluff. Chug-a-chug, chuff-chuff. The grown-ups sit in those heavy wooden lawn chairs of the 1930s: so still, so handsome. And I, a pudgy child who will not use words yet, this soon after his mother's death, in high-sided shoes and white socks, I am shouting, yelling, in my own sort of birdsong, yelling and grumbling as I roll; stones and pebbles bite into my ribs. I am magnifying my size with the sound I make. Faster and faster I go, then either my father stops me or I curl up against a tree trunk, I'm not sure which.

The change in momentum changed everything, how the light darkened and had a name, like dusk; how the trees and faces emerged and could be named. I remember feeling large from the adventure but small as well, factually small. And because I was in my own mind no one thing, large or small or boy or son of this household, I remember the dreamlikeness of being no one, of being lifted and of being of no important weight. The smells, the grass, my father's shirt—they were more important than I was. I was no one and nothing, about to be devoured by sleep.

I take 300 milligrams of AZT and 300 milligrams of 3TC daily, and my T-cell count is over 100 again. This might be delusive, but I am grateful. I inhale pentamidine about every three weeks. I take between fifteen and twenty pills a day. The cost is astronomical, and so are the fees of the lawyers even when they shave them out of friendship. Tina Brown of *The New Yorker* and Deborah Karl said from the start they would protect us. I don't know if you can understand what such warriors' support means when you are helpless. Kindness always conveys a great deal of meaning about the universe, but perhaps it matters more, shines more brightly, in relation to this disease than to any other at the moment. I think it is because this disease makes an even greater mockery of everything one was before—mentally and physically, socially and erotically, emotionally and politically.

I wish someone would find a cure. I really don't want to die this way. (And I would like to feel my death had some meaning and was not an accident and that it belonged to me and not to those who talk about it.) But at the same time I have to confess that I haven't a great deal to complain about. I often want to go along the street, chanting *Save me, save me, save me*, but I do not do that, partly because almost every act of charity and compassion brings me some meaning and ease. My grandson Harper said, *Are you sick?* And I said, *Yes*, and then he changed the subject. When the visit ended, he made a point of telling me that he liked me quite a lot. I like him quite a lot. He was going off with his other grandfather to Kenya and South Africa for a few weeks. I told him to whisper my name to the grass when he was in Africa, and he very unsolemnly repeated my words and said he would do it.

Today I cannot find anything in my life to be proud of—love or courage or acts of generosity. Or my writing. My life has been mostly error. Error and crap. It seems to have been a load of crap to have been alive. Everything in language goes dead, in a morbid Rockettes march.

I have not been able to work for six weeks, but when I could I was working on a memoir piece about Frank O'Hara, who introduced me to the work of Pollock and Rothko. Today I was thinking about my first sight of a drip Pollock: the paint hardly dry, and the madness and vitality, the quivering beauty, the shock, the immense, immense, freshness.

I remember Chartres in 1949 before the stained glass was restored. No one I had spoken to and nothing I'd read had prepared me for the delicacy of the colors, the pale blue, a sky blue really, and the yellow.

The transcendent theater of the nave while the light outside changed moment to moment—clouds blowing over—and the colors brightening or darkening in revolving whorls inside the long, slanted beams of lady-light. I had never been *inside* a work of genius before.

I have started to die again. I made a recovery with new pills, but then collapsed. I am what is called a disconnector: some measurements of my condition are favorable and others are not, but they move in ways unrelated to one another when they should move conjointly.

I sometimes see in the mirror the strange rearrangement of an adopted child's face in preparation for entering his new household.

I find operatic arias to be very moving now—showy and subtly coarse, technically elaborate, lengthy, embarrassingly detailed and impolitic, un-American, and beyond the hemming and hawing of dialogue.

My dreams are mostly of vacations again and have a still-sweet quality; they even comment on the sweetness of the air and light in the strange, new place where I am a tourist. It is a maybe cheapened version of paradise. The dreams usually end in a gentle drowning, and then I wake.

I ought to have dinner. I haven't eaten or taken my pills—just a little suicide. I mostly live because of Ellen, although I might put on a show if any of the grandchildren were in the apartment. It is unbelievably strange to live when things are *over*, when things are done with. Poor Kundera. It is the unbearable lightness of not-being. What do you suppose an embrace of mine would be worth now?

In New York one lives in the moment rather more than Socrates advised, so that at a party or alone in your room it will always be difficult to guess at the long-term worth of anything. When I first started coming to New York, I was in college at Harvard. This was six years after the end of the Second World War. New York didn't glitter then. There were no reflecting glass buildings but, rather, stone buildings that looked stiff-sided and had smallish windows that caught sun rays and glinted at twilight: rows of corseted, sequined buildings. Driving through the streets in a convertible owned by a school friend's very rich

mother, one was presented with a series of towering perspectives leap-
ing up and fleeing backward like some very high stone-and-brick wake
from the passage of one's head. Advertising flowed past, billboards and
neon and window signs: an invitation to the end of loneliness. New
York was raunchy with words. It was menacing and lovely, the
foursquare perspectives trailing down the fat avenues, which were
transformed in the dimming blue light of the dissolving workday.
Overwhelming beauty and carelessness, the city then—one of the wonders of the world.

New York was the capital of American sexuality, the one place in
America where you could get laid with some degree of sophistication,
and so Peggy Guggenheim and André Breton had come here during
the war, whereas Thomas Mann, who was shy, and Igor Stravinsky,
who was pious, had gone to Los Angeles, which is the best place for
voyeurs. I was always crazy about New York, dependent on it, scared
of it—well, it *is* dangerous—but beyond that there was the pressure of
being young and of not yet having done work you really liked, trade-
mark work, breakthrough work. The trouble with the city's invitation
was that you were aware you might not be able to manage: you might
drown, you might fall off the train, whatever metaphor you preferred,
before you did anything interesting. You would have wasted your life.
One worked hard or not at all, and tried to withstand the constant
demolishing judgment. One watched people scavenge for phrases in
other people's talk—that hunt for ideas which is, sometimes, like
picking up dead birds. One witnessed the reverse of glamour—that
everyone is jealous. It is not a joke, the great clang New York. It is the
sound of brassy people at the party, at all parties, pimping and doing
favors and threatening and making gassy public statements and being
modest and blackmailing and having dinner and going on later. (It
was said you could get anyone to be disliked in New York merely by
praising that person to someone nervous and competitive.) Literary
talk in New York often announced itself as the best talk in America.
People would say, "Harold, you are hearing the best in America
tonight." It would be a cutthroat monologue, disposable with in pass-

ing, practiced with a certain carelessness in regard to honesty. But then truth was not the issue, as it almost never is in New York.

Learning to write: I remember the sheer seriousness of the first acquisition of some sort of public ability, learning something; learning also the fragility of mental acquisition, the despair as this new thing slipped from my mental grasp. You become rigid in your attempt to hold the acquisition; if it stays, or more exactly, if it recurs, others join to it. Perhaps you build your daily life around this oddity. You don't let it go when people talk to you or when fucking or when people tease your deepest attention. *You are a cold person,* people say of this trait.

I am an addict of language, of storytelling and of journalism. I read, not frenziedly anymore, but constantly. I long to love other people's words, other people for their words, their ideas. I do dearly love conversation as a self-conscious, slightly or greatly social climber's art. I love to talk, and I prefer it by a large amount if nothing depends on the talk, not money or sex or invitations—just the talk, like experiments in pure science, or as a funny mix of chemical and electrical investigation that has to be immediately comprehensible—and immediately comprehended—and in which no one can dominate, and dexterity really is all.

Telephoning is a wonderful waste of mind, the vocal do-jiggers, all of it lost as soon as said. And behold the little faxes. The little faxes devour the tender gripes.

As someone who is ill, I feel I have only dubious rights to interrupt anyone else's life, and I try to control access to my own time. I do not like to watch people wrestle with the fact of who I am and with my death and what it means to them, but if one is open about having the disease, such reactions and intrusions are inevitable. I did not really expect to live this long. I do not think I am reasonable, but I do not care if I am reasonable or not.

I have tried some of the new drugs. There is an as-yet-untried one called saquinavir and to get it I entered a lottery for patients with very low T-cell counts, a salvage drawing, I think it's called. I won a lottery once before, in the fourth grade. This time it appears there will be a delay: a special hospital board has been set up to review the lottery and the allotment of the drug—I think it is mostly to prevent doctors from being trapped by sympathy. Or self-importance. There is a rumor that the drug, a protease inhibitor, besides being the weakest of the PI's, is difficult to manufacture. There may well be a shortage and a delay, which means we could all die before we try it anyway.

For me, neurotic (if that word still has meaning) or not, illness had never been a useful reality, never a landscape (or kingdom) of increased sensitivity or heightened storytelling. I remember thinking a year or so ago that if my strength went it would not be possible to think, to write. I have no gift for sickness. And I am not graceful in my dependence.

I did apologize to Ellen once. I said I was sorry, really sorry, to do this to her, to be so much work, and after a rather long pause, she said, "Harold, you were always this much work. All that is different is that I give you meals in bed and I cry when you are in pain. But you were always work."

And I am still writing, as you see. I am practicing making entries in my journal, recording my passage into nonexistence. This identity, this mind, this particular cast of speech, is nearly over.

Late Fall 1995

I am at the end of the list of AIDS drugs to take. I wake frightened now; it is a strange form of fright—geometric, limited, final.

Being ill like this combines shock—*this time I will die*—with a pain and agony that are unfamiliar, that wrench me out of myself. It is like visiting one's funeral, like visiting loss in its purest and most monumental form, this wild darkness, which is not only unknown but which one cannot enter as oneself. Now one belongs entirely to nature, to time: identity was a game. It isn't cruel what happens next, it is merely a form of being caught. Memory, so complete and clear or so evasive, has to be ended, has to be put aside, as if one were leaving a chapel and bringing the prayer to an end in one's head. It is death that goes down to the center of the earth, the great burial church the earth is, and then to the curved ends of the universe, as light is said to do.

Call it the pit, the melodramatic pit: the bottomless danger in the world is bottomed with blood and the end of consciousness. Yet I don't wake angry or angrily prepared to fight or to accuse. (Somehow I was always short of rage. I had a ferocity and will but without rage. I often thought men stank of rage; it is why I preferred women, and homosexuals.) I awake with a not entirely sickened knowledge that I am merely young again and in a funny way at peace, an observer who is aware of time's chariot, aware that the last metamorphosis has occurred.

I am in an adolescence in reverse, as mysterious as the first, except that this time I feel it as a decay of the odds that I might live for a while, that I can sleep it off. And as an alteration of language: I can't say *I will see you this summer*. I can't live without pain, and the strength I draw on throughout the day is Ellen's. At times I cannot entirely believe I ever was alive, that I ever was another self, and wrote—and loved or failed to love. I do not really understand this erasure. Oh, I can comprehend a shutting down, a great power replacing me with someone else (and with silence), but this inability to have an identity in the face of death—I don't believe I ever saw this written about in all the death scenes I have read or in all the descriptions of old age. It is curious how my life has tumbled to this point, how my memories no longer apply to the body in which my words are formed.

Perhaps you could say I did very little with my life, but the *douceur*, if that is the word, Tallyrand's word, was overwhelming. Painful and light-struck and wonderful.

I have thousands of opinions still—but that is down from millions—and, as always, I know nothing.

I don't know if the darkness is growing inward or if I am dissolving, softly exploding outward, into constituent bits in other existences: micro-existence. I am sensible of the velocity of the moments, and entering the part of my head alert to the motion of the world I am aware that life was never perfect, never absolute. This bestows contentment, even a fearlessness. Separation, detachment, death. I look upon another's insistence on the merits of his or her life—duties, intellect, accomplishment—and see that most of it is nonsense. And me, hell, I am a genius or I am a fraud, or—as I really think—I am possessed by voices and events from the earliest edge of memory and have never existed except as an Illinois front yard where these things play themselves out over and over again until I die.

It bothers me that I won't live to see the end of the century, because, when I was young, in St. Louis, I remember saying to Marilyn, my sister by adoption, that that was how long I wanted to live: seventy years. And then to see the celebration. I remember the real light in the room; I say real because it is not dream light. Marilyn is very pretty, with a bit of self-display, and chubby, and she does not ever want to be old like Gramma. If she is alive, she would be in her seventies now; perhaps I would not recognize her on the street.

I asked everyone—I was six or seven years old—I mean everyone, the children at school, the teachers, women in the cafeteria, the parents of other children: How long do you want to live? I suppose the secret to the question was: What do you enjoy? Do you enjoy living? Would you try to go on living under any circumstances?

To the end of the century, I said when I was asked. Well, I won't make it.

True stories, autobiographical stories, like some novels, begin long ago, before the acts in the account, before the birth of some of the people in the tale. So an autobiography about death should include, in my case, an account of European Jewry and of Russian and Jewish events–pogroms and flights and murders and the revolution that drove my mother to come here. (A family like mine, of rabbis, trailing across forty centuries, is a web of copulations involving half the world and its genetic traces, such that I, wandering in the paragraphs of myself, come upon shadows on Nuremburg, Hamburg, St. Petersburg.) So, too, I should write an invocation to America, to Illinois, to *corners* of the world, and to immigration, to nomadism, to women's pride, to lecheries, and, in some cases, to cautions. I should do a riff on the issues of social class as they combine with passionate belief and self-definition, a cadenza about those people who insist categorically that they, not society, not fixed notions, will define who they are. My life, my work, my feelings, my death reside with them.

My own shadows, the light of New York, sometimes become too much now; I pull the shades. I have been drawing spaceships for my grandsons.

I feel very well, and for a week now, as part of some mysterious cycle, I have felt very happy. Also, today, for no particular reason, I am enormously conceited about my writing. Everyone is more interested in my death. I cannot be bothered with my death except as it concerns my books. When I write it out like this, it is a pose, but inside me, it is very real, very firm, this state, very firm for a while. Actually, all my states are now very precarious, just as if I were dancing except that the motion is that of time, or of my time, and it is this time that might, stumble and fall, might seem to—that is what I mean by precarious.

The world still seems far away. And I hear each moment whisper as it slides along. And yet I am happy—even overexcited, quite foolish. But *happy*. It seems very strange to think one could enjoy one's death. Ellen has begun to laugh at this phenomenon. We know we are absurd, but what can we do? We are happy.

Me, my literary reputation is mostly abroad, but I am *anchored* here in New York. I can't think of any other place I'd rather die than here. I would like to do it in bed, looking out my window. The exasperation, discomfort, sheer physical and mental danger here are more interesting to me than the comfort anywhere else. I lie nested at the window, from which I can see midtown and its changing parade of towers and lights; birds flying past cast shadows on me, my face, my chest.

I can't change the past, and I don't think I would. I don't expect to be understood. I like what I've written, the stories and two novels. If I had to give up what I've written in order to be clear of this disease, I wouldn't do it.

One may be tired of the world—tired of the prayer-makers, the poem makers, whose rituals are distracting and human and pleasant but worse than irritating because they have no reality—while reality itself remains very dear. One wants glimpses of the real. God is an immensity, while this disease, this death, which is in me, this small, tightly defined pedestrian event, is merely real, without miracle—or instruction. I am standing on an unmoored raft, a punt moving on the flexing, flowing face of a river. It is precarious. The unknowing, the taut balance, the jolts and the instability spread in widening ripples through all my thoughts. Peace? There was never any in the world. But in the pliable water, under the sky, unmoored, I am traveling now and hearing myself laugh, at first with nerves and then with genuine amazement. It is all around me.

from Mountains of Tartary
by Eric Shipton

*Eric Shipton (1907–1977), like his friend H.W.
Tilman, loved covering new ground. Shipton in
1940 was appointed British Consul General in
Kashgar, China. He was desperate to explore
the peaks he could see from the roof of his
house, but local police forbade him to do so.
Undaunted, Shipton crept off one morning
before dawn for a brief "climbing holiday."*

There are those, I believe, who imagine that the number of unexplored and unclimbed mountains is fast running out; that given reasonably peaceful conditions, quicker and cheaper transport, in a generation or so, half a century at most, all the peaks of the world will have been scaled, and that, even in the more remote ranges, mountaineers wishing to tread new ground will have to "invent" new ways of approach. That must indeed be a gloomy prospect. But I defy even the most pessimistic mountaineer to travel far in the highlands of Central Asia and still to hold that view. He may come to wonder, as I have often wondered, whether in a century and a half of mountaineering, one-tenth of the summits of the world have as yet been reached.

For the first thirty years of this century, the huge panorama of ice-mountains seen from Ranikhet contained only one peak (Trisul) that had been climbed. Those mountains are the most easily accessible in the Himalaya. Imagine, if you can, several hundred such ranges. One of them I can see from the roof of my house in Kashgar. From here on a clear day I can count a score of peaks without name, without position on any map, unmeasured. Not amorphous desert hills that no one can want to climb anyway; not the 25,000-foot giants that would demand the tiresome organization of "high camps" and "assault parties"; not "aiguilles", "nordends" or subsidiary summits (I could use the word hundreds if I included those). They are peaks of Alpine stature and form, each rising from its own system of glacier valleys and supported by its own complex of granite face and ice-ridge. Any one of them could be climbed by a competent party, after due reconnaissance and failure, from a camp barely above the pine forest. Many of them would offer problems as attractive as any in the Alps. Yet I doubt whether by the end of the twentieth century much more will be known about these peaks, in climbing terms, than is known today. Not because of "iron curtains"; not because they lie far from the offices and homes of those interested in these matters; but simply because of the vastness of the field for new mountaineering adventure of which they form so small a part.

It may well be objected that the existence of such a field is scant consolation to those whose brief holidays confine them to overcrowded Alpine peaks. But, even so, it is well for them to contemplate this wider background, to realize that the future of mountaineering does not consist only in the unending development of gymnastic technique, and that though the advance of modern means of transport may shrink the world to lamentably small proportions, it should also continue, for a very long time to come, to open an ever-expanding field of mountaineering enterprise. Let us not waste our sympathy on posterity; there will be enough for them as there is for us.

On even the most familiar journeys in this part of the world, unexplored ranges are such a commonplace, so much the order of the marching day, that to cross a side-stream whose source is known usually calls for excited comment; a peak distinguished with a name stands like a lighthouse in a limitless sea. This is enchanting, no doubt, but overfamiliarity wuth these conditions has, I find, one unfortunate and rather disconcerting result. I appear to have lost a good deal of my interest in climbing mountains. Not entirely; but much of the rapturous enthusiasm seems to have gone. I recall, for example, my intense eagerness to make the second ascent of Mount Kenya, which for some months was a ruling passion of my life, and with some sadness contrast it with the nonchalance with which I gaze at a view of half a dozen peaks, greater in height, equally beautiful in form. I am not alone in this. I have often remarked, for example, how little members of the Mount Everest expeditions used to avail themselves of the opportunity, for many of them unique, of climbing virgin peaks around the Base Camp or in Sikkim. The excuse was rarely valid that the exhaustion of high climbing or lack of time prevented them. Everest has all too seldom allowed us to exhaust ourselves on her higher reaches; few, surely, have calculated their time with such precision as to have deny themselves an extra week, even if as much were needed.

How, then, are we to explain this away? Is it an ugly reflection upon the purity of our motive? Is the fame of a mountain a necessary part of the stimulus that makes us wish to climb it? Must we be able to point out our conquest to an appreciative audience and say "I climbed that"? Do we wonder, even subconsciously, what is the use of climbing one of a range of a thousand mountains that nobody has even heard of? I have tried to account for this disturbing tendency in myself by the reflection that mountain-climbing has its roots in a desire to explore; that given the genuine article, the substitute loses much of its allure. There is a good deal of truth in this, but the explanation is far from being entirely satisfactory. It cannot be claimed that much exploration was done on the later Everest expeditions. It does not account for the fact that in my present mood I would undoubtedly be more stirred by a view of the Peuterey Ridge than by a ridge of twice the size of an unknown mountain. Nor does it explain my acute feelings of envy when I read a friend's account of his ascent of the Guggi Route or of the Viereselgrat. Such things should be paltry beside my own opportunities, if not my exploits. But they often seem a great deal more desirable. I have wondered if this is not due to my advancing years; whether I am not becoming an armchair mountaineer, ready to envy but not to act. But I think I can honestly (if eagerly) reject this explanation. For I am satisfied that were I to visit the Alps again, my enthusiasm for climbing peaks would be little or no less than it was twenty years ago. Unfortunately, in that period I have only had one brief opportunity of putting the speculation to the test. I found, in those days, infinite satisfaction in being once more in country, every inch of which was accurately mapped, the smallest buttress named. I set out to climb a third-rate mountain as eagerly as though it had been my first expedition with rope and axe.

It seems, then, that we must look for some deeper reason for the failure of these unknown mountains to attract us to their remote and lonely summits; for we must at all costs avoid the indictment of a competitive spirit. An analogy might perhaps be allowed in the case of rock-climbing. Does the Lakeland expert gaze with longing at the great rock walls of the Lauterbrunnen Valley as he passes them in the train? Would he be consumed by an irresistible desire to force his way up one of an infinite number of possible routes on a twenty-mile-long precipice flanking the path up the Hunza Valley? Would he not be overcome by a feeling of cold futility if he tried? Like most analogies it exaggerates the case; and, of course, it will be argued that while there are great peaks to be climbed, one does not bother with minor buttresses, that, in fact, as mountain-climbing is a substitute for mountain exploration, so cliff-climbing is a substitute for mountain-climbing. This, too, may be allowed, but again I find it an unsatisfactory explanation. There *is* some quality about a buttress on Scafell that urges us to climb it, which is lacking in a cliff that is less well-known by reason of the very profusion of precipices in which it is set. So, I find, it is with mountains themselves. Some kind of intimacy, either personal or historical, seems to be necessary, without which we are oppressed by an overwhelming sense of loneliness and awed by the insignificance of our achievement.

The best way to cure a mountaineer of such unhealthy introspection is to deny him access to the mountains. Until my first tour in Kashgar, I had never been in a position of being able to gaze month after month at mountains with little or no prospect of reaching them. It was not an unmitigated torment. There was so much joy and solace in just looking at them in their never-ending variety of cloud and colour setting, that I certainly would not have wished them away. The memory that there had been periods in my life when I was completely satisfied by physical contact with great peaks was an enormous help in curbing regret and in preventing it from spoiling the contemplation of that remarkable view.

Even so, there were times when the craving to reach the mountains was almost intolerable. For in those days in Kashgar I was living in a police state. Moreover, I and my fellow-nationals were lucky enough to be fulfilling that important political role performed by the Jews under Hitler and by the bourgeoisie during the French Revolution. A scapegoat is apparently necessary to a dictatorship, at least in its earlier years. Later, of course, the species is liable to become extinct through failure of the authorities to observe even the most elementary rules of game preservation, and the ruling clique must seek or invent some external object for its righteous abuse. The excellent band of Swedish missionaries who had done such fine work here for the best part of half a century and had won the universal respect and liking of the local population, being more vulnerable to attack, had succumbed a couple of years before. The Indian traders clung to life with unreasonable tenacity, and we stayed to support them. Between us we served their purpose. Any official or private individual whom the authorities found it convenient to remove, was at once found to have been friendly with, or spying for, the British Consulate-General. I discovered later that our sinister influence had spread far and wide: in distant cities that no Indian trader or member of our staff had visited for a quarter of a century; among Kirghiz tribesmen in remote mountain valleys, who had never set eyes upon our humble establishment. The resulting boycott was tiresome, but I found it easy to bear compared to the confinement to a ten-mile radius in the midst of this country of such boundless opportunity.

At length, after nearly a year, I could stand it no longer, and I decided to slink away in secret to the nearest mountains. At the time I attributed the success of my plan to my cleverness in its execution. I later discovered that, a thousand miles away in the Provincial capital, forces were at work which were to result in a complete political *volte-face*, and which ended for a time that ugly spell of totalitarian rule. But for this, I am more than doubtful whether I would have achieved my innocent design. However that may be, I left Kashgar before dawn one morning in September in a covered country cart, together with Lhakpa Tenzing and a Hunza servant, and after two long days' travel reached the Kirghiz settlement of Bostan Terek, sixty miles to the west.

The first day's march was through the south-westward extension of the Kashgar oasis, along dusty country roads, flanked by willows, irrigation channels and fields, to Opal. This I thought was the danger-point, and though we passed through the bazaar in the dusk, I was fully expecting to be challenged and asked for our papers. However, we got through without a hitch, spent the night at the edge of the oasis, and were off again by dawn the next morning. Once out in the desert beyond Opal I breathed a sigh of relief, for I then felt fairly safe from pursuit. It was a long, hot, waterless march, utterly monotonous, over gently rising ground, rocky and scored by innumerable dry water-courses. But the mountains were in view, and though we seemed to be moving infinitely slowly, they were gradually getting nearer. Though we could see Bostan Terek the whole time, it was not easy to find the track, and once off it the going was terribly rough for our clumsy cart. We were still five or six miles from our destination when night fell. Luckily we found a spring of water and, as there was plenty of dry tamarisk wood, we made a pleasant camp. We reached Bostan Terek early on the third morning.

We were sure of a friendly reception, for the Swedish missionaries had made a summer resort in the valley, to which they had come in relays each year. I knew that they had been very well liked, and that I would benefit from a reflection of that popularity; but, even so, I was not prepared for the warmth of the welcome we received. Every family seemed to vie with each other to entertain us. If their hospitality had not been so charmingly simple and genuine, it might have been embarrassing. They seemed to think that our arrival heralded a return to the good old days. We spent the remainder of the morning drinking milk in various *akois* and talking to our hosts. It was wonderful to be away from the atmosphere of fear and suspicion, that in those days ruled in the large oases. I spent the afternoon shooting chikor (hill partridge) of which there were thousands in the foot-hills nearby. I shot some dozens without any difficulty and distributed them to our hosts.

Bostan Terek is one of the eastern valleys of the Kashgar Range, a northerly continuation of the Pamirs. The river flowing down it from the glaciers at its head disappears when it leaves the foot-hills, under the thirty-mile-wide band of coarse alluvial deposits which we had just crossed. The water emerges again in springs, helps to irrigate the Opal oasis and eventually flows into the Yarkand River. At the foot of the valley there is enough water for the cultivation of quite a wide area of fields, where the Kirghiz grow wheat and barley. Like most of the Kirghiz of these parts they are semi-nomadic grazing their flocks on the high pastures during the summer and living at the foot of the valley in winter. I have often wondered why these semi-nomads, who always inhabit the same valley, continue to live in *akois,* moving them from the arable land to the various levels of pasture and back again according to the season. It would be easy enough for them to build stone and timber houses at each place, which would far outlast their frail tents, and save the continual transport back and forth. They have told me that they dislike houses as they are difficult to keep clean and are apt to become vermin-ridden.

The following day Lhakpa and I set off up the valley, together with two Kirghiz and a couple of yaks we had hired to carry our baggage. After we had passed through the cultivated area, we climbed up onto the wide, grassy ridge of an ancient moraine. To the left, across the gorge cut by the river, the southern flank of the valley was covered with fir forest for several miles, until it merged into sheer granite cliffs. Beyond, the valley floor climbed in a series of wide, grassy terraces into the heart of the ice-mountains. We camped in a pleasant little hollow by a spring at a height of about thirteen thousand feet. From there, during the following week, Lhakpa and I did a series of climbs of varying difficulty. I had brought my dog, Khombu, with me. We had, of course, to leave him tied up when we set off each morning, telling the Kirghiz to let him free when we had been gone an hour. Each evening as we came off the glaciers we would start shouting and he would come up to meet us.

It was a perfect place for a climbing holiday. A short way above our camp the valley opened out into a wide circle of granite peaks between 17,000 feet and 18,500 feet high. Several glaciers draining from these met in the centre and flowed a short way down the main valley. The highest peak was a lovely twin-headed one which formed a prominent landmark in the view from Kashgar. I had hoped to attempt it after we had got into some sort of training on the smaller mountains. It looked very difficult indeed. It was built of a remarkable complexity of sharp granite ridges divided by steep ice-couloirs and hanging glaciers. Each day we studied it from a new angle, hoping to find some way through its formidable defences. But each aspect looked more forbidding than the last, and at length I decided reluctantly to abandon any idea of attempting it. We had neither the time nor the facilities for exploring the western aspect of the mountain, and the standard of climbing involved in an attempt on any route on the eastern side was obviously higher than anything we were likely to reach on this visit.

The second-highest peak in the group was also a very fine one, which resembled the Dent Blanche seen from the upper Zinal valley. The side of it facing the cirque was a granite precipice standing some four thousand feet sheer above the glacier. But just beyond a high col on the main watershed I had caught a profile glimpse of a face in its upper part which seemed to offer a possible route. The lower part was hidden behind the col. So on the sixth day, after we had done several climbs, we set out to reconnoitre.

The way to the col led through a glacier bay shut in by the great rock walls of the highest and the second-highest peaks, and thence up a long snow-couloir. As we were making our way up the glacier bay there was an eclipse of the sun. At this point it was not a total eclipse (the edge of the belt of totality was about a hundred miles to the north), but it was sufficiently complete to produce a weird effect of deep twilight. We reached the col before noon. From it we saw the whole of the face of our mountain. The lower part was an easy snow-slope which we could reach without any difficulty by climbing a couple of hundred feet down beyond the col. The upper part consisted of a band of broken rocks, split by a very steep snow- or ice-couloir. Above the rocks an ice-dome formed the summit of the mountain. To reach it from our camp would involve a climb of more than five thousand feet. But the difficult section was comparatively small. Much depended upon the quality of the snow on the lower part of the face.

We started the next morning just before dawn. Like each of its predecessors, it was a lovely day. Although as soon as the sun rose we were in its light, it was very cold and the snow remained frozen hard all the way up to the col. We made much better time than on the previous day. But on the face of the mountain beyond the col the snow deteriorated extraordinarily quickly, and before we had gone a thousand feet up we were sinking in well above our knees. This was an unpleasant surprise, for after at least a week of fine weather, and probably much longer, I could see no reason for such a depth of soft snow. The slow, upward struggle consumed hours of time, with almost imperceptible results.

As we approached on the rocks, the slope became steeper and the snow firmer. We had intended to climb the couloir which split the rock face, but as we came nearer to it we saw that it was composed of hard, blue ice. It was tremendously steep and it would have taken us at least six hours to cut steps to the top of it. As it was already nearly one o'clock by the time we reached the foot of the rocks, this was clearly out of the question. The rocks themselves did not look too difficult. We chose a line and started to climb them. Here we met with our third disappointment. The rocks were completely rotten, coated with ice and a great deal steeper than they had appeared from below. It was the kind of ground, common on broken, ice-covered rocks, where it appears that if one can only overcome the next ten feet it will be much easier and where this appearance always turns out to be wrong. We climbed some way up a nasty little gully and were defeated by a slippery scoop, only ten feet high, at its top. With great difficulty we traversed across to a rib to the left. Here we found that the rock was firmer and comparatively free from ice. I decided that we should give the rib a trial and if we failed to climb it we should abandon the attempt.

After a couple of pitches the rib steepened a lot and the climbing became very difficult. But by then we were only a hundred feet below the base of the ice-dome forming the summit. I led off in a determined attempt to reach it, supposing that the difficulties would then be over. I had already conceived the idea of glissading down the ice-couloir as an alternative to climbing down the rocks. Though it was steep and narrow and composed entirely of ice, there was a perfect run out at the bottom and providing we kept our feet we could not come to any harm. The idea appealed to me so much that I pressed my efforts on the upper part of the rib a good deal farther than I ought to have done. I climbed very slowly. It was difficult all the way and there was absolutely no stance, let alone a belay to which I could bring Lhakpa. I had almost reached the ice when the rope came taut behind me. I could not possibly have held Lhakpa, who in any case said, very wisely, that in the circumstances he would rather not follow. I had either to retreat or unrope and go on to the top, perform my wild glissade and then return to fetch Lhakpa, who fortunately was in a comfortable position. The prospect of climbing down the way I had come was so abhorrent that I decided on the latter course.

I unroped and threw down the end, thus effectively burning my boats. I then climbed the remaining few feet to the top of the rocks. Here to my dismay I found that my difficulties were by no means over. The base of the ice-dome was flush with the top of the rocks and there was no ledge between the two. Moreover, for the first four feet the ice was vertical, before it gradually began to slope back. At the top of the rib there was one foot-hold, flat but only large enough to take the sole of one boot. With infinite caution, by a sort of "mantelpiece" movement, I managed, after two attempts, to stand with my left foot on this. It was a horrible position, for at first there was nothing to hold on to, and the bulge of the ice seemed to be pushing me outwards off my balance. I remember wondering how many times I would bounce if I fell, before reaching the snow-slope below. I swung my axe above my head and dug the pick into the ice. That helped matters, but it was not a permanent relief and I had to face the unpleasant task of cutting a step in the ice. Fortunately, immediately to my right, the face of the ice, though still vertical, receded in conformity with the contour of the rock, which allowed me to swing my axe much more freely than would otherwise have been the case. First I cut a handhold well above the four-foot vertical section, and then, holding on to this with my gloved left hand, began work on the step. It was very laborious; for the step had to be large, as it would be awkward to step into it, and also knee-room had to be fashioned above. After every dozen or so strokes I had to rest my right arm. Also my left foot was getting very tired and I had often to relieve the pressure on it by anchoring my axe in the ice-slope above and leaning on it and the hand-hold. I must have worked on that step for well over half an hour before I was satisfied with it. I had cut it too high for convenience and had a struggle to get on to it. But once there, the relief was intense. The weight at last off my left foot, I could lean forward over the ice-bulge. The second and third steps were easy to make, and after that I was standing squarely on the ice-slope above. Soon, as the angle eased off, there was a covering of firm snow on the ice, and presently I could stop cutting and kick steps instead. I almost ran up the last slope, and five minutes later I reached the top of the mountain.

It was a quarter-past four. The air was calm, and the sun was still quite warm. I was still feeling the blissful relief of no longer being plastered against the ice-bulge. To this was now added the thrill of reaching the summit, of which I had several times during the day almost abandoned hope, and which latterly had become merely a way of escape. For a moment I almost forgot the unpleasant prospect of the glissade to which I was now committed. I would like to have sat for an hour studying the view. But I could not afford more than ten minutes; as it was, there was no chance of getting back to camp before dark. To the south, the peaks of the Kungur and Chakragil massifs were clear. But the best part of the view was to the north where stood the highest mountain of the Bostan Terek group. I was only a little lower than its twin summits, and its clean-cut, sweeping ridges stood out, magnificently defined in the slanting sunlight. I had no camera with me. In those days in Sinkiang cameras were strictly forbidden and it would have been asking for trouble to carry one.

It was nearly half-past four by the time I started the descent. I walked a little way along the wide summit ridge, and then started diagonally down to the right until I was immediately above the ice-couloir. A shout came from below and, looking down, I saw that Lhakpa had already climbed down to the snow-slope below the rocks. I cut a few steps down until I could get a clear view of the whole length of the couloir. It was dead straight, but very narrow in its middle section. It was essential that I should start exactly above this narrow part, for, once started, I could not possibly control the direction of my glissade. I cut a large platform from which to start, and stood for a few minutes contemplating the prospect with a sinking heart. It was much more frightening than I had expected. The ice was tremendously steep; Lhakpa and the blessed snow-slope looked miles away down; though the length of the couloir was not more than a few hundred feet; the two crags projecting from its sides half-way down allowed distressingly little room for error. However, there was nothing for it but to take the plunge, and the sooner I did so, the sooner I would get it over. It was at least, very simple; all I had to do was to keep my head, keep my legs and my body absolutely rigid, and hang on to my ice-axe for all I was worth. I leant hard back with my right hand almost on the ferrule of the axe (even so I seemed to be standing almost upright) and let my feet slip out of the step. The next moment I seemed to be falling through space with hardly any contact on the ice. The rushing wind caught my breath, but at the same time I felt as if I were shouting at the top of my voice. It seemed endless; but I was dimly aware of the rock promontories rushing up towards me, and then past me, one on either side. I had no time to realize that my aim through the narrow section had been true before a wave of snow rushed up and blinded me. Then after a while I felt my pace slacken. I dug my heels in, came to a halt and sank down on the snow, completely winded.

For the second time in about an hour I experienced a glorious sense of relief. The summit had been reached and the somewhat unorthodox descent of the only difficult part achieved. Nothing remained but a long but easy downward journey in the soft evening light. While I lay on the snow-slope recovering my breath, Lhakpa came across to join me. My hat had disappeared. I made no attempt to look for it. We roped up and plunged on down the slope. The slight rise from the foot of the face to the col demanded unwelcome effort, but the snow in the couloir beyond was sufficiently firm for a gentle glissade. Darkness fell as we were making our way over the rough, moraine-covered lower glacier. But soon we had the camp-fire to guide us. Khombu came up to meet us in answer to our shouts. The Kirghiz, bless them, had a pot of boiling water ready for us, and tea was soon made.

a c k n o w l e d g m e n t s

Many people contributed to this anthology and I thank them all.

At Thunder's Mouth Press and Avalon Publishing Group:
Neil Ortenberg, Susan Reich, Dan O'Connor and Ghadah Alrawi
offered indispensable help.

At Balliett & Fitzgerald Inc.:
Sue Canavan designed another beautiful book. Production editor
Maria Fernandez cheerfully oversaw production with help from
Meghan Murphy and Paul Paddock. Jodi Brandon proofread the
manuscript with care and skill. Will Balliett offered friendship and
guidance and a chance to participate in this wonderful series.

At the Thomas Memorial Library in Cape Elizabeth, Maine:
Thanks to all the librarians, but especially to Susan Sandberg who
worked to locate and borrow countless books from across the country.

At the Writing Company:
Nate Hardcastle, a funny and gentle soul, helped gather selections,
facts and materials and kept me on schedule.

At Shawneric.com:
The unflappable Shawneric Hachey secured permissions and scanned
copy, and lent his marvelous eye to the task of choosing photographs.

Among family and friends:
My mother Ellen Brodkey helped with permission to reprint the
excerpt by Harold Brodkey.
Clint Willis, series editor of Adrenaline Books and my husband of 20
years, encouraged and supported me, as he always has done.
My sons Abner and Harper Willis renewed my spirit every day.

We gratefully acknowledge all those who gave permission for written material to appear in this book. We have made every effort to trace and contact copyright holders. If an error or omission is brought to our notice we will be pleased to remedy the situation in future editions of this book. For further information, please contact the publisher.

Excerpt from *The Lost Tribe*, copyright © 1996 by Edward Marriott. Reprinted by permission of Henry Holt and Company, LLC. ❖ "An Evening Among Headhunters", excerpted from *An Evening Among Headhunters* by Lawrence Millman. Copyright © 1998 by Lawrence Millman. Used by permission of Lumen Editions, Cambridge, Mass. ❖ "Lost City of the Lukachukais", excerpted from *Escape Routes* by David Roberts, copyright © 1997 by David Roberts. Text from the book, *Escape Routes* by David Roberts included with permission of the publisher, The Mountaineers, Seattle, WA. ❖ Excerpt from *Antisuyo: The Search for the Lost Cities of the Amazon* by Gene Savoy, copyright © 1970, Gene Savoy. Permission to excerpt *Antisuyo: The Search for the Lost Cities of the Amazon* granted by Gene Savoy, c/o The Andean Explorer's Foundation & Ocean Sailing Club, 643 Ralston St., Reno, NV 89503, c/o Elizabeth Berney, Esq., The Literary Resources Agency, 48 Carriage Road, Great Neck, NY 11024. ❖ "Cahill Among the Ruins in Peru", excerpted from *Jaguars Ripped My Flesh* by Tim Cahill, copyright © 1987 by Tim Cahill. Reprinted with permission of Barbara Lowenstein Associates, New York. ❖ Excerpt from *Snow on the Equator* by H. W. Tilman, copyright © 1983 by Joan A. Mullins and Pamela H. Davis. Text from the book, *The Seven Mountain-Travel Books* included with permission of the publishers, The Mountaineers, Seattle, WA, and Bâton Wicks, London. ❖ Excerpt from *In Trouble Again* by Redmond O'Hanlon. U.S. Rights: copyright © 1988 by Redmond O'Hanlon, used by permission of Grove/Atlantic, Inc.; World English rights excluding U.S.: copyright © 1998 by Redmond O'Hanlon, reprinted by permission of The Peters Fraser Dunlop Group Limited. ❖ Excerpt from *Adventures in the Unknown Interior of America* by Alvar Núñez Cabeza de Vaca. Reprinted with the permission of Scribner, a Division of Simon & Schuster from *Adventures in the Unknown Interior of America*, translated and annotated by Cyclone Covey. Copyright © 1961 by Macmillan Publishing Company. ❖ Excerpt from *The Dogs of Paradise* by Abel Posse. Reprinted with the permission of Scribner, a

b i b l i o g r a p h y

The selections used in this anthology were taken from the editions listed below. In some cases, other editions may be easier to find. Hard to find or out-of-print titles often can be acquired through inter-library loan services. Internet sources also may be able to locate these books.

Brodkey, Harold. *This Wild Darkness: The Story of My Death*. New York: Henry Holt & Company, 1998.

Cabeza de Vaca, Alvar Núñez. *Adventures in the Unknown Interior of America*. New York: Collier Books, 1961.

Cahill, Tim. *Jaguars Ripped My Flesh*. New York: Bantam Doubleday Dell, 1987.

Finkel, Michael. "Crazy in the Congo". Washington, D.C.: *National Geographic Adventure*, April 2000.

Long, John. *Gorilla Monsoon*. Helena, MT: Chockstone Press, 1989.

Marriott, Edward. *The Lost Tribe*. New York: Henry Holt and Company, 1997.

Mazuchelli, Nina. *The Indian Alps and How We Crossed Them*. New York: Dodd, Mead, and Company, 1876.

Millman, Lawrence. *An Evening Among Headhunters*. Cambridge, MA: Lumen Editions, 1998.

Nansen, Fridtjof. *Farthest North*. New York: Greenwood Press, 1968.

O'Hanlon, Redmond. *In Trouble Again*. New York: Vintage Books, 1988.

Posse, Abel. *The Dogs of Paradise*. New York: Antheneum, 1989.

Roberts, David. *Escape Routes*. Seattle, WA: The Mountaineers, 1997.

Savoy, Gene. *Antisuyo: The Search for the Lost Cities of the Amazon*. New York: Simon & Schuster, 1970.

Shipton, Eric. *Eric Shipton: The Six Mountain-Travel Books*. Seattle, WA: The Mountaineers, 1985.

Tilman, H. W. *The Seven Mountain-Travel Books*. Seattle, WA: The Mountaineers, 1997.

Wetherell, W. D. *Upland Stream*. New York: Little, Brown & Company, 1991.